PTOLEMY'S TETRABIBLOS

PTOLEMY'S TETRABIBLOS

OR

QUADRIPARTITE

BEING

FOUR BOOKS

OF THE

INFLUENCE OF THE STARS

NEWLY TRANSLATED FROM THE GREEK PARAPHRASE OF PROCLUS

WITH

A PREFACE, EXPLANATORY NOTES

AND

AN APPENDIX

CONTAINING

EXTRACTS FROM THE ALMAGEST OF PTOLEMY

AND THE WHOLE OF HIS

CENTILOQUY

TOGETHER WITH

A Short Notice of Mr. Ranger's Zodiacal Planisphere

AND AN EXPLANATORY PLATE

By J. M. ASHMAND

NEW EDITION

> "Ye stars, which are the poetry of Heaven!
> If, in your bright leaves, we would read the fate
> Of men and empires,—'tis to be forgiven."
>
> LORD BYRON.

SYMBOLS & SIGNS
North Hollywood, CA 91607

ISBN NO. 0-912504-31-5
LC NO. 76-41123

COPYRIGHT © 1976 BY SYMBOLS & SIGNS

Published by

SYMBOLS & SIGNS

P.O. BOX 4536
NORTH HOLLYWOOD, CALIFORNIA 91607

PRINTED IN U.S.A.

TO THE

AUTHOR OF "WAVERLEY"

THIS TRANSLATION

OF A

WORK CONTAINING THE BEST ACCREDITED PRINCIPLES

OF

ASTROLOGY

IS DEDICATED

With the most profound admiration of his unrivalled Talents

WHICH COULD ALONE HAVE RESTORED

INTEREST TO THE SPECULATIONS

OF AN

ANTIQUATED SCIENCE

ADVERTISEMENT

THE use recently made of Astrology in the poetical machinery of certain works of genius (which are of the highest popularity, and above all praise), seems to have excited in the world at large a desire to learn something of the mysteries of that science which has, in all former ages, if not in these days, more or less engaged reverence and usurped belief. The apparent existence of such a general desire has caused the completion of the following Translation, and its presentation to the public; although it was originally undertaken only in part, and merely to satisfy two or three individuals of the grounds on which the now neglected doctrines of Astrology had so long and so fully maintained credit.

TABLE OF CONTENTS

CONTENTS

PREFACE

OF all sciences, whether true or false, which have at any time engaged the attention of the world, there is not one of which the real or assumed principles are less generally known, in the present age, than those of Astrology. The whole doctrine of this science is commonly understood to have been completely overturned; and, of late, people seem to have satisfied themselves with merely knowing the import of its name. Such contented ignorance, in persons, too, sufficiently informed in other respects, is the more extraordinary, since Astrology has sustained a most conspicuous part throughout the history of the world, even until days comparatively recent. In the East, where it first arose, at a period of very remote antiquity,[1] and whence it

---

[1] Sir Isaac Newton has the following remarks in regard to the origin of Astrology :—" After the study of Astronomy was set on foot for the use of navigation, and the Ægyptians, by the heliacal risings and settings of the stars, had determined the length of the solar year of 365 days, and by other observations had fixed the solstices, and formed the fixed stars into asterisms, all which was done in the reigns of Ammon, Sesac, Orus, and Memnon," (about 1000 years before Christ), " it may be presumed that they continued to observe the motions of the planets, for they called them after the names of their gods; and Nechepsos, or Nicepsos, King of Sais," [772 B.C.], " by the assistance of Petosiris, a priest of Ægypt, invented astrology, grounding it upon the aspects of the planets, and the qualities of the men and women to whom they were dedicated[2]; and in the beginning of the reign of Nabonassar, King of Babylon, about which time the Æthiopians, under Sabacon, invaded Ægypt " [751 B.C.], " those Ægyptians who fled from him to Babylon, carried thither the Ægyptian year of 365 days, and the study of astronomy and astrology, and founded the æra of Nabonassar, dating it from the first year of that king's reign " [747 B.C.], " and beginning the year on the same day with the Ægyptians for the sake of their calculations. So Diodorus : ' *they say that the Chaldæan in Babylon, being colonies of the Ægyptians, became famous for astrology, having learned it from the priests of Ægypt.*' "—Newton's Chronology, pp. 251, 252.

Again, in p. 327 : " The practice of observing the stars began in Ægypt in the days of Ammon, as above, and was propagated from thence, in the reign of his son Sesac, into Afric, Europe, and Asia, by conquest; and then Atlas formed the sphere of the Libyans " [956 B.C.], " and Chiron that of the Greeks [939 B.C.]; and the Chaldæans also made a sphere of their own. But astrology

[2] It is maintained by astrologers, that the planets, *having been observed* to produce certain effects, were *consequently* dedicated to the several personages whose names they respectively bear.

xi

came to subjugate the intellect of Europe, it still even now holds sway. In Europe, and in every part of the world where learning had " impress'd the human soil," Astrology reigned supreme until the middle of the 17th century. It entered into the councils of princes, it guided the policy of nations, and ruled the daily actions of individuals. All this is attested by the records of every nation which has a history, and

was invented in Ægypt by Nichepsos, or Necepsos, one of the Kings of the Lower Ægypt, and Petosiris his priest, a little before the days of Sabacon, and propagated thence into Chaldæa, where Zoroaster, the legislator of the Magi, met with it : so Paulinus ;

> ' Quique magos docuit mysteria vana Necepsos.' "

The arcana of Astrology constituted a main feature in the doctrines of the Persian Magi ; and it further appears, by Newton's Chronology, p. 347, that Zoroaster (although the æra of his life has been erroneously assigned to various remoter periods) lived in the reign of Darius Hystaspis, about 520 B.C., and assisted Hystaspes, the father of Darius, in reforming the Magi, of whom the said Hystaspes was Master. Newton adds, p. 352, that " about the same time with Hystaspes and Zoroaster, lived also Ostanes, another eminent Magus : Pliny places him under Darius Hystaspis, and Suidas makes him the follower of Zoroaster : he came into Greece with Xerxes about 480 B.C., and seems to be the Otanes of Herodotus. In his book, called the Octateuchus, he taught the same doctrine of the Deity as Zoroaster."

Having quoted thus far from Newton, it seems proper to subjoin the following extract from the " Ancient Universal History : "—" In the reign of Gushtasp " [the oriental name of Darius Hystaspis], " King of Persia, flourished a celebrated astrologer, whose name was Gjamasp, surnamed Al Hakim, or the wise. The most credible writers say that he was the brother of King Gushtasp, and his confidant and chief minister. He is said to have predicted the coming of the Messiah ; and some treatises under his name are yet current in the East. Dr. Thomas Hyde, in speaking of this philosopher, cites a passage from a very ancient author, having before told us that this author asserted there had been among the Persians ten doctors of such consummate wisdom as the whole world could not boast the like. He then gives the author's words : ' Of these, the sixth was Gjamasp, an astrologer, who was counsellor to Hystaspis. He is the author of a book intitled *Judicia Gjamaspis*, in which is contained his judgment on the planetary conjunctions. And therein he gave notice that Jesus should appear ; that Mohammed should be born ; that the Magian religion should be abolished, etc. ; nor did any astrologer ever come up to him.' [*E. lib. Mucj. apud Hyde.*] Of this book there is an Arabic version, the title of which runs thus : The Book of the Philosopher Gjamasp, containing Judgments on the Grand Conjunctions of the Planets, and on the Events produced by them. This version was made by Lali ; the title he gave it in Arabic was Al Keranai, and he published it A.D. 1280. In the preface of his version it is said that, after the times of Zoroaster, or Zerdusht, reigned Gushtasp, the son of Lohrasp,[1] a very

---

[1] This seems to be a mistake of the Arabian author, for Gushtasp was identical with Darius Hystaspis, and Lohrasp [otherwise Cyaxares] was father of Darius the Mede, who was overcome by Cyrus, 536 B.C.—See Newton.

by none more fully than by those of England. Yet, with these striking facts before their eyes, the present generation seem never, until now, to have inquired on what basis this belief of their forefathers was established, nor by what authority the delusion (if it was one) could have been for so many ages supported. Among a thousand persons who now treat the mention of Astrology with supercilious ridicule, there is scarcely one who knows distinctly what it is he laughs at, or on what plea his ancestors should stand excused for having, in their day, contemplated with respect the unfortunate object of modern derision.

powerful prince; and that in his reign flourished in the city of Balch, on the borders of Chorassan, a most excellent philosopher, whose name was Gjamasp, author of this book; wherein is contained an account of all the great conjunctions of the planets which had happened before his time, and which were to happen in succeeding ages; and wherein the appearances of new religions and the rise of new monarchies were exactly set down. This author, throughout his whole piece, styles Zerdusht, or Zoroaster, our Prophet. [D'Herbelot, Bibl. Orient. Art. Gjamasp.] The notion of predicting the rise and progress of religions from the grand conjunctions of the planets, has been likewise propagated in our western parts : Cardan was a bold assertor of this doctrine. The modern Persians are still great votaries of astrology, and although they distinguish between it and astronomy, they have but one word to express astronomer and astrologer ; viz. *manegjim*, which is exactly equivalent to the Greek word ἀστρολογος. Of all the provinces of Persia, Chorassan is the most famous for producing great men in that art ; and in Chorassan there is a little town called Genabed, and in that town a certain family which, for 6 or 700 years past, has produced the most famous astrologers in Persia ; and the king's astrologer is always either a native of Genabed, or one brought up there. Sir John Chardin affirms that the appointments in his time for these sages amounted to six millions of French livres per annum.—Albumazar of Balch (scholar of Alkendi, a Jew, who was professor of judicial astrology at Bagdad, in the Caliphate of Almamoum[1]) became wonderfully famous. He wrote expressly from the Persian astrologers, and it may be from the works of Gjamasp, since he also reports a prediction of the coming of Christ in the following words : viz. ' In the sphere of Persia, saith Aben Ezra, there ariseth upon the face of the sign Virgo a beautiful maiden, she holding two ears of corn in her hand, and a child in her arm : she feedeth him, and giveth him suck, &c. This maiden,' saith Albumazar, ' we call Adrenedefa, the pure Virgin. She bringeth up a child in a place which is called Abrie [the Hebrew land], and the child's name is called Eisi [Jesus].' This made Albertus Magnus believe that our Saviour, Christ, was born in Virgo ; and therefore Cardinal Alliac, erecting our Lord's nativity by his description, casteth this sign into the horoscope. But the meaning of Albumazar was, saith Friar Bacon, that the said virgin was born, the Sun being in that sign, and so it is noted in the calendar ; and that she was to bring up her son in the Hebrew land. [Mr. John Gregory's Notes on various Passages of Scripture.]"—*Ancient Universal History, vol.* 5, *pp.* 415 *to* 419.

[1] This caliph reigned in the earlier part of the 9th century, and caused Ptolemy's Great Construction to be translated into Arabic, as hereafter mentioned.

The general want of information on these points, and the indifference with which such want has been hitherto regarded, cannot surely be attributed solely to the modern disrepute of the science ; for mankind have usually, in every successive age, exercised great industry in tracing all previous customs, however trifling or obsolete, and in examining all sorts of creeds, however unimportant or erroneous, whenever there has appeared any striking connection between such matters and historical facts ; and, since astrology is most unquestionably blended intimately with history, it therefore becomes necessary to seek for some further hypochesis, by which this ignorance and indifference may be accounted for.

Perhaps astrology has been conceived to have borne the same relation to astronomy as alchymy did to chymistry. If such has been the notion, it has certainly been adopted in error, for a modern chymist is still almost an alchymist : it is true that he no longer delays his work in deference to the planets, nor does he now try to make gold, nor to distil elixir of earthly immortality ; but nevertheless he still avails himself, to a certain degree, of the same rules and the same means as those of the old alchymist : he is still intent upon the subtle processes of Nature, and still imitates her as far as he can. He reduces the diamond to charcoal by an operation analogous to that by which the alchymist sought to transmute lead into gold ; and he mainly differs from the alchymist only in having assured himself that there is a point beyond which Nature forbids facsimiles. Not so slightly, however, does the astronomer differ from the astrologer, but *toto cœlo :* the astrologer considered the heavenly bodies and their motions merely as the mechanism wherewith he was to weave the tissue of his predictions ; and astronomy is no more an integral part of astrology, than the loom is of the web which has been woven by it. To have an idea of what alchymy was, it is sufficient to have an idea of chymistry ; but astronomy, in itself, will never give a notion of astrology, which requires additional and distinct consideration.

It may be urged, that in the present day a general idea of this by-gone and disused science is quite sufficient for everybody not professedly antiquarian. Such an assertion would doubtless never be controverted, provided the proposed general idea might comprehend the truth. But the present actual general idea of astrology is by no means so comprehensive ; indeed, nothing can well be more inaccurate, or even more false : it seems to have been adopted not from the elements of the science itself, but from trite observations made by writers against the science ; and consequently the world now wonders at the lamentable defect of understanding that could ever have permitted belief in it— forgetting that astrology has been consigned to neglect, not in consequence of any *primâ facie* palpability in its imputed fallacies, nor indeed of any special skill or acuteness on the part of its professed adversaries, but rather in consequence of the sudden and astonishing growth of other undoubted sciences, with which it has been presumed to be incompatible, and which during the thousands of years of the reign of astrology were either unborn, or still slumbering in continued infancy.[1]

The words " professed adversaries," which have just now been used, are of course not intended to be applied to those mighty explorers of Nature's laws and man's powers, who, in their lofty career, may have made an incidental swoop at the pretensions of astrology. Directly engaged in more exact pursuits, they stopped not to dissect this their casual prey, which, after having been thus struck by eagles, was left to regale crows and daws, and these, in their convivial loquacity, accused their unfortunate victims of crimes incapable of being committed, and of offences which had never been imagined. Of the real faults of their victim these garrulous bipeds seem not to have been aware, or, if aware, they seem to have considered them as not sufficiently prominent. Nor was this want of candour or information absolutely confined to the mere vulgar herd of vituperative scribblers, for even the sparkling essay against astrology, written by Voltaire (in his irrepressible desire to convince the world that he was *au fait* in everything), proves only that the writer, though the most generally informed man of his time, had mistaken the really assailable points of the object of his attack.

The author of the present Translation has no intention now of either advocating or impugning the doctrines of the science of which his Translation discourses : his purpose is a different one. He has that sort of respect for " the dead, which are really dead," which, although it does not incline him to " praise " them " *more* than the living, which are yet alive," is still sufficient to incite him to endeavour to avert the imputation of idiot credulity, to which their faith in astrology seems now to subject them in the general opinion of the enlightened " living." And, while he disclaims all idea of presuming to offer any argument on either side of the question, as to the validity of the science, he must still, at the

---

[1] To this view of the case, the following remarks seem not inapplicable : they are taken from a periodical work of deserved reputation :—

" The study of astrology itself, as professing to discover, by celestial phenomena, future mutations in the elements and terrestrial bodies, ought, perhaps, not to be despised.[2] The theory of the tides, for example, is altogether an astrological doctrine, and, long before the days of Sir Isaac Newton, was as well understood as it is at this moment. The correspondence alleged by the ancient physicians to exist between the positions of the Moon and the stages of various diseases, is so far from being rejected by the modern faculty, that it has been openly maintained."[3] The writer then recounts sundry incidents, asserted by the astrologers to be dependent on the Moon, and he adds these words : " The fact of these allegations might be so easily ascertained, that it is surprising they should still be pronounced incredible, and *denied* rather than *contradicted*."

[2] " Sir Christopher Heydon's Defence of Astrology, p. 2, edit. 1603."
[3] " Dr. Mead on the Influence of the Sun and Moon upon Human Bodies. See also Edinb. Rev. vol. 12, p. 36—Balfour on Sol-Lunar Influence." *Blackwood's Magazine for Dec.*, 1821, *Part 2, No. 59.*

same time, confess his admiration of the ingenuity and contrivance manifest in its construction, and avow his readiness to believe that all its harmonized complications might have easily held dominion over some of the strongest minds in that darker period when it flourished.

In executing here the desire of attempting to vindicate the ancient credence in astrology, an elaborate disquisition would surely be not only unnecessary, but misplaced : it seems sufficient to refer the reader to the work of which the following is a translation, and to these undisputed facts—that the science was formerly inculcated by the highest and most erudite authorities of the period—that it was insisted on by votaries in all parts of the world, attesting and producing instances of its truth ;— and, moreover, that it was so finely and beautifully put together, as to cause the only deficiency of one small, though most important, link in its whole chain of argument, to be undetected by dull minds, and readily supplied by enthusiastic genius. For centuries after centuries all branches of learning were either made subservient to astrology, or carried on in close alliance with it ; and many of the illustrious names which it recalls to our recollection are gratefully reverenced even by modern science. The genius of Roger Bacon, although he was the first of that school of natural philosophy which acknowledges none but experimented truths, was nevertheless bowed to the doctrines of judicial astrology; and his greater Namesake, who after an interval of several centuries succeeded to him in giving proper direction to the mental energy, was still an arguer in favour of celestial influences : it may be, therefore, fairly inferred, that the subtle spell which had strength to enthrall " stuff " so " stern," could have been of no weak or vulgar order, but that it was sufficiently potent and refined to interest and amuse even the present age.[1]

[1] In the 51st No. of the Quarterly Review, Art. " *Astrology and Alchymy*," the following observations are made :—

" Certainly, if man may ever found his glory on the achievements of his wisdom, he may reasonably exult in the discoveries of astronomy ; but the knowledge which avails us has been created solely by the absurdities which it has extirpated. Delusion became the basis of truth. Horoscopes and nativities have taught us to place the planet in its sure and silent path ; and the acquirements which, of all others, now testify the might of the human intellect, derived their origin from weakness and credulity " (p. 181). Again ; " Astrology, like alchymy, derives no protection from sober reason ; yet, with all its vanity and idleness, it was not a corrupting weakness. Tokens, predictions, prognostics, possess a psychological reality. All events are but the consummation of preceding causes, clearly felt, but not distinctly apprehended. When the strain is sounded, the most untutored listener can tell that it will end with the key-note, though he cannot explain why each successive bar must at last lead to the concluding chord. The omen embodies the presentiment, and receives its consistency from our hopes or fears." (p. 208).

It may, perhaps, be difficult to assent to all of the propositions involved in these extracts ; but there are among them some which are clearly unquestionable.

In this little volume will be found the whole of the elements of astrology, and the entire ground-work of those stupendous tomes in folio and quarto on the same subject, which were produced in myriads during the 16th and 17th centuries, for the due mystification of the then world. The present volume is addressed equally to the general reader, as well as to the votary of pure astrology, if any such there be ; to the one it offers amusement ; for the other, it should contain the most glowing interest. Even to the speculative metaphysician it will furnish food for contemplation ; for, in addition to its peculiar hypothesis of cause and effect, it develops many of those apparent incongruities of character so often united in the same individual ; and this development, even although adapted to the doctrine of the stars, still merits attention ; inasmuch as the phenomena of which it treats (in whatever way they may be produced or regulated) will ever remain in actual existence.

The only English translation of Ptolemy's Tetrabiblos, hitherto published, appears to have been first set forth in 1701, under the name of " The Quadripartite." That publication has been long removed from general sale ; and its gross misinterpretation of the author, caused by the carelessness or ignorance of Whalley and his assistants, by whom it was produced, has rendered most of its pages unintelligible : its absence is, therefore, scarcely to be regretted. The second edition of the same translation, professing to be " revised, corrected, and improved," and published by Browne and Sibley, in 1786, was not, in any one instance, purified from the blunders and obscurities which disgraced its predecessor : it seems, in fact, less excusable than the former edition, of which it was merely a reprint, without being at all corrected, not even in certain typographical *errata* which the former printer had been zealous enough to point out in his final page. Even this second publication, worthless as it intrinsically is, can rarely now be met with, and, like the former, only at a very heavy price.

The present Translation has been made from Proclus's Greek Paraphrase of Ptolemy's original text ; the edition followed is that of the Elzevirs, dated in 1635.[1] But, in the course of translation, continual references have been also had to various editions of the original text, in order to ascertain the proper acceptation of doubtful passages. The editions thus inspected were that by Camerarius, printed at Nuremberg in 1535 ; that by Melancthon, printed at Basle in 1553 ; and that by Junctinus, printed, with his own enormous commentaries, at Lyons, in 1581. Independently of these references, the present translation has

---

[1] This edition was printed in double columns, one containing Proclus's Greek Paraphrase, the other the Latin translation of Leo Allatius ; and William Lilly (no light authority in these matters) thus wrote of it in the year 1647 : " Indeed Ptolemy hath been printed in folio, in quarto, in octavo, in sixteens : that lately printed at Leyden " [where the Elzevirs were established] " I

been collated with the Latin of Leo Allatius, and with two other Latin translations : one printed at Basle, together with a translation of the Almagest in 1541 ; the other by itself at Perugio, in 1646.[1] The Translator has devoted all this extreme care and attention to his labours, in the wish to render Ptolemy's astro-judicial doctrine into English as

conceive to be most exact; it was performed by Allatius." To the said edition is prefixed an anonymous address to the reader, in Latin, and to the following effect :—

" I have reckoned it part of my duty to give you, benevolent reader, some short information as to the publication of this little work, which, having hitherto existed only in Greek,[2] is now, in its Latin dress, accessible to the curiosity of all persons. This Paraphrase of Proclus on the Tetrabiblos of Ptolemy was translated a few years ago by Leo Allatius, a Greek by birth, eminently skilled in the learning of his own nation, as well as in Latin literature, and already celebrated for other writings in both languages. He lives, I have understood, in Rome, in the family of Cardinal Biscia, and holds some office in the Vatican Library. He undertook his present work, however, for his own private gratification, and that of certain friends ; but when writings compiled with this view have once quitted their author's hands, it will often happen that they have also, at the same time, escaped his control. So this offspring of Allatius, having emerged from Rome, arrived at Venice, from whence it was forwarded to me by a certain great personage of illustrious rank, in order that I might cause it to be printed. The names of Ptolemy and Proclus, so celebrated among mathematicians and philosophers, besides the subject of the work itself, seemed to me a sufficient warrant for committing it to the press. Whereupon I delayed not to avail myself of the advantages I possessed in having access to our excellent and most accurate typographers, the Elzevirs, and I earnestly solicited them to publish it : they, in their love for the commonwealth of letters, took upon themselves the charge of printing it in the form you see. You will learn from it, inquisitive Reader, how much power the stars have over the atmosphere and all sublunary things : for the stars, and those brighter bodies of heaven, must not be imagined to be idle. The whole doctrine of the stars is not, however, here treated of, but only that distinct part of it which the Greeks call judicial and prognostic, and which, while confined within certain limits is as entertaining as it is useful, and is partly considered to be agreeable to nature. Bnt should it pretend to subject to the skies such things as do not depend thereupon, and should it invite us to foresee by the stars such things as are above the weakness of our apprehension, it will assuredly deserve to be reprehended as a vain and empty art, which has been demonstrated in many learned books by

[1] This translation from the Perugio press has been serviceable in presenting certain various readings ; but it does not seem to possess any other peculiar merit. It professes to be a translation from the original text of Ptolemy ; and so likewise does the translation printed at Basle, as above quoted.

[2] This assertion is applicable only to Proclus's Paraphrase. There were several prior translations of the original Tetrabiblos in Latin and Arabic ; and it appears by an extract from the Bibliotheca Græca of Fabricius [which will be found in a subsequent page], that a Latin version, done from the Arabic, was printed at Venice as early as the year 1493.

purely and perfectly as possible ; and, with the same view, he has likewise added, in an Appendix, certain extracts from such parts of the
Almagest as were found to be referred to in his present work.   Further
illustration is also given by notes gathered from the " Primum Mobile "
of Placidus,[1] and from a variety of other sources whence any elucidation
of the text might be derived.   Even Whalley's " Annotations " (to use
his own grandiloquent designation) have occasionally yielded information, not altogether unimportant, although generally incomplete.

It seems improper to close this Preface (notwithstanding the bulk
it has already attained), without annexing the following short notice
of the life and works of the great man from whom the Tetrabiblos has
emanated.

Claudius Ptolemy was born at Pelusium, in Ægypt, and became an

the great Picus of Mirandola.   The Chaldæans, Genethliacs, and Planetarians,
have been always held in disrepute, because they professed to know not only
more than they actually did know, but also more than is allowed to man to
know.   Even Ptolemy, while he employs himself in his present work upon the
Doctrine of Nativities, is scarcely free from the charge of superstition and
vanity : perhaps, in a Pagan, this may be forgiven ; but it is hardly to be toler-
ated, that persons professing Christianity should be led away by such an empty
study, in which there is no solid utility, and the whole pleasure of which is
puerile.   Finally, I warn you that some persons doubt whether this was really
produced by Ptolemy[2] : nevertheless, it has certainly appeared to Porphyry
and Proclus (who were doubtless great philosophers, although hostile to the
Christian faith) to be worthy of receiving elucidation by their Commentaries
upon it.[3]   Peruse it, however, friendly reader, with caution, having first shaken
off the weakness of credulity, for the sinew of wisdom is not to believe rashly.
Farewell."

In addition to the remarks made in the foregoing address regarding Leo
Allatius, it may be observed that he was appointed Keeper of the Vatican
Library by Pope Alexander VII, with whom he was in high favour.   It is said
of him, that he had a pen with which he had written Greek for forty years, and
that he shed tears on losing it.   Another story of him states, that the Pope had
often urged him to take holy orders, that he might be advanced in the church,
and one day asked him why he had not done so : " Because," said Allatius, " I
would be free to marry."—" Why, then, do you not marry ? "—" Because I
would be free to take orders."—*Chalmer's Biographical Dictionary.*

[1] It appears by the printed works of this author, that he was named Didacus
Placidus de Titis.   He was a native of Bologna, by profession a monk, and was
styled Mathematician to the Archduke Leopold William of Austria.   He wrote
in the earlier part of the 17th century, and his work, now cited, is considered
to contain the most successful application of Ptolemy's astrological rules to
practice.   The original is extremely scarce ; but a new English edition, by
Cooper, may be had of the Publishers of this work.

[2] The reader is again referred to the extract from Fabricius (inserted in a
subsequent page), containing that learned person's account of this book among
the other works of Ptolemy.

[3] Their Commentaries were printed at Basle, in 1559.

illustrious disciple of the school of Alexandria, in which city he flourished during the reign of Adrian and that of Antoninus Pius. The date of his birth has been commonly assigned to the 70th year of the Christian æra ; but the accuracy of this date seems questionable ; for he has himself noted in one part of his works, that Antoninus reigned twenty-three years. He must have, therefore, survived that prince ; and, as it is not probable that he continued his scientific labours until after ninety years of age, which he must have done had he been born about the year 70, because Antoninus died in the year 161, it seems that his birth would be more properly ascribed to some later period. Moreover, it is asserted by the Arabians, that he died in the 78th year of his age ; and a similar statement is also made by Luca Gauricus, in the dedication of his version of the Almagest[1] to Dominico Palavicini : Gauricus has, however, placed his death in the year 147, which does not accord with the fact of his having survived Antoninus.

Ptolemy has recorded that he observed, at Alexandria, an eclipse of the Moon, in the 9th year of Adrian ; and that he made many observations upon the fixed stars in the 2nd year of Antoninus Pius : whence it may be concluded, that his observations upon the heavens were principally made during the period from A.D. 125 to A.D. 140, or thereabouts ; and it also follows, of course, that the supposition, entertained by some authors, of his identity with the Ptolemy who was always in attendance upon Galba, as his personal astrologer, and who promised Otho that he should survive Nero and obtain the empire, is entirely without foundation. To Gauricus's[2] version of the Almagest there is also another dedication, addressed to Pope Sixtus, and composed by George Trapezuntius, describing Ptolemy as " *regiâ stirpe oriundum,*" and explaining that he had, " with a truly regal mind," applied himself to the sciences, because the ancient sceptre of the Ptolemies had previously passed into the hands of Cleopatra, and because the kingdom of Ægypt had been since reduced to the state of a Roman province. The authentic details of the circumstances of Ptolemy's life are, however, extremely few. It is said that he was distinguished among the Greeks by the epithets " most wise," and " most divine," on account of his great learning ; and, according to the Preface to Whalley's translation of the Tetrabiblos, the Arabians report that " he was extremely abstemious, and rode much on horseback " ; adding, that although he was " spruce in apparel," yet his breath was not remarkable for an agreeable odour.

The errors of the Ptolemaic theory of the universe have now been long discarded ; but there are many points in which modern sciences, and modern astronomy in particular, have reaped incalculable benefits from the labours and researches of its great founder. He has preserved

---

[1] Printed at Basle, 1541.
[2] Chalmer's Biographical Dictionary.

and transmitted to us the observations and principal discoveries of re-moter periods, and has enriched and augmented them with his own. He corrected Hipparchus's catalogue of the fixed stars, and formed tables for the calculation and regulation of the motions of the Sun, Moon, and planets. He was, in fact, the first who collected the scattered and detached observations of Aristotle, Hipparchus, Posidonius, and others on the economy of the world, and digested them into a system, which he set forth in his Μεγαλη Συνταξις or Great Construction, divided into thirteen books, and called, after him, the Ptolemaic System. This and all his other astronomical works are founded upon the hypothe-sis, that the earth is at rest in the centre of the universe, and that the heavenly bodies, stars, and planets, all move round it in solid orbs, whose motions are all directed by one *primum mobile*, or first mover, of which he discourses at large in the " Great Construction." In that work he also treats of the figure and divisions of the earth, of the right and oblique ascensions of the heavenly bodies, and of the motions of the Sun, Moon, and planets ; and he gives tables for finding their situations, latitudes, longitudes, and motions : he treats also of eclipses, and the methods of computing them ; and he discourses of the fixed stars, of which he furnishes a numerous catalogue, with their magnitudes, lati-tudes, and longitudes.[1]

It has been truly said, that " Ptolemy's order, false as it was, enabled observers to give a plausible account of the motions of the Sun and Moon, to foretell eclipses, and to improve geography[2] ; " or, in other words, that it represented the actual phenomena of the heavens as they really appear to a spectator on the earth. It is therefore clear that Ptolemy's astrology is just as applicable to modern and improved astronomy as it was to his own.[3]

---

[1] In France, about the beginning of the 16th century, Oronce Finé, the Royal Reader, attempted, under the patronage of Francis I, to produce an astronomical clock, in which everything moved according to the principles of Ptolemy. It was kept, about fifty years ago, in the monastery of St. Geneviéve, at Paris. In Lilly's Catalogue of Astrological Authors, Orontius Finæus is mentioned as the writer of a work on the twelve houses of heaven, printed in Paris, 1553.

[2] *Spectacle de la Nature.*

[3] The objection which has been urged against astrology, that the signs are continually moving from their positions, cannot invalidate this conclusion. That objection has, in fact, no real existence ; for Ptolemy seems to have been aware of this motion of the signs, and has fully provided for it in the 25th Chapter of the 1st Book of the Tetrabiblos. From that chapter it is clear that the respective influences he ascribes to the twelve signs (or divisions of the zodiac) were considered by him as appurtenant to the *places* they occupied, and not to the *stars* of which they were composed. He has expressly and repeatedly declared that the point of the vernal equinox is ever the beginning of the zodiac, and that the 30 degrees following it ever retain the same virtue as that which he has in this work attributed to Aries, although the stars forming Aries may

In the year 827[1] the "Great Construction" was translated by the Arabians into their own language, and by them communicated to Europe. It is through them that it has been usually known by the name of the Almagest. In the 13th century, the Emperor Frederic II caused it to be translated from the Arabic into Latin, and Sacrobosco[2] was consequently enabled to write his famous work upon the sphere. It was not, however, until about the end of the 15th century that the "Great Construction" was translated into Latin from the *original* text ; and this important service was rendered to science by Purbach, a professor of philosophy at Vienna, who learned the Greek tongue at the instigation of Cardinal Bessarion. By means of this translation, the Ephemerides of George Müller, surnamed Regiomontanus, a disciple of Purbach's, were first composed. The Greek text of the Almagest, or Great Construction, was first published at Basle, by Simon Grynæus, in 1538 ; and it was again printed at the same place in 1551, with certain other works of Ptolemy.[3] The rest of Ptolemy's works connected with astronomy, and now extant, are the Tetrabiblos, or Four Books of the Influence of the Stars[4] (now translated) ; the Centiloquy, or Fruit of his Four Books, being a kind of supplement to the former ; and the Significations of the Fixed Stars. The last is merely a daily calendar,

---

have quitted those degrees : the next 30 degrees are still be accounted as Taurus, and so of the rest. There is abundant proof throughout the Tetrabiblos, that Ptolemy considered the virtues of the *constellations* of the zodiac distinctly from those of the *spaces* they occupied.

[1] The French say 813, but 827 is the date given by English chronologists.

[2] This scientific man was a Mathurine Friar, and a professor in the University of Paris : he died in 1256. It is pointed out in the Edinburgh Review, No. 68, that he was a native of Yorkshire, and his real name John Holywood, euphonized, in Paris, into Sacrobosco.

[3] Chalmers.—The Tetrabiblos was among these works.

[4] To such readers as may be curious to know in what manner this book was promulgated in Europe, after the revival of letters, the following extract from the Bibliotheca Græca of Fabricius will furnish information :—

"Lib. IV. Cap. XIV. §4. Τετραβίβλος, Σύνταξις Μαθηματικη *Quadri-partitum, sive quatuor libri de apotelesmatibus et judiciis astrorum, ad Syrum* (h). Græce primum editi a *Joachimo Camerario*, cum versione suâ duorum priorum librorum, et præcipuorum e reliquis locorum. Norimb. 1535, 4to.—Hinc cum versione *Phil.* Melancthonis, qui in præfat. ad Erasmum Ebnerum Senatorem Norimbergensem testatur se editionem Camerarii multis mendis purgasse, tum numeros in locis apheticis tam Græci quam Latini textus emendasse. Basil, 1553, 8vo.—*Latine* pridem verterat *Ægidius Tebaldinus*, sive latino-barbaré ex Hispanica versione, Alfonsi Castellæ Regis jussu, ex Arabico (i) confectâ. Vertit et *Antonius Gogava*, Lovan. 1548, 4to ; Patavii, 1658, 12mo ; Pragæ, 1610, 12mo. Commentario illustravit *Hieron. Cardanus* prioribus duobus libris Camerarii, posterioribus Gogavæ versione servatâ, Basil, 1554, fol. ; 1579, fol. ; Lugd. 1555, 8vo, et in Cardani opp.—*Georgii Vallæ* commentarius, anno 1502 editus, nihil aliud est, quam Latina versio scholiorum

showing the risings and settings of the stars, and the nature of the weather
thereby produced.   There are likewise extant his geographical work
(which has rendered important service to modern geographers), and also
his celebrated book on Harmonics, or the Theory of Sound.

Proclus, to whom the world is indebted for the improved text of the
Tetrabiblos,[1] was born at Constantinople, in the year 410.   He studied

Græcorum, sive exegeseos jejunæ *Demophili* in tetrabiblon, quæ cum
Porphyrii sive *Antiochi* isagoge, Græce et Latine, addita *Hieron Wolfii*
versione, lucem vidit Basil. 1559, fol.   In his scholiis Dorotheus allegatur, p. 48,
110, et 139 ; Cleopatra, p. 88 ; Porphyrius Philosophus, p. 169.   Meminit et
auctor Petosiridis ac Necepso, p. 112 :—λεγει δε παλαιον τον Νεχεψω (ita leg.
pro χεψω ut p. 112) και Πετοσιριν, ουτοι γαρ πρωτοι το δι ασρολογιας
εχηπλωσαν προγνωςικον[2] Paraphrasin tetrabibli a *Proclo* concinnatam Græce
edidit Melancthon, Basil. 1554, 8vo.   Græce et Latine cum versione suâ
Leo Allatius, Lugd. Batav. 1654,[3] 8vo.   Locum Ptolemæi e codice Græco
MS. in collegio Corporis Christi Oxon, feliciter restituit Seldenus, p. 35 ad
Marmora Arundeliana.   Haly Heben Rodoan Arabis commentarium laudat
Cardanus, cum Demophilo Latine editum."

" (h) Schol. Græc.—Προσφωνει τω Συρω ο Πτολεμαιος το βιβλιον, προς
ον και τας αλλας αυτου πασας πραγματειας προσεφωνησεν.   Λεγουσι δε τινες
ως πεπλασαι αυτο το του Συρω ονομα.   Αλλοι δε οτι ου πεπλασα,, αλλ' ιατρος
ην ουτος αχθεις και δια τουτων των μαθηματων.

" (i) Selden. Uxor Hebr. p. 342. Cæterum de Alphonsi Regis curâ in
promovenda Arabica Quadripartiti versione, vide, si placet, Nic : Antonium
in Bibl. veteri Hispana, t. 2, p. 55, vel Acta Erud. A. 1697, p. 302.   Latino
versio ex Arabico facta lucem vidit Venet, 1493, fol.   Viderit porro Gassendus
qui in Philosophia Epicuri, ubi contra Astrologos disputat. t. 2, p. 501. con-
tendit tetrabiblon indignum esse Ptolemæi genio et subdititum.   Equidem Jo.
Pico judice, l. 1, contra Astrologos, p. 285, Ptolemæus *malorum* sive Apoteles-
maticorum est *optimus*."

[1] It will be seen by the preceding note, that Proclus's Paraphrase of the
Tetrabiblos should properly be considered as superior to the other readings
of that book ; since it appears, on the authority of Fabricius, that Melancthon,
after having been at the pains of correcting and republishing, in 1553 (with
his own emendations), the edition of Camerarius, containing the reputed
original text, still deemed it advisable, in the following year, to edit Proclus's
Paraphrase. This Paraphrase must, therefore, necessarily have had claims to
his attention not found in the text he had previously edited.[4]

[2] " Nechepsos and Petosiris are anciently spoken of, for they first explained
prognostication by Astrology."

[3] This was perhaps a reprint of the edition of 1635, from which the present
translation has been made ; unless there may have been an error of the press
in stating 1654 instead of 1635, which seems probable, as the edition of 1635
is unnoticed by Fabricius.

[4] " Ptolemy addresses the book to Syrus, to whom he has also addressed all
his other treatises. Some say that this name of Syrus was feigned ; others,
that it was not feigned, but that he was a physician, and educated in these
sciences."

at Alexandria and at Athens, and became very eminent among the later Platonists. He succeeded Syrianus, a celebrated philosopher, in the rectorship of the Platonic school at Athens, and died there in 485.[1] He was a most voluminous author, in poetry as well as in prose. Among his works there are Hymns to the Sun, to Venus, and to the Muses ; Commentaries upon several pieces of Plato, and upon Ptolemy's Tetrabiblos[2] ; an Epitome or Commendium of all the Astronomical Precepts demonstrated in the Almagest ; and elements of Theology and Natural Philosophy. He was in dispute with the Christians on the question of the eternity of the world, which he undertook to prove in eighteen elaborate arguments. A late writer in a certain periodical work has erroneously identified him with another Proclus, who was in favour with the Emperor Anastasius, and who destroyed the ships of Vitalianus, when besieging Constantinople in 514, by burning them with great brazen mirrors, or *specula*.

Signs of the Zodiac.

♈	Aries	♎	Libra
♉	Taurus	♏	Scorpio
♊	Gemini	♐	Sagittarius
♋	Cancer	♑	Capricorn
♌	Leo	♒	Aquarius
♍	Virgo	♓	Pisces

---

[1] Chalmer's Biographical Dictionary.

[2] It will, of course, be understood that this Commentary is distinct from his Paraphrase, now translated.

PTOLEMY'S TETRABIBLOS

OR

FOUR BOOKS

OF THE

INFLUENCE OF THE STARS

BOOK THE FIRST

CHAPTER I

PROEM

THE studies preliminary to astronomical prognostication, O Syrus! are two : the one, first alike in order and in power, leads to the knowledge of the figurations of the Sun, the Moon, and the stars ; and of their relative aspects to each other, and to the earth : the other takes into consideration the changes which their aspects create, by means of their natural properties, in objects under their influence.

The first mentioned study has been already explained in the Syntaxis[1] to the utmost practicable extent ; for it is complete in itself, and of essential utility even without being blended with the second ; to which this treatise will be devoted, and which is not equally self-complete. The present work shall, however, be regulated by that due regard for truth which philosophy demands : and since the material quality of the objects acted upon renders them weak and variable, and difficult to be accurately apprehended, no positive or infallible rules (as were given in detailing the first doctrine, which is always governed by the same immutable laws) can be here set forth : while, on the other hand, a due observation of most of those general events, which evidently trace their causes to the Ambient, shall not be omitted.

It is, however, a common practice with the vulgar to slander everything which is difficult of attainment, and surely they who condemn the first of these two studies must be considered totally blind, whatever arguments may be produced in support of those who impugn the second. There are also persons who imagine that whatever they

[1] The Almagest, or *Magna Constructio*.

themselves have not been able to acquire, must be utterly beyond the reach of all understanding ; while others again will consider as useless any science of which (although they may have been often instructed in it) they have failed to preserve the recollection, owing to its difficulty of retention.   In reference to these opinions, therefore, an endeavour shall be made to investigate the extent to which prognostication by astronomy is practicable, as well as serviceable, previously to detailing the particulars of the doctrine.

CHAPTER II

KNOWLEDGE MAY BE ACQUIRED BY ASTRONOMY TO A CERTAIN EXTENT

THAT a certain power, derived from the æthereal nature, is diffused over and pervades the whole atmosphere of the earth, is clearly evident to all men.   Fire and air, the first of the sublunary elements, are encompassed and altered by the motions of the æther.   These elements in their turn encompass all inferior matter, and vary it as they themselves are varied ; acting on earth and water, on plants and animals.[1]

[1] The following extract from an old geographical work, framed on the rules of Ptolemy, explains the system on which this action of the æther is made to depend :—

"Chap. 2.   The world is divided into two parts, the elemental region and the æthereal.   The elemental region is constantly subject to alteration, and comprises the four elements ; earth, water, air and fire.   The æthereal region, which philosophers call the fifth essence, encompasses, by its concavity, the elemental ; its substance remains always unvaried, and consists of ten spheres ; of which the greater one always spherically environs the next smaller, and so on in consecutive order.   First, therefore, around the sphere of fire, GOD, the creator of the world, placed the sphere of the Moon, then that of Mercury, then that of Venus, then that of the Sun, and afterwards those of Mars, of Jupiter, and of Saturn.   Each of these spheres, however, contains but one star : and these stars, in passing through the zodiac, always struggle against the *primum mobile*, or the motion of the tenth sphere ; they are also entirely luminous.   In the next place follows the firmament, which is the eighth or starry sphere, and which trembles or vibrates (*trepidat*) in two small circles at the beginning of Aries and Libra (as placed in the ninth sphere) ; this motion is called by astronomers the motion of the access and recess of the fixed stars." (Probably in order to account for the procession of the equinoxes.)   "This is surrounded by the ninth sphere, called the chrystalline or watery heaven, because no star is discovered in it.   Lastly, the *primum mobile*, styled also the tenth sphere, encompasses all the before-mentioned æthereal spheres, and is continually turned upon the poles of the world, by one revolution in twenty-four hours, from the east through the meridian to the west, again coming round to the east.   At the same time, it rolls all the inferior spheres round with it, by its own force ; and there is no star in it.   Against this *primum mobile*, the motion of the other spheres, running from the west through the meridian to the east,

The Sun, always acting in connection with the Ambient, contributes to the regulation of all earthly things : not only by the revolution of the seasons does he bring to perfection the embryo of animals, the buds of plants, the spring of waters, and the alteration of bodies, but by his daily progress also he operates other changes in light, heat, moisture, dryness and cold ; dependent upon his situation with regard to the zenith.

The Moon, being of all the heavenly bodies the nearest to the Earth, also dispenses much influence ; and things animate and inanimate sympathize and vary with her. By the changes of her illumination, rivers swell and are reduced ; the tides of the sea are ruled by her risings and settings ; and plants and animals are expanded or collapsed, if not entirely at least partially, as she waxes or wanes.

The stars likewise (as well the fixed stars as the planets), in performing their revolutions,[1] produce many impressions on the Ambient. They cause heats, winds, and storms, to the influence of which earthly things are conformably subjected.

And, further, the mutual configurations of all these heavenly bodies, by commingling the influence with which each is separately invested, produce a multiplicity of changes. The power of the Sun however predominates, because it is more generally distributed ; the others either co-operate with his power or diminish its effect : the Moon more frequently and more plainly performs this at her conjunction, at her first and last quarter, and at her opposition : the stars act also to a similar purpose, but at longer intervals and more obscurely than the Moon ; and their operation principally depends upon the mode of their visibility, their occultation and their declination.

From these premises it follows not only that all bodies, which may be already compounded, are subjected to the motion of the stars, but also that the impregnation and growth of the seeds from which all bodies proceed, are framed and moulded by the quality existing in the Ambient at the time of such impregnation and growth. And it is upon this principle that the more observant husbandmen and shepherds are accustomed, by drawing their inferences from the particular breezes which may happen at seed-time and at the impregnation of their cattle, to form predictions as to the quality of the expected produce. In short, however unlearned in the philosophy of nature, these men can foretell, solely by their previous observation, all the more general and

---

contends. Whatever is beyond this, is fixed and immovable, and the professors of our orthodox faith affirm it to be the empyrean heaven which GOD inhabits with the elect."—Cosmographia of Peter Apianus (named Benewitz), dedicated to the Archbishop of Saltzburg, edited by Gemma Frisius, and printed at Antwerp 1574.

[1] It will be recollected that the Ptolemaic astronomy attributes motion and a regular course to those stars which we now call fixed, but which the Greeks merely termed απλανεις, *undeviating*.

usual effects which result from the plainer and more visible configurations of the Sun, Moon, and stars. It is daily seen that even most
illiterate persons, with no other aid than their own experienced observation, are capable of predicting events which may be consequent on the
more extended influence of the Sun and the more simple order of the
Ambient, and which may not be open to variation by any complex
configurations of the Moon and stars towards the Sun. There are,
moreover, among the brute creation, animals who evidently form
prognostication, and use this wonderful instinct at the changes of the
several seasons of the year, spring, summer, autumn, and winter ; and,
also, at the changes of the wind.

In producing the changes of the seasons, the Sun itself is chiefly the
operating and visible cause. There are, however, other events which,
although they are not indicated in so simple a manner, but dependent
on a slight complication of causes in the Ambient, are also foreknown by
persons who have applied their observation to that end. Of this kind,
are tempests and gales of wind, produced by certain aspects of the Moon,
or the fixed stars, towards the Sun, according to their several courses, and
the approach of which is usually foreseen by mariners. At the same
time, prognostication made by persons of this class must be frequently
fallacious, owing to their deficiency in science and their consequent in-
ability to give necessary consideration to the time and place, or to the
revolutions of the planets ; all which circumstances, when exactly
defined and understood, certainly tend towards accurate foreknowledge.

When, therefore, a thorough knowledge of the motions of the stars,
and of the Sun and Moon, shall have been acquired, and when the situation of the place, the time, and all the configurations actually existing
at that place and time, shall also be duly known ; and such knowledge
be yet further improved by an acquaintance with the natures of the
heavenly bodies—not of what they are composed, but of the effective
influences they possess ; as, for instance, that heat is the property of the
Sun, and moisture of the Moon, and that other peculiar properties
respectively appertain to the rest of them ;—when all these qualifications for prescience may be possessed by any individual, there seems
no obstacle to deprive him of the insight, offered at once by nature and
his own judgment, into the effects arising out of the quality of all the
various influences compounded together. So that he will thus be competent to predict the peculiar constitution of the atmosphere in every
season, as, for instance, with regard to its greater heat or moisture, or
other similar qualities ; all which may be foreseen by the visible position
or configuration of the stars and the Moon towards the Sun.

Since it is thus clearly practicable, by an accurate knowledge of the
points above enumerated, to make predictions concerning the proper
quality of the seasons, there also seems no impediment to the formation
of similar prognostication concerning the destiny and disposition of
every human being. For by the constitution of the Ambient, even at

the time of any individual's primary conformation, the general quality
of that individual's temperament may be perceived ; and the corporeal
shape and mental capacity with which the person will be endowed at
birth may be pronounced ; as well as the favourable and unfavourable
events indicated by the state of the Ambient, and liable to attend the
individual at certain future periods ; since, for instance, an event
dependent on one disposition of the Ambient will be advantageous to a
particular temperament, and that resulting from another unfavourable
and injurious. From these circumstances, and others of similar import, the possibility of prescience is certainly evident.

There are, however, some plausible assailants of this doctrine, whose
attacks although greatly misapplied seem yet worthy of the following
observations.

In the first place, the science demands the greatest study and a constant attention to a multitude of different points ; and as all persons
who are but imperfectly practised in it must necessarily commit frequent mistakes, it has been supposed that even such events as have been
truly predicted have taken place by chance only, and not from any
operative cause in nature. But it should be remembered that these
mistakes arise, not from any deficiency or want of power in the science
itself, but from the incompetency of unqualified persons who pretend to
exercise it. And, besides this, the majority of the persons who set
themselves up as professors of this science, avail themselves of its name
and credit for the sake of passing off some other mode of divination ;
by that means defrauding the ignorant, and pretending to foretell many
things which from their nature cannot possibly be foreknown ; and
consequently affording opportunities to more intelligent people to
impugn the value even of such predictions as can rationally be made.
The reproach, however, thus brought upon the science is wholly
unmerited ; for it would be equally just to condemn all other branches
of philosophy, because each numbers among its professors some mischievous pretenders.

Secondly, it is not attempted to be denied that any individual,
although he may have attained to the greatest possible accuracy in the
science, must still be liable to frequent error, arising out of the very
nature of his undertaking, and from the weakness of his limited capacity
in comparison with the magnitude of his object. For the whole theory
of the quality of matter is supported by inference rather than by positive
and scientific proof ; and this is caused principally by the concretion
of its temperament out of a multitude of dissimilar ingredients. And,
although the former configurations of the planets have been observed
to produce certain consequences (which have been adapted to configurations now taking place), and are, after long periods, and in a greater
or less degree, resembled by subsequent configurations, yet these subsequent configurations never become exactly similar to those which have
preceded them. For an entire return of all the heavenly bodies to the

exact situation in which they have once stood with regard to the earth will never take place, or at least not in any period determinable by human calculation, whatever vain attempts may be made to acquire such un-attainable knowledge.[1] The examples referred to for guidance being therefore not exactly similar to the existing cases to which they are now applied, it must naturally follow that predictions are sometimes not borne out by the events. Hence arises the sole difficulty in the con-sideration of events produced by the Ambient. For no other con-current cause has been hitherto combined with the motion of the heavenly bodies; although the doctrine of nativities, particularly that part of it relating to peculiar individual temperament, demands also the consideration of other concomitant causes, which are neither trifling nor unimportant, but essentially potent in affecting the in-dividual properties of the creatures born. Thus the variety in seed has the chief influence in supplying the peculiar quality of each species; for, under the same disposition of the Ambient and of the horizon, each various kind of seed prevails in determining the distinct formation of its own proper species; thus man is born, or the horse is foaled; and by the same law are brought forth all the other various creatures and productions of the earth. It is also to be remembered, that considerable variations are caused in all creatures by the respective places where they may be brought forth: for although, under the same disposition of the Ambient, the germs of the future creatures may be of one species, whether human or of the horse, the difference in situation, of the places in which they are generated, produces a dissimilarity in the body and spirit of one from the body and spirit of another: and in addition to this it must be considered that different modes of nurture, and the variety of ranks, manners, and customs, contribute to render the course of life of one individual greatly different from that of another[2]; con-

---

[1] There seems reason to suppose that this was a favourite speculation among the ancients. In Scipio's Dream, as related by Cicero, the phantom of his illustrious grandfather is made to speak of this entire return of all the celestial bodies to some original position which they once held, as being the completion of the revolution of one great universal year: and the phantom adds, " but I must acquaint you that not one-twentieth part of that great year has been yet accomplished."

This quotation is from memory, and perhaps may not be verbally correct.

[2] In this passage the author seems to have anticipated, and exposed the absurdity of an argument now considered very forcible against astrology: viz. that "if the art were true, then any two individuals born under the same meridian, in the same latitude, and at the same moment of time, must have one and the same destiny; although one were born a prince, and the other a mendicant." Such a monstrous conclusion is nowhere authorized by any astrological writer; it is, on the contrary, always maintained by all of them, that the worldly differences and distinctions, alluded to in the text, inevitably

sequently, unless every one of these varieties be duly blended with the causes arising in the Ambient, the prejudgment of any event will doubtless be very incomplete. For, although the greatest multiplicity of power exists in the Ambient, and although all other things act as concurrent causes in unison with it, and can never claim it as a concurrent cause in subservience to them, there will still, nevertheless, be a great deficiency in predictions attempted to be made by means of the heavenly _____ alone, without regard to the other concurrent causes just now _____ to.

_____ ese circumstances, it would seem judicious neither to deny _____ practicability of prescience, because prognostications _____ derived are sometimes liable to be fallacious ; nor, on _____ admit that all events, whatever, are open to previous _____ inquiry could in all cases be securely conducted _____ to mere inference, and as if it were not limited _____ mere human abilities. The art of navigation, _____ ed, although it is in many points incomplete ; _____ t predictions are frequently imperfect cannot _____ he art of prescience : the magnitude of its _____ lance that it bears to a divine attribute, should _____ commendations, and receive the utmost regard and attention. And, since no weakness is imputed to a physician, because he inquires into the individual habit of his patient, as well as into the nature of the disease, no imputation can justly attach to the professor of prognostication, because he combines the consideration of species, nurture, education and country, with that of the motion of the heavens : for as the physician acts but reasonably, in thus considering the proper constitution of the sick person as well as his disease ; so, in forming predictions, it must surely be justifiably allowable to comprehend in that consideration every other thing connected with the subject in addition to the motion of the heavens, and to collect and compare with that motion all other co-operating circumstances arising elsewhere.

prevent this exact resemblance of destiny ; and all that they presume to assert is, that, in their respective degrees, any two individuals, so born, will have a partial similarity in the leading features of their fate. Whether their assertion is *uniformly* borne out, I will not take upon me to determine, but it would be unfair not to subjoin the following fact :—

In the newspapers of the month of February, 1820, the death of a Mr. Samuel Hemmings is noticed : it was stated that he had been an ironmonger, and prosperous in trade ; that he was born on the 4th of June, 1738, at nearly the same moment as his late Majesty, and in the same parish of St. Martin's-in-the-Fields ; that he went into business for himself in October, 1760 ; that he married on the 8th September, 1761 ; and finally, after other events of his life had resembled those which happened to the late King, that he died on Saturday, the 29th January, 1820.

These coincidences are, at least, highly remarkable.

CHAPTER III

THAT PRESCIENCE IS USEFUL

IT appears, then, that prescience by astronomy is possible under certain adaptation; and that alone it will afford premonition, as far as symptoms in the Ambient enable it to do so, of all such events as happen to men by the influence of the Ambient. These events are, from their commencement, always in conformity with the spiritual and corporeal faculties, and their occasional affections; as well as with the shorter or longer duration of those affections. They are also conformable with other things which, although not actually in man's immediate person, are still absolutely and naturally connected with him : in connection with his body they are applicable to his estate, and his conjugal cohabitations; in connection with his spirit, they relate to his offspring[1] and his rank; and they are also connected with all fortuitous circumstances which may occasionally befall him.

That the foreknowledge of these can be attained has already been demonstrated; and it remains to speak of the utility of the attainment. First, however, let it be said in what respect and with what view it is proposed to draw advantage from this science; if it be considered in its tendency to promote the good of the mind, no object more advantageous can surely be wanting to induce the world to rejoice and delight in it, since it offers an acquaintance with things divine and human : if it be considered in respect to the benefits it is capable of conferring on the body, its utility in this view also, will be found on comparison to excel that of all other arts conducive to the comforts of life, for it is of more general application and service than all the others together. And, although it may be objected to the art of prescience, that it does not co-operate towards the acquirement of riches or glory, let it also be remembered that the same objection attaches to every other art and science; since there it not one which can of itself produce either riches or glory, not yet is there one which is on that plea deemed useless : it seems, therefore, that the science of prognostication, with its high qualifications and its aptitude to the most important objects, does not, in any greater degree, deserve to be condemned.

In general, however, the persons who attack and reprobate it as being useless, do not pay due regard to the manner in which it becomes necessary; but deny its utility on the specious argument that it is

---

[1] The Greek word for this, γοναι, though found in the Elzevir edition from which this translation is made, does not appear in other copies; the Basle edition of 1553 says merely, η τε τιμη και το αξιωμα, "*honour and rank*," which is the sense also given in the Latin translation of Perugio, 1646, without any mention of "*offspring*."

superfluous and puerile to attempt to foreknow things which must inevitably come to pass : thus considering it in a mode at once abstracted, unlearned, and unfair. For, in the first place, this fact ought to be kept in view, that events which necessarily and fully happen, whether exciting fear or creating joy, if arriving unforeseen, will either overwhelm the mind with terror or destroy its composure by sudden delight ; if, however, such events should have been foreknown, the mind will have been previously prepared for their reception, and will preserve an equable calmness, by having been accustomed to contemplate the approaching event as though it were present, so that, on its actual arrival, it will be sustained with tranquillity and constancy.

In the next place, it must not be imagined that all things happen to mankind, as though every individual circumstance were ordained by divine decree and some indissoluble supernal cause ; nor is it to be thought that all events are shown to proceed from one single inevitable fate, without being influenced by the interposition of any other agency. Such an opinion is entirely inadmissable ; for it is on the contrary most essential to observe, not only the heavenly motion which, perfect in its divine institution and order, is eternally regular and undeviating ; but also the variety which exists in earthly things, subjected to and diversified by the institutions and courses of nature, and in connection with which the superior cause operates in respect to the accidents produced.

It is further to be remarked that man is subject, not only to events applicable to his own private and individual nature, but also to others arising from general causes. He suffers, for instance, by pestilences, inundations, or conflagrations, produced by certain extensive changes in the Ambient, and destroying multitudes at once ; since a greater and more powerful agency must of course always absorb and overcome one that is more minute and weaker. In great changes, therefore, where a stronger cause predominates, more general affections, like those just mentioned, are put in operation, but affections which attach to one individual solely are excited when his own natural constitution peculiar to himself may be overcome by some opposing impulse of the Ambient, however small or faint. And in this point of view it is manifest that all events whatsoever, whether general or particular, of which the primary cause is strong and irresistible, and against which no other contrary agency has sufficient power to interpose, must of necessity be wholly fulfilled ; and that events indicated by a minor cause must of course be prevented and annihilated, when some other agency may be found contending for an opposite effect ; if, however, no such opposing agency can be found, they also must be fulfilled, in due succession to the primary cause. Nevertheless, the fulfilment of events thus indicated must not be ascribed solely to the vigour of the cause producing them, nor to any inevitable fate, but rather to the absence of any opposing influence capable of prevention. And thus, with all things whatsoever

B

which trace their causes and origin to nature, the case is exactly similar ; for stones,[1] plants, animals, wounds, passions, and diseases, all will of necessity operate on man to a certain degree ; and they fail to do so, if antidotes be found and applied against their influence.

In exercising prognostication, therefore, strict care must be taken to foretell future events by that natural process only which is admitted in the doctrine here delivered ; and, setting aside all vain and unfounded opinions, to predict that, when the existing agency is manifold and great, and of a power impossible to be resisted, the corresponding event which it indicates shall absolutely take place ; and also, in other cases, that another event shall not happen when its exciting causes are counteracted by some interposing influence. It is in this manner that experienced physicians, accustomed to the observation of diseases, foresee that some will be inevitably mortal, and that others are susceptible of cure.

Thus, when any opinion is given by the astrologer with respect to the various accidents liable to happen, it should be understood that he advances nothing more than this proposition ; viz. that, by the property inherent in the Ambient, any conformation of it, suitable to a particular temperament, being varied more or less, will produce in that temperament some particular affection. And it is also to be understood that he ventures this opinion with the same degree of confidence, as that with which a physician may declare that a certain wound will increase or grow putrid ; or a man acquainted with metals say that the magnet[2] will attract iron. But neither the increase nor putrefaction of the wound nor the magnet's attraction of iron, is ordained by any inevitable law, although these consequences must necessarily follow, in due obedience to the first principles of the existing order of nature, when no means of prevention can be found and applied. But, however, neither of these consequences will take place, when such antidotes shall be presented as will naturally prevent them—and a similar consideration should be given to the predictions of the astrologer—because, if garlick be rubbed

---

[1] In allusion to the sympathetic powers anciently attributed to certain stones.

[2] Whalley, in translating this chapter, makes the following remark on this mention of the magnet : "However much later it was that the loadstone became known in Europe, what is mentioned of it in this chapter makes it evident that it was known in Ægypt, where Ptolemy lived, in his time."—That worthy translator forgot (if indeed he ever knew) that the loadstone's property of attracting iron was known to Thales, and commented on by Plato and Aristotle, all of whom lived some centuries, more or less, before Ptolemy. It is its polarity that was not known until the 11th or 12th century ; and the French say that the earliest notice of that polarity is found in a poem of Guyot of Provence, who was at the Emperor Frederick's Court at Mentz in 1181.— See the French Encyclopædia, &c.

on the magnet, iron will experience no attraction;[1] and if proper medicines be applied to the wound, it will cease to increase or to putrefy. And therefore all events which happen to mankind take place also in the regular course of nature, when no impediments thereto are found or known : but again, on the other hand, if any impediments or obstructions be found in the way of events which may be predicted by the regular course of nature to happen, such events will either not take place at all, or, if they should take place, will be much diminished in their force and extent.

The same order and consequence exist in all cases, whether the events have a general or only a particular operation ; and it may therefore well be demanded, why prescience is believed to be possible as far as it regards general events, and why it is allowed to be serviceable in preparing for their approach ; while in particular instances its power and use are altogether denied. That the weather and the seasons, and the indications of the fixed stars, as well as the configurations of the Moon, afford means of prognostication, many persons admit ; and they exercise this foreknowledge for their own preservation and comfort, adapting their constitutions to the expected temperature, by cooling and refreshing things for the summer, and by warm things for the winter. They also watch the significations of the fixed stars, to avoid dangerous weather, in making voyages by sea ; and they notice the aspects of the

---

[1] Respecting the effect here asserted to be produced on the magnet by garlick, I have found the following mention in a book called " The Gardener's Labyrinth," printed at London in 1586. " Here also I thought not to ouerpasse the maruellous discord of the adamant-stone and garlike, which the Grœkes name to be an Antipatheia or naturall contrarietie betweene them ; for such is the hatred or contrarietie between these two bodies (lacking both hearing and feeling), that the adamant rather putteth away, than draweth to it, iron, if the same afore be rubbed with garlike ; as Plutarchus hath noted, and, after him, Claudius Ptolemæus. Which matter, examined by diuers learned, and founde the contrarie, caused them to judge, that those skilful men (especially Ptolemie) ment the same to be done with the Egyptian Garlike ; which Dioscorides wrote to be small garlike, and the same sweete in taste, possessing a bewtifull head, tending unto a purple colour. There be which attribute the same to Ophioscoridon, which Antonius Microphonius Biturix, a singular learned man, and wel practised in sundry skilles, uttered this approoued secrete to a friend whom he loued."

In the same book, the " Ophioscoridon " is thus spoken of : " There is another wild garlike which the Greekes name Ophioscoridon ; in English Ramsies ; growing of the owne accord in the fallow fieldes."

Cornelius Agrippa (according to the English translation) has stated that the presence of the diamond also neutralizes the attractive power of the magnet. But as that great magician was somewhat inclined to quibbling, it is not impossible that by the word he uses for " diamond " (viz. adamas) he may mean the adamant or loadstone ; which would reduce his assertion merely to this, that one magnet will counteract another.

Moon, when at the full, in order to direct the copulation of their herds and flocks, and the setting of plants or sewing of seeds : and there is not an individual who considers these general precautions as impossible or unprofitable. Still, however, these same persons withhold their assent to the possibility of applying prescience to particular cases ; such, for instance, as any particular excess or diminution of cold or heat, whether arising out of the peculiar temperament producing the original cold or heat, or from the combination of other properties ; nor do they admit that there are any means of guarding against many of these particular circumstances. And yet, if it be clear that persons, who prepare themselves by cooling things, are less affected by any general heat of the weather, there seems no reason for supposing that a similar preparation would not be equally effectual against any particular conjuncture oppressed by immoderate heat. It appears, however, that this idea, of the impracticability of attaining foreknowledge of particular circumstances, must originate solely in the mere difficulty of the acquirement ; which difficulty is certainly rendered peculiarly arduous by the necessity of conducting the enquiry with the greatest accuracy and precision : and to this it must be added, that, as there is rarely found a person capable of arranging the whole subject so perfectly that no part of the opposing influence can escape his attention, it frequently happens that predictions are not properly regulated by due consideration of that opposing influence, and that the effects are at once considered fully liable to be brought to pass, agreeably to the primary agency and without any intervention. This defect, of not sufficiently considering the opposing influence, has naturally induced an opinion that all future events are entirely unalterable and inevitable. But, since the foreknowledge of particular circumstances, although it may not wholly claim infallibility, seems yet so far practicable as to merit consideration, so the precaution it affords, in particular circumstances, deserves in like manner to be attended to ; and, if it be not of universal advantage, but useful in few instances only, it is still most worthy of estimation, and to be considered of no moderate value. Of this, the Ægyptians seem to have been well aware ; their discoveries of the great faculties of this science have exceeded those of other nations, and they have in all cases combined the medical art with astronomical prognostication. And, had they been of opinion that all expected events are unalterable and not to be averted, they never would have instituted any propitiations, remedies, and preservatives against the influence of the Ambient, whether present or approaching, general or particular. But, by means of the science called by them Medical Mathematics, they combined with the power of prognostication the concurrent secondary influence arising out of the institutions and courses of nature, as well as the contrary influence which might be procured out of nature's variety ; and by means of these they rendered the indicated agency useful and advantageous : since their astronomy pointed out to them the kind of temperament liable to be acted upon, as well as the events about to proceed from the Ambient, and the peculiar influence of those events, while their medical skill made them acquainted with everything suitable or unsuitable to each of the effects to be procured. And it is by this process that remedies for present and preservatives against future disorders are to be acquired : for, without astronomical knowledge, medical aid would be most frequently unavailing; since the same identical remedies are not better calculated for all persons whatsoever, than they are for all diseases whatsoever.[1]

The practicability and utility of prescience having been thus far briefly explained, the ensuing discourse must be proceeded with. It commences, introductorily, with an account of the efficient properties of each of the heavenly bodies, taken from the rules of the ancients, whose observations were founded in nature. And, first, of the influences of the planets and of the Sun and Moon.

CHAPTER IV

THE INFLUENCES OF THE PLANETARY ORBS

THE Sun[2] is found to produce heat and moderate dryness. His magnitude, and the changes which he so evidently makes in the seasons, render his power more plainly perceptible than that of the other heavenly bodies ; since his approach to the zenith of any part of the earth creates a greater degree of heat in that part and proportionately disposes its inhabitants after his own nature.

The Moon principally generates moisture ; her proximity to the earth renders her highly capable of exciting damp vapours, and of thus operating sensibly upon animal bodies by relaxation and putrefaction. She has, however, also a moderate share in the production of heat, in consequence of the illumination she receives from the Sun.

Saturn produces cold and dryness, for he is most remote both from the Sun's heat and from the earth's vapours. But he is more effective in the production of cold than of dryness. And he and the rest of the planets derive their energy from the positions which they hold with regard to the Sun and Moon ; and they are all seen to alter the constitution of the Ambient in various ways.

Mars chiefly causes dryness, and is also strongly heating, by means of his own fiery nature, which is indicated by his colour, and in consequence of his vicinity to the Sun ; the sphere of which is immediately below him.

---

[1] This seems to explain the origin of the old alliance between medicine and astrology, so universally preserved until almost within the last century.

[2] It will be recollected that the Ptolemaic hypothesis considers the Sun as a planetary orb, in consequence of his apparent progress through the zodiac.

Jupiter revolves in an intermediate sphere between the extreme cold of Saturn and the burning heat of Mars, and has consequently a temperate influence : he therefore at once promotes both warmth and moisture. But, owing to the spheres of Mars and the Sun, which lie beneath him, his warmth is predominant : and hence he produces fertilizing breezes.

To Venus also the same temperate quality belongs, although it exists conversely ; since the heat she produces by her vicinity to the Sun is not so great as the moisture which she generates by the magnitude of her light, and by appropriating to herself the moist vapours of the earth, in the same manner that the Moon does.

Mercury sometimes produces dryness, and at other times moisture, and each with equal vigour. His faculty of absorbing moisture and creating dryness proceeds from his situation with regard to the Sun, from which he is at no time far distant in longitude ; and, on the other hand, he produces moisture, because he borders upon the Moon's sphere, which is nearest to the earth ; and, being thus excited by the velocity of his motion with the Sun, he consequently operates rapid changes tending to produce alternately either quality.

CHAPTER V

BENEFICS AND MALEFICS

OF the four temperaments or qualities above mentioned, two are nutritive and prolific, viz. heat and moisture ; by these all matter coalesces and is nourished : the other two are noxious and destructive, viz. dryness and cold ; by these all matter is decayed and dissipated.

Therefore, two of the planets, on account of their temperate quality, and because heat and moisture are predominant in them, are considered by the ancients as benefic, or causers of good : these are Jupiter and Venus. And the Moon also is so considered for the same reasons.

But Saturn and Mars are esteemed of a contrary nature, and malefic, or causers of evil : the first from his excess of cold, the other from his excess of dryness.

The Sun and Mercury are deemed of common influence, and productive either of good or evil in unison with whatever planets they may be connected with.

CHAPTER VI

MASCULINE AND FEMININE

THERE are two primary sexes, male and female ; and the female sex partakes chiefly of moisture. The Moon and Venus are therefore said to be feminine, since their qualities are principally moist.

The Sun, Saturn, Jupiter, and Mars are called masculine. Mercury is common to both genders, because at certain times he produces dryness, and at others moisture, and performs each in an equal ratio.

The stars, however, are also said to be masculine and feminine, by their positions with regard to the Sun. While they are matutine and preceding the Sun, they are masculine ; when vespertine and following the Sun, they become feminine.[1]

And they are further regulated in this respect by their positions with regard to the horizon. From the ascendant to the mid-heaven, or from the angle of the west to the lower heaven, they are considered to be masculine, being then oriental : and in the other two quadrants, feminine, being then occidental.

CHAPTER VII

DIURNAL AND NOCTURNAL

THE day and the night are the visible divisions of time. The day, in its heat and its aptitude for action, is masculine :—the night, in its moisture and its appropriation to rest, feminine.

Hence, again, the Moon and Venus are esteemed to be nocturnal ; the Sun and Jupiter, diurnal ; and Mercury, common ; since in his matutine position he is diurnal, but nocturnal when vespertine.

Of the other two planets, Saturn and Mars, which are noxious, one is considered to be diurnal, and the other nocturnal. Neither of them, however, is allotted to that division of time with which its nature accords (as heat accords with heat), but each is disposed of on a contrary principle : and for this reason, that, although the benefit is increased when a favourable temperament receives an addition of its own nature, yet, the evil arising from a pernicious influence is much mitigated when dissimilar qualities are mingled with that influence. Hence the coldness of Saturn is allotted to the day, to counterbalance its heat ; and the dryness of Mars to the night, to counterbalance its moisture. Thus each of these planets, being moderated by this combination, is placed in a condition calculated to produce a favourable temperament.[2]

---

[1] " Astronomers call the planets matutine, when, being oriental from the Sun, they are above the earth when he rises ; and vespertine, when they set after him." Moxon's Mathematical Dictionary.

[2] Whalley here appends the following note : " To this chapter may be properly added, that a planet is said to be diurnal, when, in a diurnal nativity, above the earth ; and, in a nocturnal nativity, under the earth : but nocturnal, when, in a nocturnal nativity, above the earth ; or, in a diurnal nativity, under the earth."

CHAPTER VIII

THE INFLUENCE OF POSITION WITH REGARD TO THE SUN

THE respective powers of the Moon and of the three superior planets are either augmented or diminished by their several positions with regard to the Sun.

The Moon, during her increase, from her first emerging to her first quarter, produces chiefly moisture; on continuing her increase from her first quarter to her full state of illumination, she causes heat; from her full state to her third quarter she causes dryness; and from her third quarter to her occultation she causes cold.

The planets, when matutine, and from their first emerging until they arrive at their first station, are chiefly productive of moisture; from their first station until they rise at night, of heat; from their rising at night until their second station, of dryness; and from their second station until their occultation, they produce cold.[1]

But it is also sufficiently plain that they must likewise cause, by their intermixture with each other, many varieties of quality in the Ambient: because, although their individual and peculiar influence may for the most part prevail, it will still be more or less varied by the power of the other heavenly bodies configurated with them.

CHAPTER IX

THE INFLUENCE OF THE FIXED STARS

NEXT in succession, it is necessary to detail the natures and properties of the fixed stars; all of which have their respective influences, analogous to the influences of the planets: and those stars which form the constellations of the zodiac require to be first described.

Aries. The stars in the head of Aries possess an influence similar in its effects to that of Mars and Saturn: those in the mouth act similarly to Mercury, and in some degree to Saturn; those in the hinder foot, to Mars; those in the tail, to Venus.

---

[1] Although all the positions mentioned in this paragraph are not applicable to Venus and Mercury, which can never rise at night, that is to say, at sunset, and although the author in the beginning of the chapter speaks only of the Moon and the three superior planets, there yet seems no reason why the orbits of Venus and Mercury should not be similarly divided by their inferior and superior conjunctions, and their greatest elongations.

The following is from Whalley: "The first station, in this chapter mentioned, is when a planet begins to be retrograde; and the second station when, from retrogradation, a planet becomes direct. They" (the planets) "begin to rise at night when in opposition to the Sun."

Taurus. Those stars in Taurus, which are in the abscission of the sign, resemble in their temperament the influence of Venus, and in some degree that of Saturn : those in the Pleiades are like the Moon and Mars. Of the stars in the head, that one of the Hyades which is bright and ruddy, and called Facula,[1] has the same temperament as Mars : the others resemble Saturn, and, partly, Mercury ; and those at the top of the horns are like Mars.

Gemini. The stars in the feet of Gemini have an influence similar to that of Mercury, and moderately to that of Venus.

The bright stars in the thighs are like Saturn : of the two bright stars on the heads, the one, which precedes and is called Apollo,[2] is like Mercury ; the other which follows, called Hercules,[3] is like Mars.

Cancer. The two stars in the eyes of Cancer are of the same influence as Mercury, and are also moderately like Mars. Those in the claws are like Saturn and Mercury. The nebulous mass in the breast, called the Præsepe, has the same efficacy as Mars and the Moon. The two placed on either side of the nebulous mass, and called the Asini, have an influence similar to that of Mars and the Sun.

Leo. Of the stars in Leo, two in the head are like Saturn and partly like Mars. The three in the neck are like Saturn, and in some degree like Mercury. The bright one in the heart, called Regulus,[4] agrees with Mars and Jupiter. Those in the loins, and the bright one in the tail, are like Saturn and Venus : those in the thighs resemble Venus, and, in some degree, Mercury.

Virgo. The stars in the head of Virgo, and that at the top of the southern wing, operate like Mercury and somewhat like Mars : the other bright stars in the same wing, and those about the girdle, resemble Mercury in their influence, and also Venus moderately. The bright one in the northern wing, called Vindemiator, is of the same influence as Saturn and Mercury : that called Spica Virginis is like Venus and partly Mars : those at the points of the feet and at the bottom of the garments are like Mercury, and also Mars, moderately.

Libra.[5] Those stars at the points of the claws of Scorpio operate

---

[1] The little Torch ; now known by the name of Aldebaran.
[2] Castor.   [3] Pollux.   [4] Cor Leonis.
[5] Called by the ancients χηλαι, Chelæ, or the *claws* of Scorpio ; which sign they made to consist of 60 degrees, omitting Libra. Thus Virgil in the first Georgic, line 33, &c.

> Quo locus Erigonen inter, Chelasque sequentes
> Panditur : ipse tibi jam brachïa contrahit ardens
> Scorpius, et cœli justâ plus parte reliquit.

Ovid, likewise, takes the following notice of Scorpio :—

> Porrigit in spatium signorum membra duorum.   *Met.* 2, l. 198.

like Jupiter and Mercury : those in the middle of the claws, like Saturn, and in some degree like Mars.

Scorpio. The bright stars in the front of the body of Scorpio have an effect similar to that produced by the influence of Mars, and partly to that produced by Saturn : the three in the body itself, the middle one of which, called Antares,[1] is ruddy and more luminous, are similar to Mars and moderately to Jupiter : those in the joints of the tail are like Saturn and partly like Venus : those in the sting, like Mercury and Mars. The nebula is like Mars and the Moon.

Sagittarius. The stars at the point of the arrow in Sagittarius have influence similar to that of Mars and the Moon : those on the bow, and at the grasp of the hand, act like Jupiter and Mars : the nebula in the face is like the Sun and Mars : those in the waist and in the back resemble Jupiter, and also Mercury moderately : those in the feet, Jupiter and Saturn : the four-sided figure in the tail is similar to Venus, and in some degree to Saturn.

Capricorn. The stars in the horns of Capricorn have efficacy similar to that of Venus, and partly to that of Mars. The stars in the mouth are like Saturn, and partly like Venus : those in the feet and in the belly act in the same manner as Mars and Mercury : those in the tail are like Saturn and Jupiter.

Aquarius. The stars in the shoulders of Aquarius operate like Saturn and Mercury ; those in the left hand and in the face do the same : those in the thighs have an influence more consonant with that of Mercury, and in a less degree with that of Saturn : those in the stream of water have power similar to that of Saturn, and, moderately, to that of Jupiter.

Pisces. Those stars in Pisces, which are in the head of the southern fish, have the same influence as Mercury, and, in some degree, as Saturn : those in the body are like Jupiter and Mercury : those in the tail and in the southern line are like Saturn, and, moderately, like Mercury. In the northern fish, those on its body and back-bone resemble Jupiter, and also Venus in some degree : those in the northern line are like Saturn and Jupiter ; and the bright star in the knot acts like Mars, and moderately like Mercury.[2]

---

[1] Adams's Treatise on the Globes calls this star " Kalb al Akrab, or the Scorpion's heart," and adds, that " the word Antares (if it is not a corruption) has no signification." But it should be observed that Ptolemy states that this star partakes of the nature of Mars : it seems therefore not improbable that Antares may be a regular Greek word, compounded of αντι *pro* and αρης *Mars*, and signifying *Mars's deputy*, or *lieutenant*, or *one acting for Mars*.

[2] Salmon, in his " Horæ Mathematicæ, or Soul of Astrology " (printed by Dawks, 1679) divides each sign of the zodiac into six faces of five degrees each, " because that in every sign there are various stars of differing natures " ;

CHAPTER X

CONSTELLATIONS NORTH OF THE ZODIAC

THE constellations north of the zodiac have their respective influences, analogous to those of the planets, existing in the mode described in the following list.

Ursa Minor. The bright stars in this constellation are like Saturn, and in some degree like Venus.

Ursa Major is like Mars, but the nebula under the tail resembles the Moon and Venus in its influence.

Draco. The bright stars operate like Saturn and Mars.

Cepheus is like Saturn and Jupiter.

Bootes is like Mercury and Saturn ; but the bright and ruddy star, called Arcturus, is like Mars and Jupiter.

Corona Borealis is like Venus and Mercury.

Hercules (or the Kneeler) is like Mercury.

Lyra is like Venus and Mercury.

Cygnus is like Venus and Mercury.

Cassiopeia is like Saturn and Venus.

Perseus is like Jupiter and Saturn : but the nebula, in the hilt of the sword, is like Mars and Mercury.

Auriga. The bright stars are like Mars and Mercury.

Serpentarius is like Saturn, and moderately like Venus.

Serpens is like Saturn and Mars.

Sagitta is like Saturn, and moderately like Venus.

Aquila is like Mars and Jupiter.

Delphinus is like Saturn and Mars.

Equus (or Pegasus). The bright stars are like Mars and Mercury.

Andromeda is like Venus.

Delta (or the Triangle) is like Mercury.

and he gives a particular description to each face, depending on its ascension or culmination. This seems an attempt to adapt Ptolemy's signification of the several stars, composing the different signs, to some general rule or mode of judgment : but it does not merit the implicit assent of astrologers. It is understood that Salmon was not the inventor of this division of the signs into faces, but that it came originally from the Arabian schools.

CHAPTER XI

CONSTELLATIONS SOUTH OF THE ZODIAC

THE influences of the constellations south of the zodiac, existing in a similar mode, are as follows :—

Piscis Australis. The bright star in the mouth is of the same influence as Venus and Mercury.

Cetus is like Saturn.

Orion. The stars on the shoulders operate similarly to Mars and Mercury ; and the other bright stars to Jupiter and Saturn.

Fluvius (or *Eridanus*). The last bright one is of the same influence as Jupiter ; the rest are like Saturn.

Lepus is like Saturn and Mercury.

Canis. The bright star in the mouth is like Jupiter, and partly like Mars : the others are like Venus.

Procyon.[1] The bright star is like Mercury, and in some degree like Mars.

Hydrus. The bright stars are like Saturn and Venus.

Crater is like Venus, and in some degree like Mercury.

Corvus is like Mars and Saturn.

Argo. The bright stars are like Saturn and Jupiter.

Centaurus. The stars in the human part of the figure are of the same influence as Venus and Mercury ; the bright stars in the horse's part are like Venus and Jupiter.

Lupus. The bright stars are like Saturn, and partly like Mars.

Ara is like Venus, and also Mercury in some degree.

Corona Australis. The bright stars are like Saturn and Jupiter.

The respective influences of the several stars have been observed by the ancients to operate in conformity with the mode pointed out in the foregoing distributions.[2]

---

[1] Canis Minor.

[2] "Of the fixed stars in general," Whalley says, " Those of the greatest magnitude are the most efficacious ; and those in, or near, the ecliptic, more powerful than those more remote from it. Those with north latitude and declination affect us most. Those in the zenith, influence more than others, more remote. Likewise such as are in partial conjunction with, or in the antiscions of any planets, or which rise and set, or culminate with any planet, or are beheld by any planet, have an increase of power : but of themselves the fixed stars emit no rays."

CHAPTER XII

THE ANNUAL SEASONS

THE year comprises four seasons; spring, summer, autumn, and winter; of these, the spring partakes chiefly of moisture, for on the dissipation of cold and recommencement of warmth, an expansion of the fluids takes place : the summer is principally hot, owing to the Sun's nearest approach to the zenith : the autumn is principally dry, because the recent heat has absorbed the moisture : and the winter is chiefly cold, the Sun being then at his farthest distance from the zenith.

The beginning of the whole zodiacal circle (which in its nature as a circle can have no other beginning, nor end, capable of being determined), is therefore assumed to be the sign of Aries, which commences at the vernal equinox :[1] since the moisture of spring forms a primary beginning in the zodiac, analogous to the beginning of all animal life ; which, in its first age of existence, abounds principally in moisture : the spring, too, like the first age of animal life, is soft and tender ; it is therefore suitably placed as the opening of the year, and is followed by the other seasons in appropriate succession. The summer comes second, and, in its vigour and heat, agrees with the second age of animals ; the prime of life, and the period most abounding in heat. Again, the age when the prime of life has passed away, and in which decay prepares to advancě, is chiefly abundant in dryness, and corresponds to the autumn. And the final period of old age, hastening to dissolution, is principally cold, like the winter.

CHAPTER XIII

THE INFLUENCE OF THE FOUR ANGLES

THE angles are the four cardinal points of the horizon, whence are derived the general names of the winds. With respect to their qualities, it is to be observed that the eastern point, or angle of the ascendant,

---

[1] This sentence shows the futility of the objection raised against astrology (and mentioned in the Preface to this translation) that the signs have changed and are changing places. It is clear from this sentence that Ptolemy ascribes to the 30 degrees after the vernal equinox, that influence which he has herein mentioned to belong to Aries ; to the next 30 degrees, the influence herein said to belong to Taurus ; and so of the rest of the zodiac. We should rather say that the stars have changed places, than that the parts of heaven, in which they were once situated, have done so. Ptolemy himself seems to have foreseen this groundless objection of the moderns, and has written, in the 25th chapter of this book, what ought completely to have prevented it. It has certainly been one of the misfortunes of astrology to be attacked by people entirely ignorant of its principles.

is chiefly dry in its nature; because, on the Sun's arrival therein, the damps occasioned by the night begin to be dried up : and all winds blowing from that quarter, under the common name of east winds, are arid and free from moisture.

The southern point, or angle of the mid-heaven, is the most hot ; because the Sun's meridan position, which produces greater warmth and heat, declines (in this part of the earth) towards the south. The winds, therefore, which blow from that quarter, and are commonly called south winds, are hot and rarefying.

The western point, or occidental angle, is moist ; because, when the Sun is there, the moisture, which had been overpowered during the day, recommences its operation : and the winds proceeding from thence, and commonly called west winds, are light and damp.

The northern point, or angle of the lower heaven, is the most cold ; for the Sun's meridian position in this part of the earth is far removed from it in declination : and all winds thence proceeding, under the common name of north winds, are cold and frosty.

It will, of course, be seen that a thorough acquaintance with the foregoing matters is essential in order to acquire the faculty of distinguishing temperaments in every shape and variation : since it is sufficiently obvious that the effective influence of the stars must be greatly diversified by the constitutions of the seasons, as well as those of the ages of life, and of the angles ; and also that the stars have a much stronger influence on any constitution, when there may not be in it any tendency contrary to their own, as the whole influence is then entire and unalloyed. For example, stars effecting heat operate more vigorously in constitutions of heat ; and those effecting moisture in constitutions of moisture. On the other hand, should a tendency, contrary to their own, exist in any constitution, the stars accordingly become less efficacious ; in consequence of being attempered and mixed with that contrary tendency : and this happens, for instance, when stars effecting heat are attempered by constitutions of cold, or stars producing moisture by constitutions of dryness. The influence of every star is thus modified by the proportionate admixture presented by constitutions of a nature different from its own.

In succession to the previous instructions, the following description of the natural and peculiar properties of the signs of the zodiac is annexed : the general temperaments of the signs are analogous to those of the seasons, which are respectively established under each sign, but they have, also, certain peculiar energies, arising from their familiarity with the Sun, the Moon, and the stars, which shall be hereafter specified; —and the simple and unmixed influences existing in the signs, as considered only in themselves and with regard to each other, will be first stated.

CHAPTER XIV

TROPICAL, EQUINOCTIAL, FIXED, AND BICORPOREAL SIGNS

AMONG the twelve signs, some are termed tropical, others equinoctial, others fixed, and others bicorporeal.

The tropical signs are two : viz. the first thirty degrees after the summer solstice, which compose the sign of Cancer ; and the first thirty degrees after the winter solstice, composing the sign of Capricorn. These are called *tropical,* because the Sun, after he has arrived at their first points, seems to *turn,* and to change his course towards a contrary latitude ;[1] causing summer by the *turn* he makes in Cancer, and winter by that which he makes in Capricorn.

There are also two equinoctial signs : Aries, the first after the vernal equinox ; and Libra, the first after the autumnal equinox : they are so called, because the Sun, when in the first point of either, makes the day and night equal.

Of the remaining eight signs, four are fixed, and four bicorporeal. Those signs, which severally follow immediately after the two tropical and the two equinoctial signs, are termed fixed, because, during the Sun's presence in them, the cold, heat, moisture or dryness, of the season, which commenced on his arrival in the preceding tropical or equinoctial sign, is then more firmly established : not, however, that the temperament of the season has in itself actually increased in vigour, but, having continued for some time in operation, it then renders all things more strongly affected by its influence.

The bicorporeal signs severally follow the fixed signs ; and, being thus intermediately placed between the fixed and the tropical signs, they participate in the constitutional properties of both, from their first to their last degrees.

CHAPTER XV

MASCULINE AND FEMININE SIGNS

AGAIN, among the twelve signs, six are called masculine and diurnal, and six feminine and nocturnal. They are arranged in alternate order, one after the other, as the day is followed by the night, and as the male is coupled with the female.

The commencement, it has been already said, belongs to Aries ; since the moisture of the spring forms an introduction for the other seasons. And, as the male sex governs, and the active principle takes

---

[1] In other words, the Sun then begins to diminish his declination, which, at the first points of the said signs, is at its greatest amount.

precedence of the passive, the signs of Aries and Libra are consequently considered to be masculine and diurnal. These signs describe the equinoctial circle, and from them proceed the principal variation, and most powerful agitation, of all things. The signs immediately following them are feminine and nocturnal; and the rest are consecutively arranged as masculine and feminine, by alternate order.

Masculine or feminine qualities are, however, by some persons, attributed to the signs by means of a different arrangement, and by making the sign ascending (which is also called the horoscope) the first of the masculine signs. They also consider the first tropical sign to be that in which the Moon is posited, because she undergoes more frequent and rapid changes and variations than any other heavenly body; and it is by a similar mode of reasoning that they establish the horoscope as the first masculine sign, on account of its being more immediately under the Sun. Again, certain of these persons likewise allow the alternate arrangement of the signs; while there are, again, others who do not admit it; but, instead thereof, divide the whole zodiac into quadrants, and denominate those between the ascendant and the mid-heaven, and between the western angle and the lower haven, oriental and masculine; and the other two quadrants, occidental and feminine.

There have also been other additional appellations bestowed on the signs, in consequence of their apparent formations and figures: they have been called quadrupedal, terrestrial, imperial, fruitful, and have received various other distinguishing epithets of the same sort; but these distinctions seem too unimportant to be even enumerated here, since their origin is obvious, and since, should they ever be thought serviceable towards the inference of future effects, they may be easily applied without the aid of further instruction.

CHAPTER XVI

MUTUAL CONFIGURATIONS OF THE SIGNS

THERE are certain familiarities or connections between different parts of the zodiac; and the chief of these is that which exists between such parts as are configurated with each other.

This mutual configuration attaches to all parts diametrically distant from each other, containing between them two right angles, or six signs, or a hundred and eighty degrees: it also exists in all parts at the triangular distance from each other, containing between them one right angle and a third, or four signs, or a hundred and twenty degrees; also, in all parts at the quadrate distance from each other, containing between them exactly one right angle, or three signs, or ninety degrees; and, also, in all parts at the hexagonal distance from each other, containing between them two-thirds of a right angle, or two signs, or sixty

degrees.[1] These several distances are taken for the following reasons :
the distance by diameter, however, is in itself sufficiently clear, and
requires no further explanation ; but, as to the rest, after the dia-
metrical points have been connected by a straight line, AB ; the space
of the two right angles, contained on the diameter, is then to be divided
into aliquot parts of the two greatest denominations ; that is to say,
into halves, AFC, CFB, and into thirds, AFD, DFE, EFB : there will
then be provided for the third part (AD) a super-proportion (DC),
equal to its own half ; and for the half (AC) a super-proportion (CE),
equal to its own third part ; so that the division into two aliquot parts,

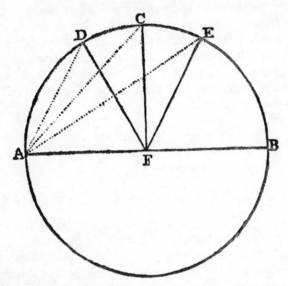

AC, CB, will make the quartile distance AC ; and the division into
three aliquot parts, AD, DE, EB, will make the sextile distance AD,
and the trinal distance AE. The respective super-proportions (on either
side of the intermediate quartile AC, formed by the one right angle
AFC), will also again make the quartile AC (if there be added to the
sextile, AD, the super-proportion DC, equal to the half of the sextile),
and the trine AE (if there be added to the quartile AC the super-proportion CE, equal to the third part of the quartile).

Of these configurations, the trine and the sextile are each called

---

[1] Whalley, in his note upon this chapter, seems to have been surprised that
no mention is made here by Ptolemy of the *conjunction ;* but he overlooked
the fact that the chapter treats only of parts of the zodiac configurated *with
each other ;* and that it was not possible for Ptolemy to conceive how any part
could be configurated *with itself.* It is, therefore, by no means wonderful
that the conjunction is not inserted here along with the rest of the aspects ;
although it is frequently adverted to in subsequent chapters, and its efficacy
particularly described.

harmonious, because they are constituted between signs of the same kind; being formed between either all feminine or all masculine signs. The opposition and quartile are considered to be discordant, because they are configurations made between signs not of the same kind, but of different natures and sexes.[1]

CHAPTER XVII

SIGNS COMMANDING AND OBEYING

ANY two signs configurated with each other at an equal distance from the same, or from either equinoctial point, are termed commanding and obeying, because the ascensional and descensional times of the one are equal to those of the other, and both describe equal parallels.

The signs in the summer semicircle are commanding; those in the winter semicircle, obeying: for, when the Sun is present in the former, he makes the day longer than the night; and, when in the latter, he produces the contrary effect.

CHAPTER XVIII

SIGNS BEHOLDING EACH OTHER, AND OF EQUAL POWER

ANY two signs, equally distant from either tropical sign, are equal to each other in power; because the Sun, when present in one, makes day and night, and the divisions of time, respectively equal in duration to those which he produces when present in the other. Such signs are also said to behold each other, as well for the foregoing reasons, as because each of them rises from one and the same part of the horizon, and sets in one and the same part.[2]

---

[1] From the tenor of this chapter it was formerly doubted whether the author intended to admit in his theory only zodiacal aspects, and to reject those which are called mundane; but Placidus has referred to the 4th Chapter of the 8th Book of the Almagest (which will be found in the Appendix to this translation) to prove that Ptolemy distinctly taught two kinds of aspect; one in the zodiac and one in the world. Whalley quotes the opinion of Placidus, which he says is farther confirmed by the 12th Chapter of the 3rd Book of this very treatise, where it is stated that the ascendant and the eleventh house are in sextile to each other; the ascendant and the mid-heaven in quartile; the ascendant and the ninth house in trine; and the ascendant and the occidental angle in opposition; all which certainly seems to be applicable to mundane aspects in particular.

[2] Whalley has a very lengthy note upon this and the preceding chapter, to show that Ptolemy here speaks of zodiacal parallels, or parallels of declination, and to point out the necessity of observing a planet's latitude, in order to ascertain its true parallels. It is, however, to be recollected, that the

CHAPTER XIX

SIGNS INCONJUNCT

ALL signs, between which there does not exist any familiarity in any of the modes above specified, are inconjunct and separated.

For instance, all signs are inconjunct which are neither commanding nor obeying, and not beholding each other nor of equal power, as well as all signs which contain between them the space of one sign only, or the space of five signs, and which do not at all share in any of the four prescribed configurations : viz. the opposition, the trine, the quartile, and the sextile. All parts which are distant from each other in the space of one sign only are considered inconjunct, because they are averted, as it were, from each other ; and because, although the said space between them may extend into two signs, the whole only contains an angle equal to that of one sign : all parts distant from each other in the space of five signs are also considered inconjunct, because they divide the whole circle into unequal parts ; whereas the spaces contained in the configurations above-mentioned, viz. the opposition, trine, quartile, and sextile, produce aliquot divisions.[1]

---

parallels now alluded to are distinct from the *mundane parallels*, which are equal distances from the horizon or meridian, and are considered by Ptolemy in the 14th and 15th Chapters of the 3rd Book of this work ; although not under the express name of mundane parallels.

[1] It has never been very clearly shown how the followers of Ptolemy have reconciled the new aspects [called the semiquadrate, quintile, sesquiquadrate, biquintile, &c.] with the *veto* pronounced in this chapter. Kepler is said to have invented them, and they have been universally adopted ; even Placidus, who has applied Ptolemy's doctrine to practice better than any other writer, has availed himself of them,[2] and, if the nativities published by him are to be credited, he has fully established their importance.

Salmon, in his "Horæ Mathematicæ," beforementioned, gives a long dissertation (from p. 403 to p. 414) on the old Ptolemaic aspects, illustrative of their foundation in nature and in mathematics ; and, although his conclusions are not quite satisfactorily drawn, some of his arguments would seem appropriate, if he had but handled them more fully and expertly ; particularly where he says that the aspects are derived " from the aliquot parts of a circle, wherein observe that, although the zodiac may have many more aliquot parts than these four (the sextile, quartile, trine, and opposition), yet those other aliquot parts of the circle, or 360 degrees, will not make an aliquot division of the signs also, which in this design was sought to answer, as well in the number 12, as in the number 360." The passage in which he endeavours to show that they are authorized by their projection, also deserves attention.

All Salmon's arguments, however, in support of the old Ptolemaic aspects, militate against the new Keplerian ones ; and so does the following extract

[2] Except the semiquadrate, which he has not at all noticed.

CHAPTER XX

HOUSES OF THE PLANETS

THOSE stars which are denominated planetary orbs have particular familiarity with certain places in the zodiac, by means of parts designated as their houses, and also by their triplicities, exaltations, terms, and so forth.

The nature of their familiarity by houses is as follows :

Cancer and Leo are the most northerly of all the twelve signs ; they approach nearer than the other signs to the zenith of this part of the earth, and thereby cause warmth and heat : they are consequently appropriated as houses for the two principal and greater luminaries ; Leo for the Sun, as being masculine ; and Cancer for the Moon, as being feminine. It has hence resulted, that the semicircle from Leo to Capricorn has been ordained solar, and the semicircle from Aquarius to Cancer, lunar ; in order that each planet might occupy one sign in each semicircle, and thus have one of its houses configurated with the Sun and the other with the Moon, conformably to the motions of its own sphere, and the peculiar properties of its nature.

Saturn, therefore, since he is cold and inimical to heat, moving also in a superior orbit most remote from the luminaries, occupies the signs opposite to Cancer and Leo : these are Aquarius and Capricorn ; and they are assigned to him in consideration of their cold and wintry nature ; and because the configuration by opposition does not co-operate towards the production of good.[1]

Jupiter has a favourable temperament, and is situated beneath the sphere of Saturn ; he therefore occupies the next two signs, Sagittarius

from the " Astrological Discourse " of Sir Christopher Heydon : " For thus, amongst all ordinate planes that may be inscribed, there are two whose sides, joined together, have pre-eminence to take up a semicircle, but only the hexagon, quadrate, and equilateral triangle, answering to the sextile, quartile, and trine irradiated. The subtense, therefore, of a sextile aspect consisteth of two signs, which, joined to the subtense of a trine, composed of four, being regular and equilateral, take up six signs, which is a complete semicircle. In like manner, the sides of a quadrate inscribed, subtending three signs, twice reckoned, do occupy likewise the mediety of a circle. And what those figures are before said to perform " (that is, to take up a semicircle) " either doubled or joined together, may also be truly ascribed unto the opposite aspect by itself ; for that the diametral line, which passeth from the place of conjunction to the opposite point, divideth a circle into two equal parts : the like whereof cannot be found in any other inscripts ; for example, the *side of a regular pentagon* " (the quintile) " *subtendeth 72 degrees, of an octagon* " (the semiquadrate) " *but 45 ; the remainders of which arcs, viz. 108 and 135 degrees, are not subtended by the sides of any ordinate figure.*"

[1] Saturn being also malefic in his nature.

and Pisces. These signs are airy and fruitful, in consequence of their trinal distance from the houses of the luminaries, which distance harmonises with the operation of good.

Mars is dry in nature, and beneath the sphere of Jupiter : he takes the next two signs, of a nature similar to his own, viz. Aries and Scorpio, whose relative distances from the houses of the luminaries are injurious and discordant.

Venus, possessing a favourable temperament, and placed beneath the sphere of Mars, takes the next two signs, Taurus and Libra. These are of a fruitful nature, and preserve harmony by the sextile distance ; and this planet is never more than two signs distant from the Sun.

Mercury never has greater distance from the Sun than the space of one sign, and is beneath all the other planets : hence he is placed nearest to both luminaries, and the remaining two signs, Gemini and Virgo, are allotted to him.[1]

CHAPTER XXI

THE TRIPLICITIES

THE familiarity existing by triplicity arises in the following mode :

The triplicity preserves accordance with an equilateral triangle, and the whole zodiacal orbit is defined by three circles, viz. that of the equinox, and those of the two tropics ; the twelve signs are, therefore, distributed among four equilateral triangles.

The first triangle, or triplicity, is formed by three masculine signs, Aries, Leo, and Sagittarius, having the Sun, Jupiter, and Mars as lords by house. Mars, however, being contrary in condition to the solar influence, this triplicity receives, as its lords, only Jupiter and the Sun. By day, therefore, the Sun claims the principal co-regency of it, and Jupiter by night. Aries is on the equinoctial circle, Leo on the summer, and Sagittarius on the winter circle. This triplicity is principally northern, owing to the concurrent dominion of Jupiter, who is fruitful and airy, and expressly connected with winds proceeding from the north ; it is, however, also north-west, in consequence of being, in

---

[1] The planets, having two houses, are said to be more powerful in one by day and in the other by night : thus,

Saturn's day house is Aquarius,		his night house Capricorn		
Jupiter's	——	Sagittarius	——	Pisces
Mar's	——	Aries	——	Scorpio
Venus's	——	Taurus	——	Libra
Mercury's	——	Gemini	——	Virgo

The above is from Whalley ; but the same disposition is to be found in all modern astrological writers.

some degree, combined with the west by means of the house of Mars, who introduces western breezes and the feminine qualities of that quarter, in consequence of his lunar condition.[1]

The second triplicity, formed by Taurus, Virgo, and Capricorn, is allotted to the dominion of the Moon and Venus, since it consists of feminine signs. The Moon rules it by night, and Venus by day. Taurus is on the summer circle, Virgo on the equinoctial, and Capricorn on the winter. This triplicity is southern, in consequence of the dominion of Venus, whose warm and moist influence produces south winds : it, however, additionally receives a mixture of the east, by means of Saturn ; for, as Capricorn is the house of that planet, and an eastern sign, Saturn becomes effective of winds from that quarter, and furnishes this triplicity with a mixture of the east, with which quarter he is further connected by means of his solar condition.[2]

The third triplicity is composed of Gemini, Libra, and Aquarius, masculine signs. It holds connection with Saturn and Mercury by containing their houses, and is therefore attributed to them, and not to Mars, to which planet it bears no relation. Saturn rules it by day, owing to his condition,[3] and Mercury by night. Gemini is on the summer circle, Libra on the equinoctial, and Aquarius on the winter. This triplicity is principally eastern, by the influence of Saturn ; but it becomes north-east by receiving also a mixture of the north from the condition of Jupiter, with which planet Saturn has, in this respect, a diurnal familiarity.[4]

The fourth triplicity, formed by Cancer, Scorpio, and Pisces, is left to the remaining planet, Mars, who has right in it by means of his house, Scorpio. But, as the signs which compose this triplicity are feminine, the Moon by night and Venus by day, through their feminine condition, govern it, together with Mars. Cancer is on the summer circle, Scorpio on the winter, and Pisces on the equinoctial. This triplicity is western, in consequence of the government of the Moon and Mars ; but it is also blended with the south by the joint dominion of Venus, and therefore becomes south-west.

---

[1] The "lunar condition" here spoken of refers to the position of Aries (Mars's house) in the lunar semicircle.

[2] Capricorn being in the solar semicircle.

[3] The reason for making Saturn diurnal lord of this triplicity may be found in Chap. vii.

[4] This familiarity seems to arise from the sextile aspect between Aquarius, the diurnal house of Saturn, and Sagittarius, the diurnal house of Jupiter.

CHAPTER XXII

EXALTATIONS

THAT which is termed the exaltation of the planets is considered by the following rules :

The Sun on his entrance into Aries is then passing into the higher and more northern semicircle ; but, on his entrance into Libra, into the more southern and lower one : his exaltation, therefore, is determined to be in Aries, as, when present in that sign, he begins to lengthen the days, and the influence of his heating nature increases at the same time. His fall is placed in Libra, for the converse reasons.

Saturn on the contrary, in order to preserve his station opposite to the Sun, in this respect, as well as in regard to their respective houses, obtains his exaltation in Libra, and his fall in Aries : since, in all cases, the increase of heat must be attended by a diminution of cold, and the increase of cold by a diminution of heat.

The Mood, again, after conjunction with the Sun in Aries, the seat of his exaltation, makes her first appearance, and begins to augment her light in Taurus, the first sign of her own triplicity, which is consequently ascribed to be her exaltation ; while Scorpio, the opposite sign, is her fall.

Jupiter, since he is efficacious in exciting fruitful breezes from the north, and since he becomes most northerly, and augments his peculiar influence when in Cancer, accordingly obtains his exaltation in that sign, and his fall in Capricorn.

Mars possesses a fiery nature, which receives its greatest intensity in Capricorn, in which sign this planet becomes most southerly ; his exaltation is therefore placed in Capricorn, in opposition to that of Jupiter, and his fall in Cancer.

Venus is of a moist nature, and becomes chiefly moist when in Pisces. Under that sign a dampness begins to be perceptible in the atmosphere, and Venus, from being in that sign, derives an augmentation of her own proper influence : her exaltation is consequently placed therein, and her fall in Virgo.

Mercury is of a nature opposite to that of Venus, and is more dry : in opposition to her, therefore, he takes his exaltation in Virgo, in which sign the autumnal dryness makes its first appearance ; and he receives his fall in Pisces.

CHAPTER XXIII

THE DISPOSITION OF THE TERMS[1]

THERE are two methods of disposing the terms of the planets, in reference to the dominion of the triplicities; one is Ægyptian, the other Chaldaic.

But the Ægyptian method preserves no regular distribution, neither in point of successive order nor in point of quantity.

In point of order it is defective, since it, in some instances, allots the first degrees of a sign to the lord of the house, in others to the lord of the triplicity, and in others again to the lord of the exaltation. By selecting examples this failure in order will easily be seen; for instance, if the order were regulated by the government of houses, for what reason should Saturn take the first degrees in Libra, since that sign is the house of Venus? or why should Jupiter take them in Aries, which is the house of Mars? If the government of triplicities were followed, for what reason should Mercury take the first degrees in Capricorn, which is in the triplicity ruled by Venus? If the government by exaltations, why should Mars take the first degrees in Cancer? that sign being the exaltation of Jupiter. And if the order were regulated even by considering the planet which possesses most of these dignities in the sign, for what reason should Mercury take the first degrees in Aquarius, in which sign he rules only by triplicity, and why not Saturn, who has government in it by house, as well as by triplicity? or why in short should Mercury, who does not possess any kind of dominion in Capricorn, receive the first degrees in that sign also? The same want of order is abundantly evident in the rest of the distribution.

An equal irregularity exists in the respective quantities of degrees allotted by the Ægyptians to the several terms of the planets. For it is by no means a proper nor sufficient demonstration of accuracy that the aggregate sum of all the numbers of every single planet amounts to the precise total requiring to be divided into portions of time; [2] since, even if it be admitted that this total, collected from every single star, is correctly asserted by the Ægyptians, it may still be objected that the same total, so collected by them, may be found in many other ways by

---

[1] In reference to the terms of the planets, Placidus has these words (according to Cooper's translation) : " The dignity of the planets in the signs and their parts, which are called the bounds and terminations " (*quasi*, terms), " have a real and natural foundation; to wit, the powerful aspect or proportional influxes to the movable points in which the stars begin to produce the primary qualities. So that, according to those things we have explained in the philosophy of the heavens, these are found to agree so well with the Ægyptian boundaries " (terms), " that they are highly deserving of admiration."

[2] This total is the 360 degrees of the zodiac, requiring to be divided according to correspondent portions of the equator; by which all time is reckoned.

interchanging the numbers in a sign. There are persons also who con-tend that in every latitude the same space of time is occupied in ascension by every star ; this, however, is manifestly wrong : for, in the first place, these persons are guided by the vulgar opinion of the plane heights of ascension, which is totally foreign to truth, and according to which, in the parallel of Lower Ægypt, the signs of Virgo and Libra would ascend each in thirty-eight degrees and a third,[1] and Leo and Scorpio each in thirty-five degrees ; when it is, on the contrary, shown by the Tables,[2] that the latter two signs occupy in their several ascensions more than thirty-five degrees each, but Virgo and Libra less. It should further be observed, that those who support this opinion seem (by so doing) not only to dispute the quantity of the terms most gener-ally received, but to be driven also to the necessity of falsifying many points ; since (as it is indispensable to keep to the same total amount of all the terms together) they make use of parts of degrees ; but even that contrivance does not enable them to reach the true point.

The old terms, admitted by many persons on the authority of former tradition, are as follows :

THE TERMS ACCORDING TO THE ÆGYPTIANS

Aries			Taurus			Gemini			Cancer			Leo			Virgo		
Jupiter	6	6	Ven.	8	8	Mer	6	6	Mars	7	7	Jup.	6	6	Mer.	7	7
Venus	6	12	Mer.	6	14	Jup.	6	12	Ven.	6	13	Ven.	5	11	Ven.	10	17
Mercury	8	20	Jup.	8	22	Ven.	5	17	Mer.	6	19	Sat.	7	18	Jup.	4	21
Mars	5	25	Sat.	5	27	Mars	7	24	Jup.	7	26	Mer.	6	24	Mars	7	28
Saturn	5	30	Mars	3	30	Sat.	6	30	Sat.	4	30	Mars	6	30	Sat.	2	30

Libra			Scorpio			Sagittarius			Capricorn			Aquarius			Pisces		
Saturn	6	6	Mars	7	7	Jup.	12	12	Mer.	7	7	Mer.	7	7	Ven.	12	12
Mercury	8	14	Ven.	4	11	Ven.	5	17	Jup.	7	14	Ven.	6	13	Jup.	4	16
Jupiter	7	21	Mer.	8	19	Mer.	4	21	Ven.	8	22	Jup.	7	20	Mer.	3	19
Venus	7	28	Jup.	5	24	Sat.	5	26	Sat.	4	26	Mars	5	25	Mars	9	28
Mars	2	30	Sat.	6	30	Mars	4	30	Mars	4	30	Sat.	5	30	Sat.	2	30

[1] The degrees here mentioned are degrees of the equator.

[2] See, in the Appendix, an extract from these tables ; the whole of which are to be found in the Almagest.

Thus, by the Ægyptian distribution, it appears that the total numbers of the degrees for each planet, added together, make 360 :—viz. for Saturn 57, Jupiter 79, Mars 66, Venus 82, and Mercury 76.

The method of the Chaldæans contains a certain simplicity of arrangement as to quantity, and preserves an order of succession rather more comformable to the dominion of the triplicities. It is, nevertheless, highly imperfect, as may be easily discovered even without being pointed out : for in the first triplicity (which the Chaldæans also attribute to the same signs ; viz. Aries, Leo, and Sagittarius), Jupiter, the lord of the triplicity, takes the first degrees ; Venus, who rules the next triplicity, follows him ; after her, in succession, are Saturn and Mercury, the lords of the triplicity of Gemini ; and lastly Mars, lord of the remaining triplicity. In the second triplicity (also allotted to the same signs, viz. Taurus, Virgo, and Capricorn), Venus stands first ; next to her, Saturn and Mercury ; after them Mars, and Jupiter last. In the other two triplicities a similar order of succession is closely followed ; and with respect to the third triplicity, which is ascribed to two lords, viz. to Saturn and Mercury, Saturn is placed first in order by day and Mercury by night.

The quantity of degrees allotted to each planet is also simply regulated in the Chaldaic method ; it diminishes in graduation from the quantity given to the planet first in order, so that each successive planet takes one degree less than that which preceded it. Thus the first planet takes eight degrees, the second seven, the third six, the fourth five, and the fifth four. By this arrangement the degrees of Saturn amount by day to 78, and by night to 66 ; the degrees of Jupiter to 72, of Mars to 69, of Venus to 75, and of Mercury by day to 66, and by night to 78—the whole amounting to 360.

Of these two distributions of the terms, that of the Ægyptians seems more to be relied on than the other ; since it has been handed down and recommended in the writings of the Ægyptian authors, and also because the degrees of the terms, in nativities rectified by them as examples, are universally in accordance with this distribution ; while, on the other hand, neither the order nor the number of the Chaldaic method has ever been recorded or explained by any writer—not even by the writers of that very nation : the accuracy of that method is consequently doubtful, and its irregularity as to the order of placing the planets is widely open to censure.

There is, however, an ancient writing which has fallen into the author's possession, and which gives a rational and consistent account of the nature of the terms ; of the order in which they are to be taken, and of the quantity belonging to each. It will be found in the subsequent chapter.

CHAPTER XXIV

THE TERMS ACCORDING TO PTOLEMY

IN arranging the order in which the planets take their terms in each sign, their exaltations, triplicities, and houses, are taken into consideration ; and whatever planet, whether benefic or malefic, may possess two rights of dominion in one and the same sign, such planet is universally placed first in order in that sign. In other cases, however, where it does not happen that a malefic possesses two rights of dominion in the sign, it is always placed last.

The lord of the exaltation is placed first ; then the lord of the triplicity; and then the lord of the house ; in regular succession, according to the series of the signs ; but it must again be remembered that any planet, having two rights of dominion in the same sign, takes precedence, as before mentioned, of those having only one. In Cancer and Leo, however, the malefics occupy the first degrees ; as those signs are the houses of the Moon and the Sun, which take no terms ; and the malefics being found to have greater potency in those signs therefore take precedence in them. Mars, consequently, receives the first degrees in Cancer, and Saturn in Leo, by which arrangement a proper order is preserved.[1]

The respective quantities of degrees for the several terms is thus determined : viz. when there is no planet found to be lord by two rights in the same sign, or in the two signs next following, each of the benefics, Jupiter and Venus, takes seven degrees ; the malefics, Saturn and Mars, take five degrees each ; and Mercury, being of common influence, takes six degrees ; thus completing the whole thirty. Since, however, there are some cases in which a planet has always a double right—(for Venus obtains the sole government of Taurus and Pisces, as the Moon does not share in the terms)—it is to be observed that when such double right (whether it exist in the same sign or in the signs next following as far as may complete a quadrant) may be possessed by any planet, that planet receives in addition one degree. The planets thus entitled were distinguished by points in the ancient writing above mentioned. And the degree, added to the quantity of the planet which exercises a double right, is subtracted from those of single right ; most generally from Saturn and Jupiter, in consequence of their slower motion.

---

[1] The cause of this disposition is that Cancer, the house of the Moon, partakes of moisture, and counteracts Mars's dryness ; while Leo, the Sun's house, is hot, and counteracts Saturn's cold.—Vide Chap. iv, and conclusion of Chap. vii of this book.

It may further be observed, that Jupiter's right, by triplicity, to the first degrees in Leo, is of course surrendered to Saturn, on the principle that the malefics have greater potency in the houses of the luminaries.

These terms are detailed in the following table :—

Aries			Taurus			Gemini			Cancer			Leo			Virgo		
Jupiter	6	6	Ven.	8	8	Mer.	7	7	Mars	6	6	Jup. Sat.	6	6	Mer.	7	7
Venus	8	14	Mer.	7	15	Jup.	6	13	Mer. Jup.	7	13	Mer.	7	13	Ven.	6	13
Mercury	7	21	Jup.	7	22	Ven.	7	20	Jup. Mer.	7	20	Sat. Ven.	6	19	Jup.	5	18
Mars	5	26	Sat.	2 4	24 26	Mars	6	26	Ven.	7	27	Jup.	6	25	Sat.	6	24
Saturn	4	30	Mars	6 4	30	Sat.	4	30	Sat.	3	30	Mars	5	30	Mars	6	30

Libra			Scorpio			Sagittarius			Capricorn			Aquarius			Pisces		
Saturn	6	6	Mars	6	6	Jup.	8	8	Ven.	6	6	Sat.	6	6	Ven.	8	8
Venus	5	11	Ven. Jup.	8 7	14 13	Ven.	6	14	Mer.	6	12	Mer.	6	12	Jup.	6	14
Mercury Jupiter	8 5	19 16	Jup. Ven.	7 8	21	Mer.	5	19	Jup.	7	19	Ven.	8	20	Mer.	6	20
Jupiter Mercury	5 8	24	Mer.	6	27	Sat.	6	25	Sat. Mars	6	25	Jup.	5	25	Mars	6 5	26 25
Mars	6	30	Sat.	3	30	Mars	5	30	Mars Sat.	5	30	Mars	5	30	Sat	4 3	30

CHAPTER XXV

THE PLACES AND DEGREES OF EVERY PLANET

THE signs have been subdivided by some persons into parts still more minute, which have been named places and degrees of dominion. Thus the twelfth part of a sign, or two degrees and a half, has been called a place, and the dominion of it given to the signs next succeeding. Other persons again, pursuing various modes of arrangement, attribute to each planet certain degrees, as being aboriginally connected with it, in a manner somewhat similar to the Chaldaic arrangement of the terms. But all these imaginary attributes cannot be herein detailed, for they receive no confirmation from nature, are not capable of being rationally demonstrated, and are, in fact, merely the offspring of scientific vanity.

The following observation, however, deserves attention, and must not be omitted.

The beginnings of the signs, and likewise those of the terms, are to be taken from the equinoctial and tropical points. This rule is not only clearly stated by writers on the subject, but is also especially evident by the demonstration constantly afforded, that their natures, influences and familiarities have no other origin than from the tropics and equinoxes, as has been already plainly shown.[1] And, if other beginnings were allowed, it would either be necessary to exclude the natures of the signs from the theory of prognostication, or impossible to avoid error in then retaining and making use of them ; as the regularity of their spaces and distances, upon which their influence depends, would then be invaded and broken in upon.

CHAPTER XXVI

FACES, CHARIOTS, AND OTHER SIMILAR ATTRIBUTES OF THE PLANETS

THE familiarities existing between the planets and the signs are such as have been already particularised.

There are also, however, further peculiarities ascribed to the planets. Each is said to be in its proper face, when the aspect it holds to the Sun, or Moon, is similar to that which its own house bears to their houses : for example, Venus is in her proper face when making a sextile aspect to either luminary, provided she be occidental to the Sun, but oriental to the Moon, agreeably to the primary arrangement of her houses.[2]

Each planet is also said to be in its proper chariot, or throne, or otherwise triumphantly situated, when it holds familiarity with the place which it actually occupies by two, or more, of the prescribed modes of connection : for when it is so circumstanced, its influence and energy are specially augmented by the familiarity it thus holds with the sign which encompasses it, and which is similar in influence and co-operates with it.

Lastly, each planet (although it may possess no familiarity with the sign encompassing it) is said to rejoice, when any connection subsists between itself and other stars of the same condition ; as, notwithstanding the distance between them, a certain sympathy and communication

---

[1] *Vide* Chapters xii and xiv of this Book.

[2] *Vide* Chapter xx. It of course follows that Saturn is in his proper face when he is five signs, or in quintile, after the Sun or before the Moon ; that Jupiter is so when in trine ; Mars when in quartile ; Venus when in sextile ; and Mercury when only one sign (or in modern phrase, in semi-sextile), after the Sun or before the Moon.

of influence is derived from their mutual resemblance. In the same manner, again, when a planet occupies a place adverse and dissimilar in condition to itself, much of its influence is dissipated and lost ; in consequence of the interposition and admixture of the other different influence, arising out of the dissimilar temperament of the sign by which it is encompassed.

CHAPTER XXVII

APPLICATION, SEPARATION, AND OTHER FACULTIES

IN all cases when the distances between planets or luminaries are but trifling,[1] the planet which precedes is said to apply to that which follows ; and that which follows to be separating from that which precedes.[2] The same rule obtains both in respect to bodily conjunction and to any other of the aspects before described ; except that, in the application and separation of the bodily conjunction, it is also essential to observe the actual latitudes of the bodies, in order to receive and consider only such a transit as may be made in the same parts of the zodiac.[3] But in the application and separation of aspects merely, the same attention is not requisite, since all the rays are uniformly converged into one focus, that is to say, into the angle of the earth,[4] and meet there alike from every quarter.

It appears, therefore, by the whole of what has been already delivered,

---

[1] This has been understood to mean, when the planets or luminaries are within each other's orbs ; Saturn's orb being 10 degrees, Jupiter's 12, Mars's 7 degrees 30 minutes, the Sun's 17 degrees, Venus's 8, Mercury's 7 degrees 30 minutes, and the Moon's 12 degrees 30 minutes.

[2] Astrologers generally agree, that the inferior planets always apply to the superior, but the superior never to the inferior, except when the inferior be retrograde. In the present instance it seems most probable that the author means the planet which is more occidental, by " the planet which precedes." He often uses " precedent " as equivalent to " occidental " in regard to the daily revolution of the heavens : and thus a planet in the first degree of Aries would precede, and be more occidental than one in the sixth degree of Aries, to which latter it would, by the regular planetary motion, be applying.

[3] On this, Whalley says that " the less the difference of latitude of the planets in conjunction, the more powerful will be the influence : for if two planets in conjunction have each considerable latitude of different denomination, the influence of such conjunction will be much lessened."

[4] Τουτ' εςι επι το κεντρον της γης. The precise meaning of the word κεντρον is " centre," rather than " angle " ; but Ptolemy uses it throughout this work, in speaking of the four angles of heaven, and I conceive he uses it here to signify an angle at, or on, the earth. The following definition of an aspect, by Kepler, strengthens my opinion : " An aspect is an angle formed on the earth, by the luminous rays of two planets ; efficacious in stimulating sublunary nature."

that the effective influence of the stars must be considered as arising not only from their own peculiar natures and properties, but also from the quality of the surrounding signs, and from configuration with the Sun and the angles ; all which has been pointed out. The influence of each planet, however, is strengthened chiefly when it may be oriental, swift and direct in its proper course and motion—for it has then its greatest power : but, on the other hand, it loses strength when occidental and slow in motion or retrograde ; as it then acts with smaller effect.[1] Its influence also receives accession or diminution, from its position with regard to the horizon ; as, if it be situated in the mid-heaven, or succedent to the mid-heaven, it is especially strong ; likewise, if it be on the actual horizon, or succedent to the horizon, it is also powerful—particularly if in the eastern quarter. Should it, however, be below the earth, and configurated with the ascendant, either from the lower heaven, or from any other part below the earth, its influence then becomes more languid ; but if, when below the earth, it hold no such configuration, it is entirely deprived of efficacy.[2]

[1] Placidus (Cooper's translation) says that " the three superiors are supposed to be stronger, if they are found to be matutine, or eastern, from the Sun ; the three inferiors, vespertine, or western ; for then they have a greater degree of light, in which consists their virtual influence, and then they are called oriental ; but occidental if otherwise. Every one knows how largely, yet to no purpose, authors have treated of the orientality of the planets."

Moxon's Mathematical Dictionary has the following words on the same subject : " Now the three superior planets are strongest, being oriental and matutine ; but the three inferior when they are occidental and vespertine. The reason is, because the first in the first case, but the last in the second, do then descend to the lowest part of their orbit, are increased in light, and approaching nearer the earth ; and so on the contrary, the inferiors matutine, the superiors vespertine are weakened."

[2] In a note on the 6th Chapter of this Book, Whalley says that, " according to Ptolemy, such as are between the ascendant and mid-heaven obtain the first place of strength, and are said to be in their oriental orientality : but, between the western horizon and the lower heaven, in their occidental orientality, which is the second place of strength : between the lower heaven and the ascendant, in their oriental occidentality, the first degree of weakness ; and between the mid-heaven and western horizon, in their occidental occidentality, the weakest place of all." This is all very pretty jargon, but certainly NOT " according to Ptolemy," who distinctly says, on the contrary, that if a planet " is on the actual horizon, or succedent to the horizon, it is also *powerful, and particularly* if in the eastern quarter." The last member of this sentence, as well as the conclusion of this 27th Chapter, shows that Ptolemy did not consider a situation between the mid-heaven and western horizon to be " the weakest place of all."

BOOK THE SECOND

CHAPTER I

GENERAL DIVISION OF THE SUBJECT

THE great and leading points, requiring to be attended to as a necessary means of introduction to the consideration of particular predictions, having been succinctly defined, the further parts of the subject, comprehending everything which may tend to facilitate prediction, and render it complete, shall now be duly proceeded in ; and, at the same time, care shall be taken to confine the whole doctrine within the limits of natural reason.

The foreknowledge to be acquired by means of Astrology is to be regarded in two great and principal divisions. The first, which may be properly called General, or Universal, concerns entire nations, countries, or cities ; and the second, denominated Particular, or Genethliacal, relates to men individually.

In considering these respective divisions, it seems proper to give priority to that which has the more general application and influence : because, in the first place, general events are produced by causes greater and more compulsatory than the causes of particular events ; secondly, because natures of more extended potency must invariably control those which are more limited in action ; and, thirdly, because particular events, or individual affections, are comprehended in those of general influence.[1] It is therefore especially necessary, in desiring to investigate particular events, to treat first of those which are general.

Again, general events are subdivided according to their operation upon entire countries, and upon certain cities or districts : one subdivision being regarded as affecting entire countries, and the other certain cities or districts only. They are also separately considered according to the causes by which they are produced ; war, pestilence, famine, earthquakes, inundations, and other similar visitations being dependent on such greater and more important causes, as arise only after considerable periods ; while slighter causes, arising more frequently, have reference only to the revolution of the seasons ; their greater or less variation in cold and heat ; the severity or mildness of the weather ; the occasional abundance or scarcity of provisions ; and other like occurrences.

Hence the consideration of those events which concern whole

---

[1] *Vide* Chap. iii, Book I, pp. 13-14.

countries, and are dependent on the greater causes (since it has a more extended scope than the other, which attaches only to certain cities, or districts, and is subject to slighter causes) takes precedence. And, for its due investigation, two essential points are to be attended to : the first is, the appropriate familiarity of the zodiacal signs and the fixed stars with the several regions which may be concerned ; and the second comprises the indications occasionally arising in those parts of the heavens where such familiarity is found : for instance, the eclipses of the Sun and Moon, and such transits as may be made by the planets, when matutine, and in their respective stations.

The nature of the sympathy between these things must, however, be explained first ; and a brief description will therefore be given of the chief peculiarities observable in whole nations ; in regard to their manners and customs, as well as to their bodily formation and temperament ; considered agreeably to their familiarity with those stars and signs whence the natural cause of their peculiarities duly proceeds.

CHAPTER II

PECULIARITIES OBSERVABLE THROUGHOUT EVERY ENTIRE CLIMATE

THE peculiarities of all nations are distinguished according to entire parallels and entire angles, and by their situation with regard to the Sun and the Ecliptic.

The climate which we inhabit is situated in one of the Northern Quadrants : but other nations, which lie under more southern parallels, that is to say, in the space between the equinoctial line and the summer tropic, have the Sun in their zenith, and are continually scorched by it. They are consequently black in complexion, and have thick and curled hair. They are, moreover, ugly in person, of contracted stature, hot in disposition, and fierce in manners, in consequence of the incessant heats to which they are exposed ; and they are called by the common name of Æthiopians. But the human race does not alone afford evidence of the violent heat in these regions ; it is shown also by all other animals and by the state of the surrounding atmosphere.

The natives of those countries which lie under the more remote northern parallels (that is to say, under the Arctic circle and beyond it[1]) have their zenith far distant from the zodiac and the Sun's heat. Their constitutions, therefore, abound in cold, and are also highly imbued with moisture, which is in itself a most nutritive quality, and, in these latitudes, is not exhausted by heat : hence they are fair in complexion, with straight hair, of large bodies and full stature. They are cold in disposition, and wild in manners, owing to the constant cold. The state of the surrounding atmosphere and of animals and plants, corresponds

---

[1] " Under the Bears," in the Greek.

c

with that of men ; who (as natives of these countries) are designated by the general name of Scythians.

The nations situated between the summer tropic and the Arctic circle, having the meridian Sun neither in their zenith nor yet far remote from it, enjoy a well-tempered atmosphere. This favourable temperature, however, still undergoes variation, and changes alternatively from heat to cold ; but the variation is never vast nor violent. The people who enjoy this kindly atmosphere are consequently of proportionate stature and complexion, and of good natural disposition : they live not in a state of dispersion, but dwell together in societies, and are civilised in their habits. Among the nations comprehended in this division, those verging towards the south are more industrious and ingenious than the others, and more adapted to the sciences : and these qualifications are engendered in them by the vicinity of the zodiac to their zenith, and by the familiarity thus subsisting between them and the planets moving in the zodiac, which familiarly gives activity and an intellectual impulse to their minds. Again, the natives of those countries which lie towards the east excel in courage, acting boldly and openly under all circumstances ; for in all their characteristics they are principally conformed to the Sun's nature, which is oriental, diurnal, masculine and dexter—(and it is plainly apparent that the dexter parts of all animals are much stronger than others)—hence results the greater courage of the inhabitants of the East. And as the Moon, on her first appearance after conjunction, is always seen in the west, the western parts are therefore lunar, and consequently feminine and sinister ; whence it follows that the inhabitants of the west are milder, more effeminate and reserved.

Thus, in all countries, certain respective peculiarities exist in regard to manners, customs and laws ; and in each it is found that some portion of the inhabitants differs partially and individually from the usual habits and condition of their race. These variations arise similarly to the variations perceptible in the condition of the atmosphere ; as, in all countries, the general state of whose atmosphere may be either hot, or cold, or temperate, certain districts are found to possess a particular temperature of their own, and to be more or less hot, or cold, by being more or less elevated than the general face of the country. So, likewise, certain people become navigators owing to their proximity to the sea, while others are equestrian, because their country is a plain ; and others, again, become domiciliated by the fertility of their soil.

And thus, in each particular climate, certain peculiar qualities are to be found, arising from the natural familiarity which it holds with the stars and the twelve signs. And although these qualities do not pervade it, in such a manner as to be necessarily exhibited by every individual native, yet they are so far generally distributed as to be of much utility in investigating particular events ; and it is highly important to take at least a brief notice of them.

CHAPTER III

THE FAMILIARITY OF THE REGIONS OF THE EARTH WITH THE TRIPLICITIES AND THE PLANETS

IT has been already stated that there are four triplicities distinguishable in the zodiac. The first, composed of Aries, Leo, and Sagittarius, is the north-west triplicity ; and Jupiter has chief dominion over it on behalf of its northern proportion ; but Mars also rules with him in reference to the west. The second, consisting of Taurus, Virgo, and Capricorn, is the south-east ; and in this triplicity Venus bears chief rule, in consequence of the southern proportion ; but Saturn also governs with her in consideration of the east. The third, composed of Gemini, Libra, and Aquarius, is north-east ; and Saturn is here the principal lord, in consequence of the eastern proportion ; Jupiter, however, governs with him in reference to the north. The fourth triplicity is constituted of Cancer, Scorpio, and Pisces, and is south-west ; it owns Mars as its principal ruler, in consideration of its western proportion ; and, on behalf of the south, it is also governed by Venus.

The four triplicities being thus established, the whole inhabited earth is accordingly divided into four parts, agreeing with the number of the triplicities. It is divided latitudinally by the line of the Mediterranean Sea, from the Straits of Hercules to the Issican Gulf, continued onwards through the mountainous ridge extending towards the east ; and by this latitudinal division its southern and northern parts are defined. Its longitudinal division is made by the line of the Arabian Gulf, the Ægean Sea, Pontus, and the lake Mæotis ; and by this line are separated its eastern and western parts.

Of the four quadrants of the earth, thus agreeing in number with the four triplicities, one is situated in the north-west of the entire earth, and contains Celto-galatia ; or, as it is commonly called, Europe. Opposed to this quadrant lies that of the south-east, towards Eastern Æthiopia ; it is called the southern part of Asia Magna. Another quadrant of the entire earth is in the north-east, about Scythia, and is called the northern part of Asia Magna. To this is opposed the quadrant of the south-west, which lies about Western Æthiopia, and is known by the general name of Libya.

Each of these quadrants contains certain parts, which, in comparison with its other parts, lie more contiguous to the middle of the earth ; and these parts, in respect of the quadrant to which they belong, have a situation opposite to the rest of that quadrant, in the same manner as that quadrant itself is situated in regard to the rest of the earth. For instance, in the quadrant of Europe, which is situated on the north-west of the whole earth, those parts of it which lie towards the middle of the earth, and near the angles of the other quadrants, are manifestly situated in the south-east of that quadrant. The like rule obtains in regard to the other quadrants. And hence it is evident that each quadrant is in familiarity with two oppositely-placed triplicities, its whole extent being adapted to the one triplicity which governs it as an entire quadrant; but its particular parts, situated about the middle of the earth, and lying, as regards the rest of the quadrant, in a direction contrary to that assigned to the whole quadrant altogether, being adapted to the other triplicity which rules the particular quadrant lying opposite to it. The planets exercising dominion in both these triplicities also hold familiarity with these particular parts; but, with the other more remote parts of any quadrant, only those planets hold familiarity which rule in the single triplicity to which the whole quadrant is allotted. With the said particular parts about the middle of the earth, Mercury also, as well as the other planets in dominion, bears familiarity, in consideration of his meditative condition and common nature.

Under this arrangement, it follows that the north-western parts of the first quadrant, or that of Europe, are in familiarity with the north-west triplicity, composed of Aries, Leo, and Sagittarius; and they are accordingly governed by the lords of that triplicity, Jupiter and Mars, vespertine. These parts, as distinguished by their appropriation to entire nations, are Britain, Galatia, Germany, Barsania,[1] Italy, Apulia, Sicily, Gaul, Tuscany, Celtica, and Spain. And, since the triplicity itself and the planets connected with it in dominion are adapted to command, the natives of these countries are consequently impatient of restraint, lovers of freedom, warlike, industrious, imperious, cleanly, and high-minded. But, owing to the vespertine configuration of Jupiter and Mars, as well as the masculine condition of the anterior parts of the triplicity, and the feminine condition of its latter parts,[2] the said nations regard women with scorn and indifference.[3] They are, however, still careful of the community, brave and faithful, affectionate in their families, and perform good and kind actions.

Among the countries before named, Britain, Galatia, Germany, and Barsania have a greater share of familiarity with Aries and Mars; and their inhabitants are accordingly wilder, bolder, and more ferocious. Italy, Apulia, Sicily, and Gaul are in familiarity with Leo and the Sun;

---

[1] Or, perhaps, Bastarnia, a part of the ancient European Sarmatia.

[2] This should probably be understood to mean in a mundane point of view, agreeably to Chaps. VI and XV, Book I. For when Aries is on the ascendant, it is, of course, oriental and masculine; and Sagittarius must consequently then be in the eighth house, occidental, and therefore feminine.

[3] The customs of nations have, in some degree, altered since Ptolemy made this severe charge against us and our brethren in the north and west of Europe. The following passage also occurs in this part of the original text :—προς δε τας συνουσιας των αρσενικων ανακινουμενοι και ζηλουντες, και μητε αισχρον μητε ανανδρον τουτο νομιζοντες. δια τουτο ουδε εκλυονται, οτι ουδε ως πασχοντες ᶜιακεινται επι τουτω, αλλα φυλαττουσι τας ψυχας ανδρειους·

and the natives of these countries are more imperious, yet kind and benevolent, and careful of the commonwealth. Tuscany, Celtica, and Spain, are connected with Sagittarius and Jupiter ; and their inhabitants are lovers of freedom, simplicity, and elegance.

The south-eastern parts of this quadrant, which are situated towards the middle of the earth, viz. Thrace, Macedonia, Illyria, Hellas, Achaia, and Crete, as well as the Cyclad Isles and the shores of Asia Minor and of Cyprus, assume, in addition, a connection with the south-east triplicity, which is composed of Taurus, Virgo, and Capricorn, and ruled by Venus and Saturn ; and, in consequence of the vicinity of these regions to the middle of the earth, Mercury likewise has a proportionate dominion over them. Hence their inhabitants, being subjected to the rulers of both triplicities, enjoy a favourable temperament of mind and of body. From Mars they imbibe their fitness for command, their courage, and impatience of restraint ; from Jupiter their love of freedom, their self-rule, their skill in guiding public affairs, and in legislation : through the influence of Venus they are also lovers of the arts and sciences, as well as of music and poetry, of public shows, and all the refinements of life ; and from Mercury they deduce their hospitality, their fondness for society and communion, their love of equity and of literature, and their power of eloquence. They are also in the highest degree conversant with sacred mysteries, owing to the vespertine figuration of Venus.

It is further to be observed of these last-named countries, that the inhabitants of the Cyclad Isles, and of the shores of Asia Minor and of Cyprus, are more particularly under the influence of Taurus and Venus, and are therefore voluptuous, fond of elegance, and over-studious in their attention to the body. The people of Hellas, Achaia, and Crete, have a stronger familiarity with Virgo and Mercury, and are therefore learned and scientific, preferring the cultivation of the mind to the care of the body. The people of Macedonia, Thrace, and Illyria, are chiefly influenced by Capricorn and Saturn ; whence they are greedy of wealth, inferior in civilization, and have no ordinances of civil polity.

The second quadrant consists of the southern division of Asia Magna. Such of its parts as are contained in India, Arriana, Gedrosia, Parthia, Media, Persia, Babylonia, Mesopotamia, and Assyria, are situated in the south-east of the whole earth, and have due familiarity with the south-east triplicity (composed of Taurus, Virgo, and Capricorn), and consequently with Venus, Mercury, and Saturn, in matutine figuration. The nature of the inhabitants of these countries is obedient to the dominion of these ruling influences ; they worship Venus under the name of Isis ; and they also pay devotion to Saturn, invoking him by the name of Mithranhelios. Many of them likewise foretell future events ; and they consecrate to the gods some of their bodily members, to which superstition they are induced by the nature of the figuration of the planets before mentioned.[1] They are, moreover, hot in constitution, amorous and lustful, fond of acting, singing, and dancing, gaudy in their dresses and ornaments; owing to the influence of Venus. Saturn, however, inclines them to simplicity of conduct; and, in consequence of the matutine figuration, they address their women publicly.[2] There are also many among them who beget children by their own mothers.[3] The matutine figurations also influence their mode of worship, which is performed by prostration of the breast; because the heart is the nobler part of the body, and, in its vivifying faculties, acts like the Sun. And, although the influence of Venus makes the people, generally speaking, finical and effeminate in their personal adornment and apparel, yet the connection which Saturn holds with them, by means of the east, still renders them great in mind, eminent in council, courageous and warlike.

It is to be remarked, that Parthia, Media, and Persia, have a more particular familiarity with Taurus and Venus; whence it follows that the dwellers in those countries wear splendid garments, and clothe the whole person entirely, except the breast; they are also fond of elegance and refinement. The countries about Babylon, Mesopotamia, and Assyria, are connected with Virgo and Mercury; their inhabitants are consequently studious of the sciences, and, among other attainments, excel in making observations on the five planets. India, Arriana, and Gedrosia, are connected with Capricorn and Saturn; the natives of these regions are, therefore, ill-formed in person, of dirty habits, and barbarous manners.

The remaining parts of this second quadrant, viz. Idumæa, Cœlesyria, Judæa, Phœnicia, Chaldæa, Orchynia, and Arabia Felix, occupy a situation in the vicinity of the middle of the earth, and in the north-west of the quadrant to which they actually belong: hence they are in familiarity with the north-west triplicity (which consists of Aries, Leo, and Sagittarius), and they have for their rulers, Jupiter and Mars, together with Mercury. By means of the figuration of these planets, the natives of the said countries are skilful in trade and all mercantile affairs, heedless of danger, yet treacherous, servile, and thoroughly fickle.

The inhabitants of Cœlesyria, Idumæa, and Judæa, are principally influenced by Aries and Mars, and are generally audacious, atheistical,[4]

---

[1] The Greek is as follows: καί τα μορια αυτων τα γεννητικα ανατιθεασι τοις θεοις· διοτι ο σχηματισμος των ειρημενων ασερων φυσει σπερματικος εσιν· Follies, similar in their kind to these, are still practised by the Faquirs of Hindostan, and by other religious sects in Asia.

[2] φανερως ποιουμενοι τας προς τας γυναικας συνουσιας·

[3] The author gives a singular reason for this incest: μισουσι δε τας (συνουσιας) προς τους αρσενας. δια τουτο και οι πλεισοι αυτων εκ των μητερων τεκνοποιουσι·

[4] The epithet is remarkable, not only as being, in the opinion of a Gentile, merited by the Jews, among other nations, but also at a period scarcely exceeding a century after their most heinous crime had been committed, expressly under

and treacherous. The Phœnicians, Chaldæans, and Orchynians, have familiarity with Leo and the Sun, and are therefore more simple and humane in disposition; they are also studious of astrology, and pay greater reverence than all other nations to the Sun. The people of Arabia Felix are connected with Sagittarius and Jupiter: the country is fertile, and abundantly productive of spices, and its inhabitants are well-proportioned in person, free in all their habits of life, and liberal in all their contracts and dealings.

The third quadrant occupies the northern division of Asia Magna. Those several parts of it which lie to the north-east of the whole earth, and comprise Hyrcania, Armenia, Mantiana, Bactriana, Casperia, Serica, Sauromatica, Oxiana, and Sogdiana, are in familiarity with the north-east triplicity, composed of Gemini, Libra, and Aquarius, and have for their rulers Saturn and Jupiter, in matutine positions; hence the inhabitants worship Jupiter and the Sun.[1] They are abundantly rich in all things: they possess much gold, and are dainty and luxurious in their diet. They are also learned in theology, skilled in magic, just in all their dealings, free and noble-minded, holding dishonesty and wickedness in abhorrence, strongly imbued with the softer affections of nature; and, in a worthy cause, they will even readily embrace death to preserve their friends. They are, furthermore, chaste in marriage, elegant and splendid in their dress, charitable and beneficent, and of enlightened intellect. All these qualities are principally produced by the matutine positions of Saturn and Jupiter, who influence the region.

Among these nations, however, Hyrcania, Armenia, and Mantiana, have a greater familiarity with Gemini and Mercury; and the inhabitants are consequently more acute in apprehension, but less tenacious of their probity. The countries about Bactriana, Casperia, and Serica, are connected with Libra and Venus; and the natives are endowed with much wealth and many luxuries, and take delight in poetry and songs. The nations about Sauromatica, Oxiana and Sogdiana, are influenced by Aquarius and Saturn; and are therefore less polished in manners, and more austere and uncouth.

The other parts of this quadrant, lying near the middle of the entire earth, consist of Bithynia, Phrygia, Colchis, Laxica, Syria, Commagene, Cappadocia, Lydia, Lycia, Cilicia, and Pamphylia. These, being situated in the south-west of their quadrant, have familiarity accordingly with the south-west triplicity, composed of Cancer, Scorpio, and Pisces,

---

the cloak of religion. It seems, however, that the Jews were charged with atheism by other writers also, and on account of their neglect of the false gods of the heathens; viz. "*falsorium deorum neglectus:* quam candem causam etiam Judæis maledicendi Tacitus habuit, et Plinius Major, cui Judæi dicuntur *gens contumeliâ numinum insignis.*" See Clark's Notes on Grotius de Verit. Relig. Christ. Lib. 2, §2.

[1] Other editions say " Saturn."

and are ruled by Mars and Venus, together with Mercury. In these countries Venus is principally worshipped ; she is invoked as the Mother of the Gods, and by various local and indigenous appellations ; Mars likewise receives adoration here, under the name of Adonis, as well as by other titles ;[1] and some of the religious services to these deities are performed by loud lamentations. The people are servile in mind, diligent in labour, yet fraudulent, knavish, and thievish ; they enter into foreign armies for the sake of hire, and make prisoners and slaves of their own countrymen : besides which, they are continually subject to intestine broils. These traits arise from the matutine figurations of Mars and Venus. It is further to be observed, that, from the circumstance of Mars receiving his exaltation in Capricorn (one of the signs of the triplicity ruled by Venus), and Venus hers in Pisces (a sign belonging to the triplicity of Mars), it thence follows that the women have strong attachments and kindly affections to their husbands, are vigilant and careful in domestic affairs, and highly industrious : they also act as servants, and labour for the men, with all due obedience, in every thing.

Bithynia, Phrygia, and Colchis, must however be excepted from sharing in this general propriety of the female character ; for, as these nations are chiefly connected with Cancer and the Moon, their male population is, generally speaking, slavish in its habits, timid and superstitious, while the greater part of the women, owing to the matutine and masculine position of the Moon, are of masculine manners, ambitious of command, and warlike. These females, like the Amazons, shun the addresses of men, and delight in the use of arms, and in manly occupations : they also amputate the right breasts of their female children for the sake of adapting them to military service, and in order that, when in combat and exposing that part of their body, they may appear to be of the male sex. Again, Syria, Commagene, and Cappadocia, are principally influenced by Scorpio and Mars ; and their inhabitants are accordingly bold, wicked, treacherous, and laborious. Lydia, Cilicia, and Pamphylia, have a greater familiarity with Pisces and Jupiter ; when their inhabitants are wealthy, of mercantile habits, living in freedom and in community, faithful to their engagements, and honest in their dealings.

The remaining quadrant is the vast tract known by the general name of Libya. Its several parts, distinguished by the particular names of Numidia, Carthage, Africa.[2] Phazania, Nasamonitis, Garamantica,

---

[1] It is usually understood that the male deity, coupled by the Phrygians with Cybele, " the mother of the Gods," was called by them Atys ; and that Adonis was the name used by the Phœnicians in addressing the associate of Venus. It has been said that these divinities were identical with the Isis and Osiris of the Ægyptians.

[2] The name of Africa was, in Ptolemy's time, limited to those parts of the coast on the Mediterranean which contained the ancient Utica, and in which Tunis now stands. Josephus says the name is derived from Afer (one of the

Mauritania, Getulia, and Metagonitis, are situated in the south-west of the entire earth, and have due familiarity with the south-west triplicity, composed of Cancer, Scorpio, and Pisces; their rulers therefore are Mars and Venus, in vespertine position. From this figuration of the planets it results that the dwellers in these regions are doubly governed by a man and a woman, who are both children of the same mother; the maɴ rules the males, and the woman the females. They are extremely hot in constitution, and desirous of women; their marriages are usually made by violence, and in many districts the local princes first enjoy the brides of their subjects: in some places, however, the women are common to all. The influence of Venus causes the whole people to delight in personal ornaments, and in being arrayed in female attire: nevertheless, that of Mars renders them courageous, crafty, addicted to magic, and fearless of dangers.

Again, however, of the above-named countries, Numidia, Carthage, and Africa, are more particularly in familiarity with Cancer and the Moon: their inhabitants, consequently, live in community, attend to mercantile pursuits, and enjoy abundantly all the blessings of nature. The natives of Metagonitis, Mauritania, and Getulia, are influenced by Scorpio and Mars, and are consequently ferocious and pugnacious in the highest degree; eaters of human flesh, utterly indifferent to danger, and so regardless and prodigal of blood, as to slay each other without hesitation on the slightest cause. The people in Phazania, Nasamonitis, and Garamantica, are connected with Pisces and Jupiter, and are accordingly frank and simple in manners, fond of employment, well disposed, fond of the decencies of life, and, for the most part, free and unrestrained in their actions: they worship Jupiter by the name of Ammon.

The other parts of this quadrant, which lies near the middle of the entire earth, are Cyrenaica, Marmarica, Ægypt, Thebais, Oasis, Troglodytica, Arabia, Azania, and Middle Æthiopia. These countries, being situated in the north-east of their quadrant, have due familiarity with the north-east triplicity (consisting of Gemini, Libra, and Aquarius), and are governed by Saturn and Jupiter, and also by Mercury. Their inhabitants, therefore, participate in the influence of all the five planets in vespertine figuration, and consequently cherish due love and reverence for the gods, and dedicate themselves to their service. They are addicted to sepulchral ceremonies; and, owing to the said vespertine position, they bury their dead in the earth,[1] and remove them from the

posterity of Abraham by Cethurah), who is stated to have led an army into Libya, and to have established himself in the country. This Afer is, of course, the same with Epher, mentioned in the fourth verse of the 25th chapter of Genesis, as a son of Midian, one of the sons of Abraham by his concubine Keturah.

[1] It does not appear why this practice should have been remarked as a national peculiarity, unless in distinction from the custom of burning the dead

C *

public eye. They use various laws and customs, and worship divers
gods. In a state of subjection, they are submissive, cowardly, abject,
and most patient ; but when they command, they are brave, generous,
and high-minded. Polygamy is frequent among them, and practised by
the women as well as the men : they are most licentious in sexual
intercourse, and allow incestuous commerce between brothers and
sisters. Both men and women are extraordinarily prolific, and correspond in this respect with the fecundity of their soil. Many of the men
are, however, effeminate and debased in mind ; in consequence of the
figuration of the malefics, together with the vespertine position of
Venus ; and some of them mutilate their persons.[1]

Among these last named countries, Cyrenaica, Marmarica, and
particularly Lower Ægypt, are chiefly influenced by Gemini and
Mercury : the natives are therefore highly intellectual and sensible,
and gifted with capacity for every undertaking ; above all, for the
attainment of wisdom, and an insight into divine mysteries. They are
also magicians, performing secret rites and ceremonies, and are in every
respect calculated for the prosecution of all scientific inquiry.[2] The
inhabitants of Thebais, Oasis, and Troglodytica, are connected with
Libra and Venus ; they are of warmer constitution, and more hasty
disposition, and enjoy life in all its plentitude and abundance. The
natives of Arabia, Azania, and Middle Æthiopia, have familiarity with
Aquarius and Saturn ; they consequently feed on flesh and fish indis-

among the Greeks and Romans. Interment is recorded as having been usual
among the Jews, and it is known to have been common among many ancient
barbarous nations.

A conjecture may perhaps be allowed, that the author, when he wrote this
passage, had in his mind the magnificent subterranean palaces, constructed for
the dead, in parts of the region in question ; some of which have been recently
made known to the modern world by the sagacity and enterprise of the
celebrated Belzoni.

[1] Τινες δε και καταφρονουσι των γεννητικων μελων.—The " contempt "
here expressed by καταφρονουσι has been taken by all translators (except
Whalley) to signify " mutilation."

[2] History warrants the high enconium here given to the natives of these
countries. Ægypt was the acknowledged mother of the arts and sciences, and
at one time the great depot of all the learning of the world : her school of
astronomy (a science which our author may be supposed to have placed in the
first rank), founded at Alexandria by Ptol. Philadelphus, maintained its superior
reputation for a thousand years. Cyrenaica gave birth to many illustrious
philosophers, and, among them, to Eratosthenes, who is said to have invented
the armillary sphere. This great man measured the obliquity of the ecliptic,
and, though he erroneously reckoned it at only 20½ degrees, it should be recollected that he lived 200 years before the Christian æra. He also measured a
degree of the meridian, and determined the extent of the earth, by means
similar to those adopted by the moderns.

TABLE SHOWING ALL THE COUNTRIES BELONGING TO EACH SIGN RESPECTIVELY

Signs.	Aries.	Taurus.	Gemini.	Cancer.	Leo.	Virgo.
Triplicity.	North West.	South East.	North East.	South West.	North West.	South East.
Quadrant of the Countries.	North West.	South East.	North East.	South West.	North West.	South East.
Countries remote from the middle of the earth.	Britain Galatia Germany Barsania	Parthia Media Persia	Hyrcania Armenia Mantiana	Numidia Carthage Africa	Italy Apulia Sicily Gaul	Mesopotamia Babylonia Assyria
Quadrant of the Countries.	South East.	North West.	South West	North East.	South East.	North West.
Countries near the middle of the earth.	Cælesyria Idumæa Judæa	Cyclades Cyprus Asia Minor	Cyrenaica Marmarica Lower Ægypt	Bithynia Phrygia Colchis	Phœnicia Chaldæa Orchynia	Hellas Achaia Crete

Signs.	Libra.	Scorpio.	Sagittarius.	Capricorn.	Aquarius.	Pisces.
Triplicity.	North East.	South West.	North West.	South East.	North East.	South West.
Quadrant of the Countries.	North East.	South West.	North West.	South East.	North East.	South West.
Countries remote from the middle of the earth.	Bactriana Casperia Serica	Metagonitis Mauritania Getulia	Tuscany Celtica Spain	India Ariana Gedrosia	Sauromatica Oxiana Sogdiana	Phazania Nasamonitis Garamantica
Quadrant of the Countries.	South West.	North East.	South East.	North West.	South West.	North East.
Countries near the middle of the earth.	Thebais Oasis Troglodytica	Syria Commagene Cappadocia	Arabia Felix	Thrace Macedonia Illyria	Arabia Azania Middle Æthiopia	Lydia Cilicia Pamphylia

criminately, and live in a state of dispersion like wild beasts; they never unite in society, but lead a wandering and savage life.

The familiarities exercised by the Planets, and by the Signs of the Zodiac, together with the manners, customs, and qualities, particular as well as general, which they produce, have now been concisely described; but in order to facilitate the knowledge and use of them, the subjoined table is inserted, to show, at one view, what countries are in connection with each sign, respectively, according to the mode above detailed.

CHAPTER IV

THE FAMILIARITY OF THE REGIONS OF THE EARTH WITH THE FIXED STARS

IN addition to the rules which have been already given, respecting the familiarity of the regions of the earth with the signs and planets, it must be observed, that all fixed stars which may be posited on any line, drawn from one zodiacal pole to the other, through such parts of the zodiac as may be connected with any particular country, are also in familiarity with that particular country.

And, with regard to metropolitan cities, it is necessary to state, that those points or degrees of the zodiac, over which the Sun and Moon were in transit, at the time when the construction of any such city was first undertaken and commenced, are to be considered as sympathizing with that city in an especial manner; and that, among the angles, the ascendant is principally in accordance with it. In certain cases, however, where the date of foundation of a metropolis cannot be ascertained, the mid-heaven in the nativity of the reigning king, or other actual chief magistrate, is to be substituted, and considered as that part of the zodiac with which it chiefly sympathizes.[1]

CHAPTER V

MODE OF PARTICULAR PREDICTION IN ECLIPSES

AFTER having gone through the necessary preliminary topics, it is now proper to speak of the manner in which predictions are to be formed and considered; beginning with those which relate to general events, affecting either certain cities, or districts, or entire countries.

The strongest and principal cause of all these events exists in the

---

[1] Whalley remarks on this passage, that the gradual progress of the fixed stars "from one sign to another, is in an especial manner to be regarded in considering the mutations, manners, customs, laws, government, and fortune of a kingdom."

ecliptical conjunctions of the Sun and Moon. and in the several transits made by the planets during those conjunctions.

One part of the observations, required in forming predictions in cases of this nature, relates to the locality of the event, and points out the cities or countries liable to be influenced by particular eclipses, or by occasional continued stations of certain planets, which at times remain for a certain period in one situation. These planets are Saturn, Jupiter, and Mars ; and they furnish portentous indications, when they are stationary.

Another branch relates to time, and gives pre-information of the period at which the event will occur, and how long it will continue to operate.

The third branch is generic ; and points out the classes, or kinds, which the event will affect.

The last part is specific ; and foreshows the actual quality and character of the coming event.

CHAPTER VI

THE REGIONS OR COUNTRIES TO BE CONSIDERED AS LIABLE TO BE COMPREHENDED IN THE EVENT

THE first of the several branches of consideration just enumerated relates to locality, and is to be exercised in the following manner :—

In all eclipses of the Sun and Moon, and especially in such as are fully visible, the place in the zodiac, where the eclipse happens, is to be noted ; and it must be seen what countries are in familiarity with that place, according to the rules laid down regarding the quadrants and the triplicities ; and in like manner it must be observed what cities are under the influence of the sign in which the eclipse happens ; either by means of the ascendant, and the situations of the luminaries at the time of their foundation, or by means of the mid-heaven of their kings or governors, actually ruling at the time of the eclipse ; although such time may be subsequent to the building of the said cities. Whatever countries or cities shall be thus found in familiarity with the ecliptical place, will all be comprehended in the event ; which will, however, principally attach to all those parts which may be connected with the identical sign of the eclipse,[1] and in which it was visible while above the earth.[2]

[1] As shown in the Table at page 51.

[2] It does not appear that the text here warrants the conclusion which Whalley has drawn from it, viz. " that wherever eclipses are not visible, they have no influence, and therefore subterranean eclipses cannot have any." Ptolemy declares, that *all* countries in familiarity with the ecliptical place will be comprehended in the event ; and, with regard to the visibility or invisibility of the eclipse, he says merely that its effects will be *principally* felt in such of the said countries as might have obtained a view of the eclipse.

CHAPTER VII

THE TIME AND PERIOD OF THE EVENT

THE second point requiring attention relates to time, and indicates the date when the event will take place, and the period during which its effect will continue : these are to be ascertained in the following manner.

It must however be premised, that as an eclipse, occurring at any particular season, cannot happen in all climates at the same temporal or solar hour,[1] so neither will the magnitude of the obscuration, nor the time of its continuance, be equal in all parts of the world. First, therefore (as is done in a nativity), the angles are to be arranged, in every country connected with the eclipse, according to the hour at which the eclipse, takes place and the elevation of the pole in that country. The time, during which the obscuration of the eclipse may continue in each country, is then to be noted in equatorial hours.[2] And, after these particulars have been carefully observed, it is to be understood that the effect will endure as many years as the obscuration lasted hours, provided the eclipse was solar ; but if lunar, a like number of months is to be reckoned instead of years.

The commencement of the effect, and the period of its general intensity, or strength, are to be inferred from the situation of the place of the eclipse with respect to the angles. For, if the ecliptical place be near the eastern horizon, the effect will begin to be manifested in the course of the first four months after the date of the eclipse ; and its general height, or intensity, will take place in, or about, the first third part of the whole extent of its duration. If the ecliptical place happen to be in or near the mid-heaven, the effect will begin to appear in the second four months, and its general intensity will occur about the second third part ; and, if the place should fall near the western horizon, the effect will begin in the third four months, and take its general intensity in the last third part of its whole duration.[3]

---

[1] Temporal or solar hours are duodecimal parts of the Sun's diurnal or nocturnal arc, and are numbered by day from sunrise to sunset ; by night, from sunset to sunrise.

[2] Equatorial hours are the twenty-four hours of the earth's revolution on its axis. Each of them is equal in duration to the passage of 15 degrees of the Equator ; and they are numbered from noon to noon. A particular explanation of the astronomical use, both of temporal and equatorial hours, is to be found in the 9th Chapter of the second Book of the Almagest ; an extract from which is given in the Appendix.

[3] The three periods of four months each, stated in this paragraph, are applicable to solar eclipses only ; for lunar eclipses, these periods may be reckoned at ten days each ; that number of days bearing the same proportion to a month, as four months to a year. On this point, Whalley, with his usual

Partial intensities, or relaxations of the effect, are, however, to be
inferred from any combinations which may happen during the intermediate period,[1] either in the actual places where the primary cause
was presented, or in other places configurated therewith.   They are
also to be conjectured by the various courses, or transits, of such planets
as co-operate in producing the effect, by being configurated with the
sign in which the primary cause was situated ; and, with this view, the
matutine, vespertine, or stationary position, or midnight culmination of
those planets must be observed ; for the effect will be strengthened and
augmented by their matutine or stationary position ; but weakened and
diminished by their being vespertine, or situated under the sunbeams,
or by their midnight culmination.

CHAPTER VIII

THE GENUS, CLASS, OR KIND, LIABLE TO BE AFFECTED

THE third division of these observations relates to the mode of distinguishing the genus, or species, of animals or things about to sustain the
expected effect.   This distinction is made by means of the conformation
and peculiar properties of those signs in which the place of the eclipse,
and the places of such fixed stars and planets, as are in dominion according to the actual sign of the eclipse, and that of the angle before it, may
be found.   And a planet, or fixed star, is to be considered as holding
dominion when circumstanced as follows.

If there be found one planet having more numerous claims than any
other to the place of the eclipse, as well as to that of the angle, being also
in the immediate vicinity of those places, and visibly applying to, or
receding from them, and having likewise more rights over other places
connected with them by configuration ; the said planet being, at the
same time, lord by house, triplicity, exaltation, and terms ; in such a
case, only that single planet is entitled to dominion.   But, if the lord
of the eclipse and the lord of the angle be not identical, then those two
planets which have most connections with each place are to be noted ;
and, of these two, the lord of the eclipse is to be preferred to the chief
dominion, " although the other is to be considered as bearing rule conjointly."[2]   And if more than two should be found, having equal pre-

---

inaccuracy, has asserted, that " in eclipses of the Moon, two days, or thereabouts,
are equal to the four months " here reckoned in eclipses of the Sun.   He adds,
however, what perhaps may be true, that " lunar eclipses are by no means so
powerful as those of the Sun, although more so than any other lunation."

[1] That is to say, from any combinations of the Sun and Moon which may
take place after the date of the eclipse, but before the close of its effect.

[2] The edition of Allatius does not contain the words here marked by inverted
commas ; but they are found in other editions of the text, and seem necessary
to complete the sense of the passage.

tensions to each place, that particular one among them which may be nearest to an angle, or most concerned with the places in question, by the nature of its condition, is to be selected for dominion.[1]

But, among the fixed stars, the chief bright one (which, during the time of the eclipse, may hold connection, in any of the nine modes of apparent configuration detailed in the First Syntaxis[2] with the angles then actually in passage), is to be admitted to dominion ; as also that one which, at the ecliptical hour, may be in an eminent situation, either having risen, or having culminated with the angle following the place of the eclipse.[3]

Having considered, according to the foregoing rules, what stars co-operate in regulating the coming event, the conformation and figure of the signs, in which the eclipse takes place and the said ruling stars may be posited, are also to be observed ; and, from the properties and characteristics of those signs, the genus or species, to be comprehended in the event, is chiefly to be inferred.

For instance, should the zodiacal constellations, and those of the ruling fixed stars out of the zodiac, be of human shape, the effect will fall upon the human race. If the signs be not of human shape, but yet terrestrial, or quadrupedal, the event would be indicated to happen to animals of similar form : the signs shaped like reptiles signify that serpents and creatures of that description will be affected ; those bearing the figure of ferocious beasts denote that the event will affect savage and destructive animals ; and those figured like tame beasts show that it will operate on animals serviceable to mankind, and of domestic character ; as intimated by the shape and figure of the signs, whether resembling horses, oxen, sheep, or any other useful animals. In addition to this, the terrestrial signs situated in the north, about the Arctic circle, indicate sudden earthquakes ; and those in the south, sudden deluges of rain. And, should the ruling places be situated in signs shaped like winged animals, as in that of Aquila, or in others of similar form, the event will take effect on birds ; and will chiefly attach to those which afford food to man. If the said places should be in signs

---

[1] "When planets, in election for Lords of the eclipse, are found of equal strength and dignity, those which are direct are to be preferred before those which are retrograde ; and the oriental before the occidental."—*Whalley's "Annotations."*

[2] That is to say, in the Almagest, Book VIII, Chap. IV ; which chapter is given, entire, in the Appendix.

[3] "In electing fixed stars, Cardan directs to observe the angle which the eclipse follows, and that which it precedes : as, if the eclipse be between the seventh house" (or occidental angle) "and the mid-heaven, the stars which are in the seventh shall be preferred ; and next, those in the mid-heaven ; but, if between the mid-heaven and the ascendant, those in the mid-heaven shall have the preference ; and next, those in the ascendant."—*Whalley's "Annotations."*

formed like creatures which swim, and in marine signs, such as Delphinus, the effect will be felt by marine animals, and in the navigation of fleets ; if in river signs, such as Aquarius and Pisces, it will attach to animals living in rivers and in fresh waters : and, if in Argo, both sea and fresh-water animals will be affected by it.[1]

Again, should the ruling places be situated in tropical or in equinoctial signs, in either case alike they presignify changes in the state of the atmosphere, at the respective season to which each sign is appropriated. For example, with regard to the season of spring and the productions of the earth, if the said places should be in the sign of the vernal equinox, they will produce an effect on the buds of the vine and fig, and of such other trees as sprout forth at that season. Should they be in the sign of the summer tropic, the event will affect the gathering and depositing of fruits ; and, with respect to Ægypt in particular, it will impede the rising of the Nile. If they should be in the sign of the autumnal equinox, they foreshow that it will operate on grain and on various sorts of herbs ; if in the sign of the winter tropic, on potherbs, esculent vegetables, and such birds and fishes as arrive in that season.

The equinoctial signs further indicate the circumstances liable to happen in ecclesiastical concerns, and in religious matters : the tropical signs give warning of changes in the atmosphere and in political affairs ; the fixed signs, of changes in institutions and in buildings ; and the bicorporeal signs show that the future event will fall alike on princes and their subjects.

Again, the ruling places situated in the east, during the time of the eclipse, signify that fruits and seeds, incipient institutions, and the age of youth, will be affected ; those, which may be in the mid-heaven above the earth announce that the coming event will relate to ecclesiastical affairs, to kings and princes, and to the middle age ; those in the west, that it will influence the laws, old age, and persons about to die.

The proportion liable to be affected, of that genus or kind on which the event will fall, is to be ascertained by the magnitude of the obscuration caused by the eclipse, and by the positions held by the operative stars in regard to the ecliptical place ; as, in vespertine position to a solar eclipse, or in matutine position to a lunar eclipse, the said stars will most usually much diminish the effect ; in opposition they render it moderate ; but in matutine position to a solar eclipse, or in vespertine to a lunar, they greatly augment and extend it.[2]

---

[1] It is perhaps unnecessary to remark, that, in speaking of ruling places, as liable to be situated in Aquila, Delphinus or Argo, Ptolemy alludes only to the places of the fixed stars in dominion : since the ecliptical place and the planets must be confined to the zodiacal signs.

[2] According to Whalley, Cardan, in reference to the nine modes of configuration, applicable to the fixed stars, says, " When a fixed star is with any planet, or in any angle, consider whether it be by any of these ways ; if not,

CHAPTER IX

THE QUALITY AND NATURE OF THE EFFECT

THE discrimination of the peculiar properties and character of the effect about to be produced, and of its good or evil nature, occupies the fourth and last division of this part of the subject.

These properties must be gathered from the power of the stars which control the ruling places, and from the contemperament created by their relative admixture with each other and with the places which they control. For, although the Sun and Moon are the acknowledged sources of all the efficacy and dominion of the stars, and of their strength or weakness, and in a certain manner regulate and command them, still, it is by the theory of the contemperament, produced by the stars in dominion, that the effect is indicated.

In order to understand the indications thus made, it is necessary to begin by attending to the following detail of the effective property of each planet—previously observing, however, that, when any circumstance is said, for the sake of brevity, to come to pass by the general influence of the five planets, their temperament, and the power and assistance they may derive from natures similar to their own, the actual continuance of their own proper constitution, or the casual combination of any analogous influence, arising from fixed stars or places in the zodiac, are all, at the same time, to be kept in view. Consequently, whenever any general remark is herein made relative to the five planets, it will likewise be necessary to bear in mind both their temperament and quality; as fully, indeed, as if the stars themselves had not been named, but only their effective quality and nature. And, it is further to be remembered, that, in every case of compound temperament, not only the combination of the planets with each other requires to be considered, but also that of such fixed stars and zodiacal places as share in the natures of the planets, by being respectively connected with them according to the familiarities already described.

Hence, when Saturn may be sole governor, he will produce disasters concomitant with cold. And, in as far as the event may apply to the human race in particular, it will induce among men lingering diseases, consumptions, declines, rheumatisms, disorders from watery humours, and attacks of the quartan ague; as well as exile, poverty, and a general mass of evils, griefs, and alarms: deaths also will be frequent, but chiefly among persons advanced in age. That part of the brute creation which

it is most weak; if it be, consider whether it be with the Sun, and not to be seen; then it is very weak. Or if it is to be seen, and is with the Sun occidental, it is indifferent. Or if it be seen, and is not with the Sun, it is stronger; or if it be seen, and is oriental, then it is strongest."

is most serviceable to man will likewise suffer, and be destroyed by disease ; and men who make use of the animals thus diseased will be infected by them, and perish with them. The atmosphere will become dreadfully chilly and frosty, unwholesome, turbid and gloomy, presenting only clouds and pestilence. Copious and destructive storms of snow and hail will descend, generating and fostering insects and reptiles noxious to mankind. In rivers, and at sea, tempests will be frequent and general, causing disastrous voyages and many shipwrecks ; and even fish will be destroyed. The waters of the sea will retire for a time, and again return and produce inundations ; rivers will overflow their banks, and cause stagnant pools ; and the fruits of the earth, especially such as are necessary to sustain life, will be lost and cut off by blight, locusts, floods, rains, hail, or some similar agency ; and the loss will be so extensive as to threaten even famine.

Jupiter, if he should be lord alone, will thoroughly improve and benefit all things. Among mankind, in particular, this planet promotes honour, happiness, content, and peace, by augmenting all the necessaries and comforts of life, and all mental and bodily advantages. It induces also favours, benefits, and gifts emanating from royalty, and adds greater lustre to kings themselves, increasing their dignity and magnanimity : all men, in short, will share in the prosperity created by its influence. With regard to the operation of the event on brutes, those which are domestic and adapted to man's service will be multiplied and will thrive ; while others, which are useless and hostile to man, will be destroyed. The constitution of the atmosphere will be healthy and temperate, filled with gentle breezes and moisture, and favourable to fruits. Navigation will be safe and successful ; rivers will rise to their just proportion ; fruit and grain, and all other productions of the earth conducive to the welfare and happiness of mankind, will be presented in abundance.

Mars, when governing alone, generally causes such mischief and destruction as are concomitant with dryness. And, among mankind, foreign wars will be excited, accompanied with intestine divisions, captivity, slaughter, insurrections of the people, and wrath of princes against their subjects ; together with sudden and untimely death, the consequence of these disturbances. Feverish disorders, tertian agues, and hæmorrhages will take place, and will be rapidly followed by painful death, carrying off chiefly youthful persons : and conflagration, murder, impiety, every infraction of the law, adultery, rape, robbery, and all kinds of violence will be practised. The atmosphere will be parched by hot, pestilential, and blasting winds, accompanied by drought, lightnings, and fires emitted from the sky. At sea, ships will be suddenly wrecked by the turbulence of the wind and strokes of lightning. Rivers will fail, springs will be dried up, and there will be a scarcity of water proper for food and sustenance. All the creatures and productions of the earth adapted to the use of man, whether beasts, grain, or fruits, will be damaged or destroyed by excessive heat, by storms of thunder and lightning, or by violent winds ; and whatever has been deposited in store will be destroyed or injured by fire, or by heat.

Venus, alone in domination, generally produces the same effects as Jupiter, yet with greater suavity and more agreeably. Glory, honour, and joy will attend mankind ; happy marriages will be contracted, and the fortunate pairs will be blest with numerous children. Every undertaking will proceed prosperously, wealth will increase, and the conduct of human life will be altogether pure, simple and pious ; due reverence being paid to all holy and sacred institutions, and harmony subsisting between princes and their subjects. The weather also will be of a favourable temperature, cooled by moistening breezes ; the air altogether pure and salubrious, frequently refreshed by fertilising showers. Voyages will be performed in safety, and be attended by success and profit. Rivers will be improved, and receive their adequate supply of waters ; and all things valuable and useful to mankind, whether animal or vegetable, will abundantly thrive and multiply.

Mercury, if possessing dominion, is usually conjoined with one or other of the planets beforementioned, and is conformed and assimilated to their natures ; yet as, in itself, it presents a certain addition to their power, this planet increases the respective impulses of them all. And, in regard to the operation of the event on mankind, it will promote industry and skill in business ; but, at the same time, thievish propensities, robberies, and plots of treachery : if configurated with the malefics, it will produce calamities in navigation, and will also cause dry and parching diseases, quotidian fever, cough, consumption, and hæmorrhage. All parts of the ceremonies and services of religion, the affairs of the executive government, as well as manners, customs, and laws, are disposed and regulated by this planet, conformably to its admixture and familiarity with each of the others. And in consequence of the dryness of its nature, arising from its proximity to the Sun, and the rapidity of its motion, it will generate in the atmosphere turbulent, sharp and varied winds, together with thunders, meteors, and lightnings, accompanied by sudden chasms in the earth, and earthquakes : by these means it not unfrequently occasions the destruction of animals and plants assigned to the service of mankind. Besides the foregoing effects, it produces, when in vespertine position, a diminution of waters, and, when matutine, an augmentation.

Each of the planets, when fully exercising its own separate and distinct influence, will properly produce the peculiar effects above ascribed to it ; but should it be combined with others, whether by configuration, by familiarity arising from the sign in which it may be posited,[1] or by

---

[1] That is to say (technically speaking), by reception, or by being posited in a sign in which another planet has a certain dignity or prerogative.

its position towards the Sun, the coming event will then happen agreeably to the admixture and compound temperament which arise from the whole communion actually subsisting among the influencing powers. It would, however, be a business of infinite labour and innumerable combinations, quite beyond the limits of this treatise, to set forth fully every contemperament and all configurations, in every mode in which they can possibly exist; and the knowledge of them must therefore be acquired by particular discrimination in every instance, under the guidance of the precepts of science. Yet the following additional remark must not be here omitted.

The nature of the familiarities, subsisting between the stars, lords of the coming event, and the countries or cities over which the event will extend, requires to be observed; for, should the stars be benefic, and their familiarity with the countries liable to sustain the effect be unimpeded by any opposing influence, they will then exercise the favourable energies of their own nature in a greater degree. And, on the other hand, when any obstacle may intervene to obstruct their familiarity, or when they themselves may be overpowered by some opposing influence, the advantages of their operation will be diminished. Again, should the stars, lords of the coming event, not be benefic, but injurious, their effect will be less severe, provided they may either have familiarity with the countries on which the event will fall, or be restrained by some opposing influence. If, however, they should have no such familiarity, and not be subjected to restraint by any others, endowed with a nature contrary to their own and possessing a familiarity with the countries in question, the evils which they produce will then be more violent and intense. And all these general affections, of whatever kind, whether good or evil, will be principally felt by those persons in whose individual nativities there may be found the same disposition of the luminaries (which are the most essential significators), or the same angles, as those existing during the eclipse which operates the general affection. The same remark equally applies to other persons, in whose nativities the disposition of the luminaries and of the angles may be in opposition to that existing during the eclipse. With respect to these coincidences, the partile agreement, or opposition, of the ecliptical place of the luminaries to the place of either luminary in a nativity, produces an effect at least capable of being guarded against.[1]

[1] In conformity to the rule laid down in Chap. VI of this Book, those individuals whose nativities may thus resemble the position of the heavens at the time of an eclipse, and who are here stated to be chiefly liable to the effects of the eclipse, will be more affected by it, if it should be visible to them.

To the precepts contained in this chapter, Placidus makes the following allusion in his remarks on the nativity of Cardinal Pancirole. " Any significator whatever, together with the other stars, whilst they are moved by a converse universal motion, change the aspect alternately, and consequently the mundane rays, as it likewise happens when they acquire parallels : the rays thus acquired

CHAPTER X

COLOURS IN ECLIPSES; COMETS, AND SIMILAR PHENOMENA

IN investigating general events, it is necessary further to observe the colours or hues displayed during an eclipse, either in the luminaries, or around them; in the shape of rods or rays, or in other similar forms. For, if these colours or hues should be black, or greenish, they portend effects similar to those produced by Saturn's nature; if white, to those operated by Jupiter; if reddish, to those by Mars; if yellow, to those by Venus; and if of various colours, to those by Mercury.

And, if the entire bodies of the luminaries be thus coloured, or should the hues extend over all the parts immediately circumjacent to the luminaries, it is an indication that the effects will attach to most parts of the region, or countries, with which the eclipse and its ruling places may be in familiarity. If, however, the colouring should not spread over the whole surface of the luminaries, nor over all the parts around them, but be limited to some particular quarter, then only such a portion of the said countries, as may be indicated by the situation of the visible hues, will be comprehended in the event.

It is also requisite to notice, with respect to general events, the risings or first appearances of those celestial phenomena called comets, whether presenting themselves at ecliptical times or at any other periods. They are displayed in the shape of beams, trumpets, pipes, and in other similar figures, and operate effects like those of Mars and Mercury; exciting wars, heated and turbulent dispositions in the atmosphere, and in the constitutions of men, with all their evil consequences. The parts of the zodiac[1] in which they may be posited when they first appear, and the direction and inclination of their trains, point out the regions or places liable to be affected by the events which they threaten; and the form of the signs indicates the quality and nature of those events, as well as the genus, class, or kind, on which the effect will fall. The

are of a long continuance, and denote a certain universal disposition of the things signified, either good or bad, according to the nature of the aspecting stars; as it happened to this Cardinal, who some years before his death was always sickly: and this observation is wonderful in the changes of the times and weather; for this principle Ptolemy adhered to in the Almagest, lib. VIII, cap. 4; and this doctrine he also mentions in the 2nd Book of Judgments, in the chapter on the Nature of Events."—(Cooper's Transalation, p. 272.)

[1] When a comet appears out of the zodiac, a line should be drawn from one zodiacal pole to the other, through the spot where it appears; and that spot is to be considered as being in familiarity with the same countries as those parts of the zodiac which may be on the same line.—*Vide* Chap. IV of this Book, relative to the manner in which fixed stars out of the zodiac hold familiarity with certain regions and countries.

time of their continuance shows the duration of their effect ; and their position, with regard to the Sun, the period when it will commence ; as, if they first appear matutine, they denote an early commencement ; but, if vespertine, that it will be late and tardy.

The general and more comprehensive parts of the consideration regarding regions, countries, and cities, having now been explained, it becomes necessary to discuss certain particular points of the same consideration ; that is to say, the annual occurrences which take place at certain fixed seasons, and the chief of which is that called the New Moon of the Year.

CHAPTER XI

THE NEW MOON OF THE YEAR

In every annual revolution made by the Sun, the first new Moon of the year is to be considered as the point of the commencement of his circuit ; this is evident not only from its denomination, but from its virtue also.[1]

The case stands thus : In the ecliptic, which, as circle, has in fact no actual or definite beginning, the two equinoctial and the two tropical points, marked by the equator and the tropical circles, are reasonably assumed as beginnings. And to obviate any doubt as to which of these four points should preferably be considered as the primary beginning (since in the regular simple motion of a circle no part of it has any apparent precedence), the appropriate quality naturally belonging to each of these four points has been taken into consideration by the writers on this subject. And the point of the vernal equinox has been consequently designated by them as the beginning of the year ; because, from that time, the duration of the day begins to exceed that of the night, and because the season then produced partakes highly of moisture, which is always a predominant quality in all incipient generation and growth. After the vernal equinox comes the summer solstice ; when the day attains its greatest length, and in Ægypt, at the same period, the rise of the Nile takes place and the Dog Star appears. Then follows the autumnal equinox, when all fruits are gathered in, and the sowing of seeds recommences anew ; lastly, comes the winter solstice, when the day proceeds from its shortest duration towards its increase.

Although the foregoing arrangement has been adopted by men of

---

[1] The Neomenia, or new Moon, was observed as a festival with much solemnity in earlier ages and by the most ancient nations. It was celebrated by the Israelites, as well as by Pagan ; and it may perhaps be gathered from the 5th and 6th verses of the 20th Chapter of the 1st Book of Samuel, that it was kept once in a year with greater ceremony than at other times : this was done, probably, at the " New Moon of the Year," as Ptolemy calls it ; or, in other words, at the new Moon nearest to the vernal equinox.

science to denote the commencement of the several seasons of the year, it yet seems to be more consonant to nature, and more consistent with the facts, that the combined positions of the Sun, and the new, or full, Moon, which happen when the Sun is nearest to the points above-mentioned, should mark the four beginnings ; and more especially if such combined positions should produce eclipses : thus, from the new or full Moon, taking place when the Sun is nearest to the first point of Aries, the spring should be dated ; from that when the Sun is nearest to the first point of Cancer, the summer ; from that when he is nearest to the first point of Libra, the autumn ; and from that when he is nearest to the first point of Capricorn, the winter. The Sun not only produces the general qualities and constitutions of the seasons, by means of which very illiterate persons are enabled, in a certain degree, to form predictions, but he also regulates the proper significations of the signs with regard to the excitation of the winds, as well as other general occurrences, more or less subjected to occasional variation. All these general effects are usually brought about by the new or full Moon which takes place at the aforesaid points, and by the configurations then exist-ing between the luminaries and the planets : but there are certain particular consequences which result from the new and full Moon in every sign,[1] and from the transits of the planets ; " and which require monthly investigation."[2]

It therefore becomes necessary to explain, in the first instance, the particular natures and attributes exercised by each sign in influencing the several constitutions of the weather, as it exists at various times of the year ; these natures and attributes shall now be immediately detailed. It will be recollected, that the particular properties of the planets and the fixed stars, as affecting the wind and the atmosphere, as well as the manner in which the entire signs hold familiarity with the winds and the seasons, have been already set forth.

CHAPTER XII

THE PARTICULAR NATURES OF THE SIGNS BY WHICH THE DIFFERENT CONSTITUTIONS OF THE ATMOSPHERE ARE PRODUCED[3]

THE sign of Aries has a general tendency, arising from the presence of the Equinox, to promote thunder and hail. Certain of its parts, however, operate in a greater or less degree, according to the nature of the stars

---

[1] That is to say, at the new and full Moon taking place during the Sun's progress through each sign.

[2] The passage marked thus " " is not in the Greek, but is found in two Latin translations.

[3] According to Wing, in his " Instructions to the Ephemerides," printed in 1652, the signs, as mentioned in this chapter by Ptolemy, are to be considered

which compose the sign : for instance, the front parts excite rain and wind ; the middle are temperate ; and those behind are heating and pestilential. The northern parts, also, are heating and pernicious, but the southern cooling and frosty.

The sign of Taurus, in its general character, partakes of both temperaments,[1] but is nevertheless chiefly warm. Its front parts, and especially those near the Pleiades, produce earthquakes, clouds and winds : the middle parts are moistening and cooling ; those behind, and near the Hyades, are fiery, and cause meteors and lightnings. The northern parts are temperate ; the southern turbulent and variable.

Gemini, in its general tendency, is temperate ; but its leading parts produce mischief by moisture ; its middle parts are entirely temperate ; its latter parts mixed and turbulent. The northern parts promote earthquakes and wind ; and the southern are dry and heating.

Cancer is, in the whole, serene and warm, but its anterior part near the Præsepe are oppressively hot and suffocating ; the middle parts are temperate, and the latter parts excite wind. And both its northern and southern parts are equally fiery and scorching.

Leo has a general tendency operative of stifling heat. The anterior parts are oppressively and pestilentially hot ; yet the middle parts are temperate ; and those behind are injurious by means of moisture. The northern parts produce variation and heat, and the southern moisture.

Virgo, in its general tendency, excites moisture and thunder. The front parts, however, are chiefly warm and noxious ; the middle temperate ; and the latter parts watery. The northern parts promote wind ; the southern are temperate.

Libra has a general tendency to produce change and variation. Its front and middle parts are temperate ; its hinder parts watery. The northern parts cause variable winds, and the southern are moistening and pestilential.

Scorpio, in its general character, is fiery and productive of thunder. The front parts cause snow ; the middle are temperate ; the latter parts excite earthquakes. Its northern parts are heating ; its southern, moistening.

Sagittarius, generally, is effective of wind. The front parts are moistening ; the middle temperate ; and the hinder parts fiery. The northern parts promote wind, and the southern variation and moisture.

---

in their quality as constellations, and not as spaces of the heavens. This opinion, however, seems to me to be erroneous ; for Ptolemy has already devoted a chapter in the 1st Book to the detail of the influences of the several stars in the respective constellations of the zodiac ; and he moreover speaks, in the present chapter, of the operation of Aries, as owing to the presence of the Equinox. This he could not have done, had he spoken of the signs as constellations instead of spaces.

[1] The temperaments here alluded to are, probably, heat and cold.

Capricorn's general tendency is to operate moisture. But its anterior parts are pernicious by means of heat, its middle parts are temperate, and its latter parts promote rain. Both its northern and southern parts are injurious by means of moisture.

Aquarius, in its general character, is cold and watery. The front parts are moistening; the middle temperate; and the latter parts productive of wind. The northern parts are heating; the southern cause snow.

Pisces, in its general character, is cold and effective of wind. The front parts are temperate ; the middle moistening; the hinder parts highly heating. The northern parts excite wind, and the southern are watery.

CHAPTER XIII

MODE OF CONSIDERATION FOR PARTICULAR CONSTITUTIONS OF THE ATMOSPHERE

THE first part of the consideration, requisite to form an estimate of the various constitutions liable to take effect in the atmosphere, applies to the general qualities pervading the several quarters of the year, and has therefore the most extended scope. In order to learn these qualities, it is necessary, in every quarter, to observe, as above directed, the new or full Moon which may happen before[1] the period of the Sun's transit through

---

[1] "*Before.*" Although I have thus Englished the word, πρo, I think it properly requires to he here rendered, by "*at*" or "*near to,*" rather than "*before.*" Firstly, because my author (in speaking of the commencement of each quarter of the year, in the 11th Chapter, p. 93), has expressly stated that "the spring is to be dated from the new or full Moon taking place when the Sun is *nearest* (εγγισα) to the first point of Aries ; the summer from that, when he is *nearest* the first point of Cancer," &c., &c. ; and (in p. 94) he states that certain general effects are brought about by the new or full Moon occurring *at* (κατα) the aforesaid points." Secondly, because, in a few lines further on, in speaking of the monthly consideration, p. 98, he again uses only εγγισα, in reference to the present passage, in which, however, he has used only πρo. Thirdly, it is a proper inference that he meant to point out here the new or full Moon which may happen *nearest* to the tropical or equinoctial points, because he has previously and explicitly taught that the principal variation of all things depends upon those points. Lastly, Allatius has here rendered the word by no other than *proximé*, which is also the word given in the Perugio Latin of 1646.

On the other hand, Whalley, in his note on the present chapter, says, that "according to this Prince of Astrologers " (meaning Ptolemy), "we are to observe the new or full Moon preceding the ingress, only, for our judgment on the succeeding quarter, and not the lunation succeeding : and the reason I conceive to be, because the lunation, which immediately precedes the ingress, carries its influence to the very position of the ingress itself, but not so that

either tropical or equinoctial point, whichever it may be ; and to arrange the angles (as in the case of a nativity) according to the degree and hour at which the new or full Moon may be found to happen, in every latitude for which the consideration may be desired. Such planets and stars as may have dominion over the places where the said new or full Moon happens, and over the following angle, are then to be noted, in the same manner as that stated with regard to eclipses. And after these preliminary steps have been attended to, a general inference may be drawn as to the proper qualities of the whole quarter ; and the intensity or relaxation of their operation is to be contemplated from the natures of the ruling planets and stars, distinguished by the faculties they possess, and by the mode in which they affect the atmosphere.

The second part of the consideration relates to each month, and requires a similar observation of the new or full Moon first taking place on the Sun's progress through each sign : and it must be remembered, that, if a new Moon should have happened at a period nearest to the Sun's transit over the past tropical or equinoctial point, the new Moon also in each succeeding sign, until the commencement of the next quarter, are to be observed ; but, if a full Moon should have so happened, then similar observation is to be made of each subsequent full Moon. The angles, also, must be duly attended to, as well as the planets and stars ruling in both the places[1] ; and especially the nearest phases, applications, and separations of the planets, and their properties. The peculiar qualities of the two places, and the winds, liable to be excited by the planets themselves and by those parts of the signs in which they may be situated, are likewise to be considered ; and also that particular wind, which is indicated by the direction of the Moon's ecliptical latitude. By the aid of these observations, and by weighing and comparing the existing vigour of each of the several properties and qualities, the general constitution of the atmosphere during each month may be predicted.

The third part of this consideration appertains to significations applying more minutely, and points out their force or weakness. In

which follows the ingress." Wing, in his Introduction to the Ephemerides (London, 1652) also says, that " for the knowledge of the weather, it is requisite to observe the conjuction or opposition of the luminaries next *preceding* the Sun's ingress into the first point of Aries."

Now, if a new or full Moon happen *immediately after* the Sun's transit or ingress, the previous full or new Moon must have happened *a fortnight before* the said transit or ingress ; and, after considering the other parts of Ptolemy's doctrine, I do not conceive, that he intended to teach, in this chapter, that a *previous* lunation, when at so great a distance before the important ingress, would have a greater influence over the ensuing quarter of the year, than a *subsequent* lunation taking place so closely after the said ingress.

[1] " *Both the places.*" These are the places of the new or full Moon, and of the following angle ; as before mentioned with regard to the quarterly consideration.

this case, the partile configurations of the Sun and Moon, at the intermediate quarters, as well as at the new or full Moon, are to be attentively
regarded ; since there is a certain variation in the constitution of the
atmosphere, which usually commences about three days before, and
sometimes, also, about three days after the Moon has equated her course
to the Sun.   The configurations effected between the Moon, at each
quarterly equation, and the planets, whether by the trine, sextile, or
other authorized distances, are also to be observed ; because the peculiar
property of the change in the constitutions of the atmosphere depends
much upon such configurations, and may be accordingly perceived by
considering the nature of the influence which the said configurated
planets and the signs exercise over the atmosphere and the winds.

The particular quality of the weather, thus produced, will be more
fully established on certain days ; especially when the brighter and more
efficacious fixed stars may be near the Sun, either matutine or vespertine ;
as, when so posited, they most frequently convert the constitution of
the atmosphere to an agreement with their own natures : and, when the
Luminaries may transit any one of the angles, a similar effect is also
produced.   At all such positions the particular constitutions of the
atmosphere are subject to variation, and thus become alternately more
intense or more relaxed in their respective qualities.   In this manner, by
certain positions of the Moon, the flux and reflux of the sea are caused :
and, when the Luminaries may be in angles, a change of the wind is
produced, according to the direction of the Moon's ecliptical latitude.

Finally, in all these considerations, it must be remembered that the
more general and first constituted cause takes precedence, and that
the particular cause comes subsequently and secondarily : and,
that the operation is in the highest degree confirmed and strengthened,
when the stars, which regulate the general effects, may be also configurated towards the production of the particular effects.

CHAPTER XIV

THE SIGNIFICATION OF METEORS

In order to facilitate prognostication in minor and more limited instances, it is important to make further observation of all remarkable
appearances occasionally visible around or near the Sun, Moon, and
stars.   And, for the diurnal state of the atmosphere, the Sun's rising
should be remarked ; for the nocturnal state, his setting ; but the
probable duration of any such state must be considered by reference
to the Sun's configuration with the Moon ; for, in most cases, each
aspect, made between them, indicates the continuance of a certain
state until another aspect shall take place.

Hence, the Sun, when rising or setting, if he shine clear and open, free from mists, gloom, and clouds, promises serene weather. But, if he have a wavering or fiery orb, or seem to emit or attract red rays, or if he be accompanied in any one part by the clouds called parhelia, or by other reddish clouds of extended figure, in the form of long rays, he then portends violent winds, chiefly liable to arise from those parts in which the said phenomena may have shown themselves. If he should be pale or lurid, and rise or set encumbered with clouds, or surrounded by halos, he indicates storms and winds coming from the quarter of his apparent situation : and, if he be also accompanied by parhelia, or by lurid or dark rays, similar effects are also threatened from the parts where those appearances may be situated.[1]

The Moon's course is to be carefully observed, at the third day before or after her conjunction with the Sun, her opposition, and her intermediate quarters ; for, if she then shine thin and clear, with no other phenomena about her, she indicates serenity ; but, if she appear thin and red, and have her whole unilluminated part visible, and in a state of vibration, she portends winds from the quarter of her latitude and declination[2] : and if she appear dark, or pale and thick, she threatens storms and showers. All halos formed around the Moon should also be observed ; for, if there appear one only, bright and clear, and decaying by degrees, it promises serene weather ; but, if two or three appear, tempests are indicated : and, if they seem reddish and broken, they threaten tempests, with violent and boisterous winds ; if dark and thick, they foreshow storms and snow ; if black and broken, tempests with both winds and snow ; and, whenever a greater number may appear, storms of greater fury are portended.

The planets, also, and the brighter fixed stars, occasionally have halos, which indicate certain effects appropriate to their tinctures, and to the nature of the stars around which they may be situated.

The apparent magnitudes of the fixed stars, and the colours of the luminous masses among them, are likewise to be remarked : for, when the stars appear brighter and larger than usual, they indicate an excitation of the wind from that quarter in which they may be situated. The nebulous mass of the Præsepe in Cancer, and others similar to it, also require observation ; as, if in fine weather they appear gloomy and

---

[1] Similar precepts may be found finely illustrated in Virgil's 1st Georgic, vide I, 433 et infra :

"Sol quoque et exoriens et cum se condit in undas
Signa dabit : "———

[2] Virgil has said almost the same thing in these beautiful lines :

"At si virgineum suffuderit ore ruborem
Ventus erit : vento semper rubet aurea Phœbe."—Georg. I, l. 430.

See also the whole passage, beginning at l. 424 :

"Si vero Solem ad rapidum Lunasque sequentes
Ordine respicies," &c.

indistinct, or thick, they thereby threaten a fall of rain ; but, if clear and in continual vibration, they announce rough gales of wind.[1]

Appearances occasionally visible in the sky, resembling the trains of comets,[2] usually indicate wind and drought ; in a degree proportionate to their multitude and continuance.

Appearances, resembling shooting or falling stars, when presented in one part only, threaten a movement of wind from that part ;[3] when in various and opposite parts, they portend the approach of all kinds of tempestuous weather, together with thunder and lightning. Clouds resembling fleeces of wool will also sometimes presage tempests ; and the occasional appearance of the rainbow denotes, in stormy weather, the approach of serenity ; in fine weather, storms. And, in a word, all remarkable phenomena, visible in the sky, universally portend that certain appropriate events will be produced, each harmonising with its proper cause, in the manner herein described.

After the forgoing brief investigation of the more limited as well as more extensive significations, regarding general events, it becomes proper to proceed to the doctrine of genethliacal prognostication, or judgments of individual nativities.

---

[1] At this place, the following sentence, not found in the Greek, is inserted in a Latin translation :

" If the northern of the two stars, situated one on each side of the Præsepe, and called the Asini, should not appear, the north wind will blow : but, if the southern one be invisible, the south wind."

[2] These coruscations are, perhaps, similar to those now known by the name of the Aurora Borealis.

[3] Virgil again :

" Sæpe etiam stellas vento impendente videbis
    Præcipites cœlo labi."—&c.   *Georg.* I, 1. 365.

A great part of the 1st Georgic consists of astrological rules for predicting the weather, closely resembling the precepts here given by Ptolemy. Virgil is said to have adopted his doctrine from Aratus.

END OF BOOK II

BOOK THE THIRD

CHAPTER I

PROEM

IN the preceding pages, such events as effect the world generally have been discussed in priority; because they are operated by certain principal and paramount causes, which are, at the same time, predominant over particular and minor events applicable only to the separate properties and natural peculiarities of individuals. The foreknowledge of these particular events is called Genethlialogy, or the science of Nativities.

It must be remembered that the causation, by which all effects, whether general or particular, are produced and foreknown, is essentially one and the same; for the motions of the planets, and of the Sun and Moon, present the operative causation of events which happen to any individual, as well as of those which happen generally; and the foreknowledge of both may be obtained by the several creatures and substances, subjected to the influence of the heavenly bodies, and by due attention to the changes produced in those natures, by the configurations displayed in the Ambient by the planetary motion.

Still, however, the causes of general events are greater and more complete than those of particular events; and, although it has been now stated, that one single identical power supplies both the causation and the foreknowledge of general as well as particular events, yet there does not belong to the two sorts of events a similar origin or beginning, at which observation of the celestial configurations must be made, for prognostication. In regard to general events, the dates of origin and commencement are many and various; for all general events cannot be traced to one origin, neither is their origin always considered by means of the matter subjected to their operation, for it may be also established by circumstances occurring in the Ambient and presenting the causation. It may, in fact, almost be said that they all originate in eminent eclipses of the Luminaries, and in remarkable transits made by the stars, at various times.

Particular events, however, which concern men individually, may be traced to one origin, single as well as manifold. Their origin is single, in respect to the primary composition of the nascent man; but it is also manifold, in respect to other circumstances subsequently indicated by dispositions in the Ambient, correlative to the primary origin. In all

particular events, the origin, or birth, of the subjected matter itself,
must, of course, be the primary origin ; and, in succession thereto, the
various beginnings of other subsequent circumstances are to be assumed.
Hence, therefore, at the origin of the subjected matter, all the properties and peculiarities of its contemperament must be observed ; and
then the subsequent events, which will happen at certain periods,
sooner or later, are to be considered by means of the division of time, or
the scale of the ensuing years.[1]

CHAPTER II

THE CONCEPTION AND THE PARTURITION, OR BIRTH ; BY WHICH LATTER EVENT THE ANIMAL QUITS THE WOMB, AND ASSUMES ANOTHER STATE OF EXISTENCE

THE actual moment, in which human generation commences, is, in
fact, by nature, the moment of the conception itself ; but, in efficacy
with regard to subsequent events, it is the parturition or birth.

In every case, however, where the actual time of conception may be
ascertained, either casually or by observation, it is useful to remark the
effective influence of the configuration of the stars as it existed at that
time ; and, from that influence, to infer the future personal peculiarities of mind and body. For the seed will, at the very first, and at once,
receive its due quality, as then dispensed by the Ambient ; and, although in subsequent periods its substance is varied by growth and
conformation, it will still, by the laws of nature, congregate, during its
growth, only such matter as may be proper to itself, and will become
more and more imbued with the peculiar property of the first quality
impressed on it at the time of conception. These precepts must always
be attended to, when that time can be ascertained.

But, if the time of conception cannot be precisely made out, that of
the birth must be received at the original date of generation ; for it is
virtually the most important, and is in no respect deficient, on comparison with the primary origin by conception, except in one view
only ; viz. that the origin by conception affords the inference of occur-
ences which take effect previously to the birth, whereas the origin by
birth can, of course, be available only for such as arise subsequently.
And, although the birth should in strictness be called the secondary
beginning, while the conception might be insisted on as the primary
beginning, it is still found to be equal to the conception in its efficacy,
and much more complete, although later in time. For the conception
may, in fact, be said to be the generation of mere human seed, but the
birth that of man himself ; since the infant at its birth acquires

---

[1] The Division of Time is subsequently laid down by the author, in the last
Chapter of the fourth Book.

numerous qualities which it would not possess while in the womb, and which are proper to human nature alone; " such, for instance, as the particular action of the senses and the movement of the body and limbs."[1] Besides, even if the position of the Ambient, actually existing at the birth, cannot be considered to assist in forming and engendering the particular shape and qualities of the infant, it is nevertheless still auxiliary to the infant's entrance into the world : because nature, after completing the formation in the womb, always effects the birth in immediate obedience to some certain position of the Ambient, corresponding and sympathising with the primary position which operated the incipient formation. It is therefore perfectly admissible, and consistent with reason, that the configuration of the stars, as it exists at the time of birth, although it cannot be said to possess any share of the creative cause, should still be considered to act in signification, as fully as the configuration at the time of conception ; because it has, of necessity, a power corresponding to that configuration which actually possessed the creative cause.

In speaking of the practicability of prognostication, in the commencement of this treatise, the intention of setting forth this part of the subject, now under consideration, in a scientific manner, has been already notified. The ancient mode of prediction, founded on the commixture of all the stars, and abounding in infinite complication and diversity, will therefore be passed over ; and, in fact, any attempt to detail it, however accurately and minutely made, in conformity to the several precepts given in the traditions relating to it, would prove unserviceable and unintelligible : it is therefore entirely abandoned. And the doctrine, now presented, comprehending every species of event liable to happen, and explaining all the effective influences generally exercised by the stars, in their separate qualities, over every species of event, shall be delivered succinctly, and in agreement with the theory of nature.

With this view, certain places in the Ambient, regulating the formation of all inferences of the events liable to affect mankind, are appointed as a kind of mark to which the whole theory of those inferences is applied, and to which the operative powers of the stars, when holding familiarity with the said places, are in a general manner directed : in the same way as, in archery, the arrow is directed to the target. And any event, which depends on the compound temperament of many various natures and influences together, must be left to the discretion of the artist, who, like the skilful archer, must himself judge of the best mode of hitting the mark.

To proceed methodically and in due order, it is proper to commence by investigating such general events as are open to consideration, and liable to have happened, or to happen, at the actual origin by birth ;

---

[1] The words, thus marked "   ", are not in the Greek, but in two Latin translations.

D

since, from that origin, all things necessary to be investigated may be gathered ; as before stated. Yet, if a previous inquiry, by means of the primary origin by conception, should nevertheless be desired and undertaken, such an inquiry may still in some degree assist prognostication ; although only in regard to properties and qualities dispensed and imbibed at the time of conception.

CHAPTER III

THE DEGREE ASCENDING

THERE frequently arises some uncertainty as to the precise time of birth, and some apprehensions lest it should not be accurately noted. In most cases, the actual minute of the hour, at which the birth happens, can only be ascertained by making a scientific observation, at the time, with an horoscopical astrolabe[1] ; for all other instruments, employed in ascertaining the hour, are almost fallacious, although used by many persons with much care and attention. The clepsydra,[2] for instance, is subject to error, because the flow of the water will, from various causes, proceed irregularly : and the sundial is often incorrectly placed, and its gnomon often distorted from the true meridian line. To obviate the difficulty arising from the inaccuracy of these instruments, it seems highly necessary to present some method by which the actually ascending degree of the zodiac may be easily ascertained, in a natural and consistent manner.

And in order to attain this essential point, it is necessary first to set down the ordinary degree which, by the Doctrine of Ascensions,[3] is found near the ascendant at the presumed hour. After this has been done, the new or full Moon, whichever it may be, that may take place next before the time of parturition, must be observed : and, if a new Moon, it will be necessary to mark exactly the degree of the conjunction of the two luminaries ; but, if a full Moon, the degree of luminary only which may be above the earth during the parturition. After this, it must be observed what planets have dominion over the said degree : and their dominion depends always on the five following prerogatives, viz. on triplicity, house, exaltation, terms, and phase or configuration[4] ;

---

[1] It is, perhaps, needless to remark that modern improvements in science have superseded the use of this and other ancient instruments here mentioned.

[2] Although the " clepsydra," or water-clock, was commonly used among the ancients for various purposes, it appears, from Martian (a Latin writer, who lived about A.D. 490), that there was also a clepsydra in special use as an astrological engine.

[3] " *The Doctrine of Ascensions*," in allusion to the method of calculating the actual position of the ecliptic.

[4] " *Phase or configuration.*" Or, holding some authorized aspect to the degree in question.

that is to say, a planet, eligible to dominion, must be connected with the degree in question either by one, or more, or all of these prerogatives.

If, therefore, there may be found any one planet properly qualified in all or most of these prerogatives, the exact degree, which it occupies in that sign in which it may be posited during the parturition, is to be remarked ; and it is then to be inferred that a degree of the same numerical denomination was actually ascending, at the precise time of birth, in that sign which appears, by the Doctrine of Ascensions, to be nearest to the ascendant.[1]

But when two planets, or more, may be equally qualified in the manner prescribed, it must be seen which of them may transit, during the parturition, a degree nearest in number to the ordinary degree shown by the Doctrine of Ascensions to be then ascending ; and that said degree, nearest in number, is to be considered as pointing out the numerical denomination of the degree actually ascending. And when the degrees of two planets, or more, may closely and equally approximate in numerical denomination to the ordinary degree found by the Doctrine of Ascensions, the degree of that planet which possesses further claims, by connection with the angles and by its own condition, is to regulate the number of the actually ascending degree.

It must however be observed, that if the actual distance of the degree, in which the ruling planet may be posited, from the ordinary degree ascending, be found to exceed its distance from the ordinary degree of the mid-heaven ; the numerical denomination, found in the way above-mentioned, is then to be considered as applicable to the actual degree in culmination ; and the other angles are to be arranged in conformity therewith.[2]

CHAPTER IV

DISTRIBUTION OF THE DOCTRINE OF NATIVITIES

AFTER due attention to the preceding instructions, the doctrine of genethliacal prognostication should be separately and distinctly considered, for the sake of order and perspicuity, in its first, second and successive divisions or heads of inquiry. It will thus be found to present a mode of investigation, at once practicable, competent and agreeable to nature.

One division is applicable only to certain circumstances established previously to the birth ; as, for instance, to those which concern the

---

[1] Or, on the ascendant.

[2] The precepts delivered in this Chapter have obtained the name of Ptolemy's Animodar : the term is probably Arabic, if it be not a corruption of the Latin words *animum*, or *animam*, *dare*, " giving animation or life " ; yet this meaning seems scarcely close enough.

parents; another to circumstances, which may be established both before and after the birth; as those respecting brothers and sisters; another to circumstances actually occurring at the very time of birth, and immediately consequent thereupon: and this head of inquiry embraces various points, and is by no means simple: and the last division relates to events liable to take place after the birth, at various periods, earlier or later; and it involves a still more diversified theory.

Thus, the questions to be solved, in regard to the actual circumstances of the birth itself, are, whether the production will be male or female; twins, or even more; whether it will be monstrous; and whether it will be reared.

The questions of the periods subsequent to the birth relate first to the duration of life (which is distinct from the question of rearing), then to the shape and figure of the body, to the bodily affections, and to injuries or defects in the members. After these, further inquiry is instituted as to the quality of the mind, and the mental affections; then, as to fortune, in regard to rank and honours as well as wealth. In succession to these, the character of the employment or profession is sought out; then, the questions relative to marriage and offspring, and to consentaneous friendship, are to be considered; then, that concerning travel; and, lastly, that concerning the kind of death which awaits the native. The question of death, although depending, in fact, upon the same influence as the question of the duration of life, seems yet to find its proper situation in being placed last in the series.

On each of the foregoing points of inquiry, the doctrine and precepts to be followed shall be thoroughly and succinctly detailed; but all idle conceits, promulgated by many persons without any foundation capable of sustaining the test of reason, shall be utterly avoided, in deference to the only true agency, which is derived from primal Nature herself. It is only upon clearly effective influences that this treatise is established: and all matters, which are open to an authorized mode of inquiry by means of the theory of the stars, and their positions and aspects with regard to appropriate places, shall be fully discussed here; but the divination by lots and numbers, unregulated by any systematic causation, must remain unnoticed.

The brief remarks, immediately following, are applicable to all cases, generally, and are now at once stated, to avoid the repetition of them under each particular division or head of inquiry.

Firstly, notice must be taken of that place in the zodiac which corresponds, according to the scheme of the nativity with the particular division of inquiry; for example, the place of the mid-heaven is adapted to questions comprised under the head of employment or profession; and the Sun's place to those relative to the concerns of the father.

Secondly, after the proper place has thus been duly ascertained, the planets holding right of dominion there, by any of the five prerogatives hereinbefore mentioned, are to be observed; and, if any one planet be found to be lord by all these prerogatives, that planet must be admitted as the ruler of the event liable to happen under that particular head of inquiry. If, however, two or three planets hold dominion, that one among them, which may have most claims to the place in question, must be selected as the ruler.

Thirdly, the natures of the ruling planet and of the signs, in which itself and the place which it thus controls may severally be situated, are to be considered as indicating the quality of the event.

Fourthly, the proportionate vigour and strength, or weakness, with which the dominion is exercised, as exhibited either by the actual cosmical position of the ruling planet, or by its position in the scheme of the nativity, will point out to what extent and with what force the event will operate. And a planet is found to be cosmically powerful when in one of its own places,[1] or when oriental, or swift in course; and it is strong in the scheme of the nativity, when transiting an angle or succedent house; especially those of the ascendant, or of the mid-heaven. But it is cosmically weaker, when not in one of its own places; or when occidental, or retarded in its course; and in respect to the scheme of the nativity, it is weak when cadent from the angles.

Lastly; the general time, about which the event will take place, is to be inferred from the ruling planet's matutine or vespertine position, in regard to the Sun and the ascendant, and from the circumstance of its being situated in an angle, or a succedent house. As, if it be matutine, or in an angle, its influence operates earlier and more promptly; but, if vespertine or in a succedent house, later and more tardily. And, in reference to this point, the quadrant which precedes the Sun, and that which precedes the ascendant, together with the quadrants opposite to these, are oriental and matutine; and the other quadrants, following the former, are occidental and vespertine.

CHAPTER V

THE PARENTS

UNDER each head of inquiry, the proposed investigation must be entered upon in the manner mentioned in the preceding chapter: and, to proceed in due order, the circumstances relating to the parents require to be first disposed of.

In conformity with nature, the Sun and Saturn are allotted to the person of the father; and the Moon and Venus to that of the mother: and the mode in which these luminaries and planets may be found posited, with reference to each other, as well as to other planets and stars, will intimate the situation of affairs affecting the parents.

Thus, for example, the degree of their fortune and wealth will be

---

[1] In House, Triplicity, Exaltation, Term or Face.

indicated by the doryphory,[1] or attendants of the luminaries. If the luminaries be accompanied (either in the same signs in which themselves are placed, or in the signs next following), by the benefics, and by such stars or planets as are of the same tendency as themselves, a conspicuous and brilliant fortune is presaged : especially, should the Sun be attended by matutine stars, and the Moon by vespertine,[2] and these stars be also well established in the prerogatives before mentioned. Likewise, if Saturn or Venus be matutine, and in proper face,[3] or in an angle, it foreshows the prosperity of either parent respectively, according to the scheme.[4] If, however, the luminaries hold no connection with the planets, and be unattended by any doryphory, the adverse fortunes of the parents, their humble state and obscurity, and then denoted ; especially, if Saturn and Venus may not be favourably constituted. The parents are also subjected to a state of vicissitude, never rising above mediocrity, when the luminaries may have a doryphory of a condition or tendency foreign to their own : as, for instance, when Mars may ascend near in succession to the Sun, or Saturn to the Moon ; or if the benefics be found constituted unfavourably, and not in conformity with their own natural condition and tendency. But should the part of fortune, as shown by the scheme of the nativity, be found in a favourable position, and in consonance with the doryphory of the Sun and Moon, the estate of the parents will then remain steady and secure. If, however, the position be discordant and adverse, or if the malefics compose the dory-phory, the parents' estate will be unproductive and even burthensome.

The probable duration of the lives of the parents is to be inferred by means of other configurations. And, in the case of the father, a long life is presaged, if Jupiter, or Venus, be in any mode whatever configurated with either the Sun, or Saturn ; or, also, if Saturn himself make an harmonious configuration with the Sun ; (that is to say, either by the conjunction, the sextile, or the trine) ; provided such configuration be fully and strongly established and confirmed :[5] and, when not so established and confirmed, although it does not actually denote a short life, yet it will not then equally presage a long life.

---

[1] Δορυφορια· This word has been heretofore rendered " *satellitium* " and " satellites," but, as these terms do not seem sufficiently precise in their meaning, and are already in use to signify the minor orbs which revolve round a principal planet, I have ventured to anglicize the Greek word ; the usual signification of which is a " bodyguard."

[2] Or, in other words, " should the stars, which attend the Sun, be such as rise *before him ;* and those, which attend the Moon, such as rise *after* her."

[3] As described in Chap. XXVI, Book I.

[4] Saturn being applicable to the father, and Venus to the mother.

[5] The Perugio Latin translation, of 1646, inserts here, " and provided Saturn and the Sun are not impeded by being posited in unfortunate or unsuitable places."

If however the planets be not posited in the manner just described ; and if Mars be elevated above,[1] or ascend in succession to the Sun, or to Saturn ; or, even, should Saturn himself not be in consonance with the Sun, but configurated with it by the quartile or opposition, and if, when thus circumstanced, both he and the Sun should be posited in cadent houses, it is then indicated that the father is liable to infirmities ; but, if in angles or succedent houses, the father will live only a short life, and suffer from various bodily injuries and diseases. The shortness of his life is particularly intimated by the position of the Sun and Saturn in the first two angles, viz. the ascendant and the mid-heaven, or in their succedent houses ; and his affliction by diseases and injuries, when they may be posited in the two other angles, the western and the lower heaven, or in the houses succedent thereto. And, if Mars be aspected to the Sun in the way before-mentioned, the father will die suddenly, or receive injury in his face or eyes ; but, should Mars be so aspected to Saturn, he will be afflicted with contractions of the muscles or limbs, and with fevers and disorders proceeding from inflammation and wounds ; or even death may be the consequence. And even Saturn himself, if badly configurated with the Sun, will also inflict disease and death on the father, by inducing such particular disorders as are incidental from watery humour.

The foregoing observations are applicable to the father, and those which follow must be attended to in the case of the mother.

Should the Sun be configurated, in any mode whatever, with the Moon or Venus, or, should Venus herself be harmoniously configurated with the Moon, either by the sextile, the trine, or the conjunction, the mother will live long.

If, however, Mars be succedent to the Moon and Venus, or in quartile or opposition to them, or, if Saturn be similarly aspected to the Moon only, and both of them be void of course or retrograde, or cadent,

---

[1] "*Elevated.*" Moxon's Mathematical Dictionary gives the following definition of this astrological term. "*Elevated.* A certain pre-eminence of one planet above another ; or, a concurrence of two to a certain act, wherein one being stronger, is carried above the weaker, and does alter and depress its nature and influence : But wherein this being *elevated* consists, there are several opinions ; some say when a planet is nearest the zenith, or meridian ; others will have it only that planet is highest ; or nearest to the Apogæon of his eccentric or epicycle. And Argol admits of all these, and several other advantages, and thence advises to collect the several testimonies, and that that planet, who has most, shall be said to be elevated above the other." According to Whalley, Cardan's opinion was that " that planet is most elevated which is more occidental and ponderous." For myself, I conceive this opinion to be inaccurate, because, if Ptolemy meant to signify only the greater occidentality of the planet, he would (as in other instances) have used the word "*preceding*" instead of "*elevated above*" ; and I incline to think, that *greater proximity to the zenith* is the truer, as well as more simple, meaning of the term " elevated."

adverse accidents and disease will attend the mother; should they, on the other hand, be swift in motion and placed in angles, they portend that her life will be short, or grievously afflicted. Their position in the oriental angles, or succedent houses, particularly denotes the shortness of her life; and, in those which are occidental, her affliction. In the same manner, should Mars be thus aspected to the Moon (and should that luminary at the same time be oriental), the mother's sudden death, or some injury in her face or eyes, will be produced: and, if the Moon be then occidental, death will be occasioned by miscarriage in parturition, by inflammation, or by wounds. Such are the effects which ensue from these aspects made by Mars to the Moon; but, should he make them to Venus, death will then take place from fever, some latent disease, or sudden sickness. Saturn's aspect[1] to the Moon, when she is oriental, inflicts on the mother disease and death from extreme colds, or fevers; but, should the Moon be occidental, the danger arises from affections of the womb, or from consumption.

In the investigation of all these circumstances, it is highly essential that the properties of the signs, in which are situated the stars actuating the influence, should be also taken into consideration; and that, by day, the Sun and Venus should be principally observed; and by night, Saturn and the Moon.

If, however, after due attention has been paid to the foregoing points, a more specific inquiry still be demanded, it will then become necessary to assume the place allotted to the naternal or maternal condition, as the case may be, for an horoscope or ascendant, in order to pursue the investigation.[2] And by this means, which in this respect will answer the purpose of a nativity, all other particulars concerning the parents may be viewed succinctly; according to the general forms hereinafter given, as adapted for practice and applicable to all events.

In these and in all other cases, the mode, in which the influences are commixed, must be carefully kept in view; and it must be observed whether any particular stars possess, in themselves alone, the operative cause, or whether others share dominion with them; and it is then to be seen which among them all are more powerful, and which of them take the lead in establishing the event: so that due inference may be

---

[1] By the quartile or opposition, as before mentioned.

[2] On this passage, Whalley remarks that "Ptolemy teacheth, from the child's nativity, to erect schemes for the father and mother, and thence to give judgment, as if it were their proper nativities; the rule is this: If the nativity be diurnal, for the father, observe the degree the Sun is in, in the child's nativity; and make that the degree ascending for the father; and conformable to that, order the cusps of all the other houses. If for the mother, use Venus. But if the nativity be nocturnal, for the father, take the place of Saturn; and for the mother, that of the Moon." Whalley adds, that what in this chapter hath relation to the parents, is what shall happen to them *after* the nativity, and not *before*."

drawn agreeably to their several natures. And should the several stars, which may happen to be combined in dominion, be also equal in power, the diversity of their several natures, and the admixture of qualities thence arising, must then be taken into consideration ; and, by fairly weighing this various admixture, the nature and quality of the future event may be apprehended.

Stars, posited separately or at a distance from each other, distribute, at their appropriate times and periods, the events operated by each : thus the earlier events are brought about by stars which are more oriental than others, and the latter events by those which are more occidental. For it is indispensably requisite that the star, under the influence of which some particular event is expected to happen, should be originally[1] connected with the place to which the inquiry, concerning that event, is allotted ; and, if such connection should not have existed, no effect of any importance an possibly be produced ; because a star does not exercise a vigorous influence, unless it was fully in communication at the beginning. But, however, the time, at which the effect will take place, is further regulated by the relative distance of the star, governing the effect, from the Sun and the angles of the world, as well as by its primary position of dominion.

CHAPTER VI

BROTHERS AND SISTERS

UNDER this head of inquiry, a general and cursory investigation, only, can be performed ; and an attempt to dive into minute particulars would be fruitless, and would prove to be merely a vain search after things not open to discovery.[2]

The place, whence inferences are drawn respecting brothers and sisters, is to be considered as being applicable only to children of the same mother, and it is consequently, agreeably to nature, presumed to be the same as the maternal place ; viz. the sign occupying the mid-heaven ; or, by day, that which contains Venus, and, by night, the Moon. This sign and its succedent are considered as indicative of the mother and her children, and the same place is therefore properly allotted to brothers and sisters.

Hence, provided this place be configurated with the benefics, there

---

[1] Or, at the actual time of nativity.

[2] In spite of this declaration of the author, it seems, by Whalley's note on this chapter, that Cardan maintained that the particular circumstances, liable to affect the brothers and sisters, might be inferred by adopting, as an ascendant, the degree of the planet holding chief dominion over the place of brethren, and erecting a scheme thereby ; in a mode similar to that allowed by Ptolemy in the case of the parents.

D *

will be several brothers and sisters : the number of them depending upon the number and positions of such benefic stars, whether in bicorporeal signs, or in signs of single form.

If, however, the malefics should be in elevation over this place, or be hostilely situated in opposition thereto, the brothers and sisters will then be few in number ; and this fewness especially follows when the malefics may surround the Sun. Should the hostile configuration be presented from the other angles,[1] and, particularly, if from the ascendant, Saturn will then represent the elder born ; and Mars, by inflicting death, will diminish the total number of brothers and sisters.[2]

Again, should the stars, which promise brethren, be favourably circumstanced as to their cosmical position, the brethren will be eminent and illustrious ; but humble and obscure, if the cosmical position be of an adverse nature. If, also, the malefic stars should be in elevation over those which give brethren, the life of the brethren will then be only of short duration.

Stars, constituted masculinely, represent brothers ; those femininely, sisters. The more oriental stars likewise represent the elder born ; and those which are more occidental, the younger.

Moreover, should the stars, which give brethren, be harmoniously configurated with that one which has dominion of the sign allotted to brethren, the brethren will be mutually friendly and affectionate ; and, if an harmonious configuration be also extended, by the same planets, to the part of fortune, the brethren will live together in communion. But, if the stars, which give brethren, should, on the contrary, be in situations unconnected with each other, or be in opposition, the brethren will then live at variance, mutually practising enmity and fraud.

CHAPTER VII

MALE OR FEMALE

AFTER the indications which regard brothers and sisters have been investigated by the foregoing rules, consonant with nature and reason, the actual native, or the person to whom the scheme of nativity is specially appropriated, demands attention ; and the first and most obvious inquiry is whether the said native will be male or female.

The consideration of this question rests not on a single basis, nor

[1] That is to say, from the angles in quartile (and therefore hostile also) to the mid-heaven.

[2] The text does not show whether it be necessary that Saturn and Mars should *both* be in the ascendant, in order to produce the effect described ; nor whether the same effect would not follow, if one of them should be in the ascendant, and the other in the occidental angle, or even in some other position.

can it be pursued in one sole direction only : it depends, on the contrary, upon the several situations of the two luminaries and the ascendant, and upon such planets as possess any prerogatives in the places of those situations ; and all these circumstances should be specially observed at the time of conception, and, in a general manner also, at that of birth.

Observation of the said three places, and of the mode in which the planets ruling them may be constituted, is wholly indispensable : it must be seen whether all, or most of them, may be constituted masculinely or femininely ; and prediction must, of course, be regulated in conformity with their disposition, so observed ; as tending to produce a male or female birth.

The masculine or feminine nature of the stars is to be distinguished in the manner already pointed out in the commencement of this treatise.[1] For instance, by the nature of the signs in which they are situated, by their relative position to each other, and also by their position towards the earth ; as when in the east, they are masculinely disposed, and, when in the west, femininely. Their relative position to the Sun also affords guidance in distinguishing them ; since, if they should be matutine, they are considered to signify the male gender ; and if vespertine, the female. Thus, from the sex chiefly prevalent, as observed by these rules, that of the native may be rationally inferred.

CHAPTER VIII

TWINS

WITH respect to the probability of the birth of twins, or a greater number at once, the same places must be observed, as those mentioned in the preceding chapter ; that is to say, the places of both luminaries and the ascendant.

When two, or all three, of the said places may be situated in bicorporeal signs, births of this kind will occur, in consequence of the combination which then arises ; especially, provided all the planets, which control those places, should also be similarly circumstanced : or although only some of them be posited in bicorporeal signs, while the rest may be placed by two or more together. Because even more than twins will be born, in a case wherein all the ruling places may be in bicorporeal signs, most of the planets being, at the same time, posited in the same way, and configurated with them. The number of children, however, to be produced at the birth, is to be inferred from the planet which exercises the right of determining the number[2] : and the sex or

---

[1] *Vide* Chapter VI, Book I.

[2] The planet here alluded to, seems to be that which may be connected with most of the ruling places.

sexes are to be predicted by means of the planets in configuration with the Sun, Moon, and ascendant.

And, should the position of the heavens be arranged so that the angle of the mid-heaven, and not that of the ascendant, may be connected with the luminaries, there will, in that case, be produced, almost always, twins ; and sometimes even more.

To speak, however, more particularly, three males will be born, as in the nativity of the Anactores,[1] when Saturn, Jupiter, and Mars may be configurated with the places before appointed, in bicorporeal signs ; and three females, as in the nativity of the Graces, when Venus and the Moon, with Mercury femininely constituted, may be configurated in like manner. When Saturn, Jupiter, and Venus may be configurated, two males and one female will be born ; as in the nativity of the Dioscuri[2]; and, when Venus, the Moon, and Mars may be so configurated, two females and one male ; as in the nativity of Ceres, Core, and Liber.[3]

In cases of this kind, however, it most usually happens that the conception has not been complete, and that the children are born with some remarkable imperfections or deformities. And, in some instances, owing to a certain concurrence of events, these numerous productions are quite extraordinary and amazing.

[1] I have looked in many other books for this word "*Anactores*" (plural of ανακτωρ), as designating three particular individuals born at the same birth ; for which signification it is here used by Ptolemy ; but my search has been in vain. Cicero has, however, written a passage, in which a word, very nearly resembling it, occurs, and which would seem to relate to the very persons alluded to by Ptolemy : viz. "The godship of the Dioscuri was established in various modes among the Greeks, and applied to various persons. One set consisted of three persons, who were styled at Athens the *Anactes*, and were the sons of Jupiter, the most ancient king, and Proserpine ; their several names were Tritopatreus, Eubuleus and Dionysius." *De Nat. Deor.*, lib. 3, cap. 21.

[2] This is the second set of the Dioscuri, as stated by Cicero : they were the children of the third, or Cretan Jupiter (the son of Saturn) and Leda ; their names were Castor, Pollux, and Helena. Helena, however, is not mentioned by Cicero.

[3] Core is a name of Proserpine ; Liber, of Bacchus. And, although the mention here made of Ceres, Proserpine and Bacchus, as being the offspring of one and the same birth, does not accord with the usual notion of the genealogy of these divinities, it seems that Ptolemy did not so represent them without some reason. For, in cap. 24, lib. 2, *De Nat. Deor.*, Cicero speaks of Liber as having been deified conjointly with Ceres and Libera (another name of Proserpine) ; and adds, that "it may be understood, from the rites and mysteries of the worship, how the deification took place." It appears also, by Davies's notes on Cicero, that Livy and Tacitus both speak of the copartnership in divinity exercised by Liber, Libera and Ceres. There is not, however, any occasion at present to dive deeper into the question of the generation of these deities ; for our author has advertised to them only to point out that so many males or females will be produced at one birth, under certain configurations of the stars.

CHAPTER IX

MONSTROUS OR DEFECTIVE BIRTHS

THE same places, as those pointed out in the two chapters last preceding, are again to be considered, in inquiring into the probability of a monstrous or defective birth. For it will be found that, at a birth of this description, the luminaries are either cadent from the ascendant, or else not in any manner configurated with it ; while, at the same time, the angles[1] are occupied by the malefics.

It therefore becomes necessary, when such a position of the heavens may occur at the time of birth, to observe forthwith the preceding new or full Moon[2] and its ruler ; as well as the rulers of the luminaries at the said time of birth. For, if all the places, in which the rulers of the luminaries, and in which the Moon herself and Mercury may be situated, at the birth, or, if most of those places should be totally inconjunct and unconnected with the places of the said preceding new or full Moon and its ruler, the birth will then be monstrous. And if it should be further found, in addition to this absence of connection, that the luminaries may be also posited in quadrupedal or bestial signs, and the two malefics in angles, the birth will in that case not be human. And should the luminaries, when so circumstanced, be not at all supported by any benefic planet, but only by malefics, the creature born will be wholly indocile, wild, and of evil nature : if, however, they should receive support from Jupiter or Venus, the offspring will then be like that of dogs or cats, or other creatures held in religious veneration and used in worship[3] : but, if Mercury support the luminaries, it will resemble that of fowls, oxen, or swine, or, of other animals adapted to the service of mankind.

When the luminaries may be in signs of human shape, while other circumstances in the scheme of the nativity may exist as before described, the creature born will then be human, or will partake of human nature, although it will still be defective in some peculiar quality. And, in order to ascertain the nature of that defect, the shape and form of the signs found on the angles occupied by the malefics, as well as of those wherein the luminaries are situated, must be taken into consideration : and, if in this instance also, no benefic planet should lend support to any one of the prescribed places, the offspring produced will be utterly void of reason, and indeed indefinable.[4] If, however, it should happen, that Jupiter or Venus give support, the defect will be

---

[1] Whalley says here, " chiefly the ascendant and mid-heaven."

[2] Whichever might have been nearer in time.

[3] It is perhaps superfluous to mention that the two kinds of animals here named (as well as many others) were venerated by the Ægyptians.

[4] The Greek says " enigmatical."

veiled by a specious outward appearance, similar to that of herma-
phrodites, and of those persons called Harpocratiaci,[1] or others of like
imperfections. And should Mercury also give support, in addition to
that of Jupiter or Venus, the offspring will then become an interpreter
of oracles and divinations ; but, if Mercury support alone, it will be
deaf and dumb,[2] although clever and ingenious in its intellect.

CHAPTER X

CHILDREN NOT REARED

THE question which now remains to be considered, in order to complete
the investigation of circumstances taking place simultaneously with the
nativity, or immediately consequent thereon, is, whether the child,
then born, will or will not be reared.

This inquiry is to be handled distinctly from that regarding the
duration of life, although there is an apparent connection between
them. The questions themselves are, indeed, similar ; for it is much
the same thing to inquire whether the child will be nurtured, or how
long it will live ; and the only distinction, between these two questions,
arises from the different modes in which they are treated. For instance, the inquiry into the duration of life is to be pursued only in
cases wherein there is allotted to the native some space of time, not less
in duration than a solar period ; that is to say, a year. Therefore, since
time is also measured by smaller portions, such as months, days, and
hours, and since the question, whether the native will or will not be
reared, belongs to cases wherein some exuberance of evil influence
threatens speedy destruction, and where life is not likely to endure
throughout a whole year, the inquiry into the duration of life must
consequently involve a more multifarious consideration, than that
which relates to rearing ; which may be at once disposed of, in a more
general and summary manner.

Thus, if either of the two luminaries be in an angle, and one of the
malefics be either in conjunction with that luminary, or else distant in
longitude from each luminary, in an exactly equal space ; so as to form
the point of junction of two equal sides of a triangle, of which sides the
two luminaries form the extremities, while, at the same time, no
benefic star may partake in the configuration, and while the rulers of the

---

[1] One Latin translation has rendered this word " stammerers " ; and, as
Harpocrates was the god of silence, Ptolemy has probably used the epithet
to signify defect of speech.

[2] " Dumb." The Greek is οδοντων εξερημενον, " *deprived of teeth*," and
Allatius has so translated it : but other translations render these words by
dumb, which, considering the nature of Mercury, seems their preferable
signification.

luminaries may be also posited in places belonging to, or controlled by, the malefics; the child, then born, will not be susceptible of nurture, but will immediately perish.

Should the configuration, made between the malefic planet and the luminaries, not exist precisely in the mode just mentioned; that is to say, should the said planet not be equally distant from both luminaries, so as to form the point of junction of two equal sides of a traingle; yet should it then happen that the rays of two malefics may nearly approach the places of the two luminaries, casting an injurious influence either on both, or only one of them, and if both the said malefics be together succedent, or in opposition, to the luminaries, or if one of them be succedent, and the other in opposition, or even if only one may particularly afflict one of the luminaries, then, in any such case, no duration of life will be allotted to the child : for the supremacy of the power of the malefics extinguishes the influence favourable to human nature, and tending to prolong existence.

Mars is exceedingly pernicious when succedent to the Sun, and Saturn when succedent to the Moon. But a converse effect takes place when either of these planets may be in opposition to the Sun or Moon, or in elevation above them; for the Sun will then be afflicted by Saturn, and the Moon by Mars; and especially so, provided the said planets should have local prerogatives in the signs containing the luminaries, or in the sign on the ascendant. And, should a double opposition exist, by the circumstance of the luminaries being placed in two opposite angles, and by the two malefics being each so posited as to be equally distant from each luminary, the child will be born almost, if not quite, dead. Nevertheless, if the luminaries should be separating from, or be otherwise configurated with benefic planets, whose rays may be projected to parts preceding the said luminaries, the child will then live as many days, or hours, as there are degrees, numbered between the prorogator[1] and the nearest malefic.

If malefics should cast their rays to parts preceding the luminaries, and benefics to parts following them, the child will be abandoned at its birth; but will afterwards meet with adoption, and will live. Yet, if the malefics should be in elevation above those benefics which are thus configurated, the child, so adopted, will lead a life of misery and servitude : if, on the contrary, the benefics should be in elevation, then whoever may adopt the deserted child will supply the place of its parents. And, provided a benefic planet should either ascend with, or near in succession to the Moon, or be applying to her,

---

[1] A prorogator is either a luminary, planet, or a certain degree of the zodiac, which determines the duration of life, or the time of the accomplishment of any event : it is hereafter fully treated of in the 13th Chapter of this Book; which shows that, in the instance now mentioned, it would be a luminary, either in the ascendant, or in the mid-heaven.

and one of the malefics be occidental, the child's own parents will, in that case, take it again under their protection.

Rules similar to the foregoing are to be observed, when more than one child is born ; for, if any one of those planets, which may be configurated towards the production of two, or even more children, should be under the west, the children will be born half dead, or deformed, and imperfect in body. And, if the planet so situated should also be beneath the malefics, the children will not be susceptible of nurture, or their life will be of the shortest span.

CHAPTER XI

THE DURATION OF LIFE

OF all events whatsoever, which take place after birth, the most essential is the continuance of life : and as it is, of course, useless to consider, in cases wherein the life of a child does not extend to the period of one year, what other events contingent on its birth might otherwise have subsequently happened, the inquiry into the duration of life consequently takes precedence of all other questions, as to the events subsequent to the birth.

The discussion of this inquiry is by no means simple, nor easy of execution ; it is conducted in a diversified process, by means of the governance of the ruling places. And the method now about to be laid down seems, of all others, the most consonant with reason, and with nature : because the influence of the prorogatory places, as well as of the rulers of those places, and the disposal of the anæretic[1] places or stars, perform the whole operation of regulating the duration of life. Each of these influences is to be distinguished in the mode pointed out in the chapters immediately ensuing.

CHAPTER XII

THE PROROGATORY PLACES

FIRSTLY, those places, only, are to be deemed prorogatory, to which the future assumption of the dominion of prorogation exclusively belongs. These several places are the sign on the angle of the ascendant, from the fifth degree above the horizon, to the twenty-fifth degree below it ; the thirty degrees in dexter sextile thereto, constituting the eleventh house, called the Good Dæmon ; also the thirty degrees in dexter quartile, forming the mid-heaven above the earth ; those in dexter

---

[1] The epithet *anæretic* is a term of art, adopted from the Greek, signifying fatal, or destructive.

trine making the ninth house, called God; and lastly, those in opposition, belonging to the angle of the west.

Secondly, among these places, the degrees which constitute the mid-heaven are entitled to preference, as being of a more potent and paramount influence: the degrees in the ascendant are next in virtue; then the degrees in the eleventh house succedent to the mid-heaven; then those in the angle of the west; and, lastly, those in the ninth house, which precedes the mid-heaven.

No degrees under the earth are, in any manner, eligible to the dominion now in question; except such only as enter into light actually above the succedent, or, in other words, with the ascendant. And any sign, although it may be above the earth, is still incompetent to partake in this dominion, if it be inconjunct with the ascendant: hence the sign which precedes the ascendant, and constitutes the twelfth house (called that of the Evil Dæmon), is incompetent; and not only for the above reason, but also because it is cadent, and because the beams cast by the stars posited therein, towards the earth, are impaired by the thick and dark exhalations arising from the earth's vapours, which produce an unnatural colour and magnitude in the appearance of stars so posited, confusing, and in some measure annihilating, their beams.

Thus far with regard to the places of prorogation.

CHAPTER XIII

THE NUMBER OF PROROGATORS, AND ALSO THE PART OF FORTUNE

AFTER due attention has been given to the instructions in the preceding chapter, the Sun, the Moon, the Ascendant, and the part of Fortune, are to be considered as the four principally liable to be elected to the office of prorogator; and their positions, together with those of such planets as rule in the places of their positions, are to be observed.

The part of Fortune is ascertained by computing the number of degrees between the Sun and the Moon; and it is placed at an equal number of degrees distant from the ascendant, in the order of the signs. It is in all cases, both by night and day, to be so computed and set down, that the Moon may hold with it the same relation as that which the Sun may hold with the ascendant; and it thus becomes, as it were, a lunar horoscope or ascendant.[1]

---

[1] The Latin translation, printed at Perugio in 1646, has here the following passage in addition: "But it must be seen which luminary may follow the other in the succession of the signs; for if the Moon should so follow the Sun, the part of Fortune is also to be numbered from the horoscope or ascendant, *according* to the succession of the signs. But if the Moon precede the Sun, the

Among the candidates for prorogation, as beforementioned, by day the Sun is to be preferred, provided he be situated in a prorogatory place ; and, if not, the Moon ; but if the Moon, also, should not be so situated, then that planet is to be elected which may have most claims to dominion, in reference to the Sun, the antecedent new Moon, and the ascendant ; that is to say, when such planet may be found to have dominion over any one of the places where these are situated, by at least three prorogatives, if not more ; the whole number being five. If, however, no planet should be found so circumstanced, the Ascendant is then to be taken.

part of Fortune must be numbered from the ascendant, *contrary* to the succession of the signs."

There is a long dissertation on the part of Fortune, in Cooper's Placidus, from pp. 308 to 318 ; and, among the directions there given for computing its situation, the following seem the most accurate and simple : viz. " In the diurnal geniture, the Sun's true distance from the east is to be added to the Moon's right ascension, and in the nocturnal, subtracted ; for the number thence arising will be the place and right ascension of the part of Fortune : and it always has the same declination with the Moon, both in number and name, wherever it is found. Again, let the Sun's oblique ascension, taken in the ascendant, be subtracted always from the oblique ascendant of the ascendant, as well in the day as in the night, and the remaining difference be added to the Moon's right ascension ; the sum will be the right ascension of the part of Fortune, which will have the Moon's declination." It is shown also by this dissertation, that the situation of the part of Fortune must be necessarily confined to the lunar parallels ; that it can but rarely be in the ecliptic ; and that its latitude is ever varying. Cooper also adds, from Cardan's Commentaries on the Tetrabiblos, that "if the Moon is going from the conjunction to the opposition of the Sun, then the Moon follows the Sun, and the part of Fortune is always under the Earth, from the ascendant ; but if the Moon has passed the opposition, she goes before the Sun, and the part of Fortune is before the ascendant, and always above the earth." This remark of Cardan's is, in effect, exactly equivalent to what is stated in the additional passage inserted in the Perugio Latin translation, and given above.

In the Primum Mobile of Placidus (Cooper's translation, p. 45), the following remark and example are given : " The part of Fortune is placed according to the Moon's distance from the Sun ; and you must observe what rays the Moon has to the Sun, for the latter ought to have the same, and with the same excess or deficiency, as the part of Fortune to the horoscope. As the Moon is to the Sun, so is the part of Fortune to the horoscope ; and as the Sun is to the horoscope, so is the Moon to the part of Fortune. So, in the nativity of Charles V, the Moon applies to the ultimate sextile of the Sun, but with a deficiency of 7° 45′ : I subtract the 7° 45′ from 5° 34′ of Scorpio, the ultimate sextile to the horoscope, and the part of Fortune is placed in 28° 9′ of Libra. N.B.—In this nativity, according to Placidus, the Sun is in the second house, in 14° 30′ of Pisces : the Moon in the ascendant, in 6° 45′ of Capricorn ; the ascendant is 5° 34′ of Capricorn ; and the part Fortune is in the ninth house, in 28° 9′ of Libra.

By night, the Moon is to be elected as prorogator, provided, in like manner, she should be in some prorogatory place ; and if she be not, the Sun : if he also be not in any prorogatory place, then that planet which may have most rights of dominion in reference to the Moon,[1] and the antecedent full Moon and the part of Fortune. But, if there be no planet claiming dominion in the mode prescribed, the Ascendant must be taken, in case a new Moon had last preceded the birth ; but, if a full Moon, the part of Fortune.

If the two luminaries, and also some ruling planet of appropriate condition, should be each posited in a prorogatory place, then, provided one luminary may be found to occupy some place more important and influential than the others, that luminary must be chosen ; but should the ruling planet occupy the stronger place, and have prorogatives of dominion suitable to the conditions of both luminaries, the planet must then be preferred to either of them.[2]

CHAPTER XIV

NUMBER OF THE MODES OF PROROGATION

WHEN the prorogator has been determined as above directed, it is also necessary to take into consideration the two modes of prorogation ; one into succeeding signs, under the projection of rays, as it is called ; and, when the prorogator may be in an oriental place, that is to say, in any place between the mid-heaven and the ascendant, this mode only is to be used. The other mode extends into signs preceding the prorogator, according to what is called horary proportion[3] ; and, in cases when the prorogator may be situated in any place receding from the mid-heaven, or, in other words, between the mid-heaven and the angle of the west, both modes of prorogation are to be adopted.

It is next to be observed, that certain degrees are anæretic ; though, in the prorogation made into signs preceding, the only degree which is strictly anæretic is that of the western horizon ; and it becomes so

---

[1] According to her position in the scheme of the nativity.

[2] Placidus, in remarking on the nativity of John di Colonna, after stating his opinion that it is an error to suppose that a malign influence to the horoscope, when the horoscope has *not* the primary signification of life is anæretic, says, that " the order and method which Ptolemy lays down for the election of a prorogator are quite absurd, unless life be at the disposal of a sole prime significator only." He proves by other arguments also, and by instances of the fact, that " *one only* signifies life, elected according to Ptolemy's method." (Cooper's translation, p. 184.)

[3] "*Horary proportion.*" So the Perugio Latin of 1646 ; the Greek word, however, is ωριμαιαν, which seems to be compounded of ωρα and ιμαω ; and, if so, the literal signification would be " extraction of hours."

because it obscures the lord of life; while other degrees, of stars
meeting with or testifying to the prorogator, both take away from and
add' to the aggregate amount of the prorogation, which would otherwise continue until the descension or setting of the prorogator. Of
these last-mentioned degrees, however, there are none properly
anæretic; since they are not borne to the prorogatory place, but, on
the contrary, that place is carried to their positions.[1] In this manner the
benefics increase the prorogation, but the malefics diminish it; and
Mercury assists the influence of either party with which he may be
configurated. The amount of the increase or diminution is indicated
by the degree, in which each star, so operating, is exactly situated; for
the number of years will depend upon, and correspond with, the horary
times[2] proper to each degree; and if the birth be by day, care must be
taken to calculate the diurnal horary times; if by night, the nocturnal.
These directions are to be understood as applicable to instances wherein
the degrees in question may be in the ascendant; if farther advanced,
a deduction proportionate to the distance is to be made, unless they
should be on the occidental horizon, in which case there can be no
remainder.

But, in the prorogation made into succeeding signs, the places of the
malefics, Saturn and Mars, are anæretic, whether meeting the prorogator bodily, or by emission of rays in quartile, from either side, or in
opposition: they are also sometimes anæretic, by a sextile ray, if in a
sign of equal power, obeying or beholding the sign of the prorogator.
And even the mere degree, in signs following, in quartile with the

---

[1] By the apparent motion of the planetary system. On this passage, Placidus
has the following observations: "In directing the significator to the west,
you must consider what stars or mundane rays are intercepted between the
significator and the west; if fortunate, add their arc to the significator's arc
of direction to the west; if unfortunate, subtract it from the same, and it
will give the arc of direction, augmented or diminished according to Ptolemy.
How largely and differently authors have spoken of this direction of the significator to the west, putting various constructions on the words of Ptolemy, is
known to every one. See Cardan in his Commentaries, Maginus in Prim. Mob.
and the Use of Legal Astrology in Physic, c. viii, where he delivers the sentiments
of Naibod. Argol censures wholly this doctrine of Ptolemy's, of directing the
moderator of life to the west, as vain and useless; but I say it is worthy of
remark, and altogether comformable to truth; because then the rays and
intermediate stars of the malign only lessen the arc of direction to the west,
and do not destroy life, when, by a right direction, the moderator or life does
not remain at the same time with the malignant planet: for, should this happen,
they kill, without any manner of doubt." (Cooper's translation, pp. 106
and 108.)

[2] "Horary times." These are the number of equatorial degrees which any
degree of the zodiac may appear, in a certain latitude on the earth, to transit
in an equatorial hour.

prorogatory place, as also the degree in sextile, if badly afflicted, which
is sometimes the case in signs of long ascension, and, still further, the
degree in trine, if in signs of short ascension, are all anæretic : so also is
the Sun's place, should the Moon be prorogatory. But, although the
meetings, which occur in the course of prorogation thus made, have,
respectively, some of them an anæretic, and other a preservative, power,
in consequence of their occurring by means of an actual transmission to
the prorogatory place[1] ; yet their anæretic tendency is not always
effectual, but only in cases where the places, so brought to the prorogatory place, may be badly afflicted. For should those places be
situated within the terms of a benefic, the operation of their anæretic
degree becomes impeded ; and it will likewise be impeded, if either
of the benefics should cast a ray in quartile, trine, or opposition,[2] to the
said anæretic degree itself, or to some other degree near in succession,
and not farther distant from it than twelve degrees, if the benefic be
Jupiter ; nor than eight, if Venus : the like impediment will also subsist, if both the prorogator and its opponent[3] should be bodies,[4] and
not have the same latitude.

Therefore, whenever there may be found two or more conflicting
configurations, auxiliary on the one hand, and hostile on the other, due
observation must be made to ascertain which party surpasses the other,
in power as well as in number. The pre-eminence in number will be, of
course, obvious, from the greater number[5] on one side than on the
other ; but, for pre-eminence in power, it must be seen whether the
stars, auxiliary or hostile as the case may be, are, on the one side, in
places appropriate to themselves, while they are not so on the other ;
and especially whether those on the one side may be oriental, and those
on the other occidental. It is also to be observed, in all cases, that not
any one of such stars, whether hostile or auxiliary, is to be left out of
the present calculation, on account of its casual position under the

---

[1] By the apparent motion of the planetary system.

[2] In reference to this passage, Placidus, in speaking of the death of Octavian
Vestrius of Rome, has these words : " the Moon is found in a parallel declination
of Mars, and Saturn with the opposition of Mars ; the sextile of Jupiter to the
Sun could give no assistance, because Jupiter is cadent, and the ray sextile is
very weak, especially when it is the principal ray : for which reason, Ptolemy,
in the chapter of Life, when he mentions the planets that are able to save in
the courses of the infortunes, does not name the sextile, but the quartile, trine,
and opposition ; because the sextile ray is feeble, particularly when it is less
than 60° : neither could Venus assist, as she was cadent from the house, and
in a sign inimical to the Sun," &c. (Cooper's Translation, p. 286.)

[3] Literally, and perhaps more properly, " its meeter."

[4] That is to say, orbs, in contradistinction to prorogations made by aspects
or degrees merely.

[5] Of the stars and places brought into configuration.

sunbeams.[1] This rule must be particularly attended to, because, even though the Moon be not prorogatory, the solar place itself becomes anæretic, if shackled by the simultaneous presence of a malefic, and not restored to freedom of operation by any benefic.

The number of years, depending on the distances between the prorogatory and anæretic places, cannot be always gathered simply and at once from the ascensional times[2] of each respective degree; but only in cases when the ascendant itself, or some other specific degree or body, actually ascending in the oriental horizon, may possess the prorogation. For, if it be desired to calculate agreeably to nature, every process of calculation that can be adopted must be directed to the attainment of one object; that is to say, to ascertain after how many equatorial times[3] the place of the succeeding body, or degree, will arrive at the position preoccupied at the birth by the preceding body, or degree: and, as equatorial time transits equally both the horizon and the meridian, the places in question[4] must be considered, in respect of their proportionate distances from both these; each equatorial degree[5] being taken to signify one solar year.

In conformity with the foregoing remarks, when it may happen that the prorogatory and preceding place may be actually on the oriental horizon, it will be proper to reckon, at once, the ascensional times which may intervene until the meeting of the degrees; because, after the same number of equatorial times, the anæreta will arrive at the prorogatory place; that is to say, at the oriental horizon. Should the prorogatory place be found on the meridian, the whole number of degrees by right ascension, in which the whole intercepted arc will transit the meridian, must then be taken. And if the prorogatory place be on the occidental horizon, the number of descensions, in which every degree of the distance will be carried down (or, in other words, the number of ascensions, in which their opposite degrees will ascend), is in that case to be reckoned.[6]

---

[1] Whalley's translation of this passage is in direct contradiction to the sense: and even that of Allatius, as well as other Latin ones, are (if strictly correct) confused in their meaning.

[2] *"Ascensional times."* These are, in other words, the number of degrees of the equator, equivalent to a certain number of zodiacal degrees, ascending in any particular latitude. They are also otherwise called the *oblique ascension* of such zodiacal degrees.

[3] *"Equatorial times"* here signify degrees of the equator, by which all time is measured.

[4] That is to say, of the preceding and of the succeeding body of degree.

[5] Which may be intercepted in the arc between them.

[6] This number is that of the oblique descensional times of the intercepted arc, or of the oblique ascensional times of the arc opposite to it. The whole of the instructions in this paragraph are fully exemplified in the following chapter.

When, however, a prorogatory and preceding place may not be situated on any one of the three aforesaid points, but in some intermediate station, it must be observed that *other* times[1] will then bring the succeeding place to the preceding one ; and *not* the times of ascension or descension, or transit of the mid-heaven, as above spoken of. For any places whatever, which have one particular position, on the same degree, in regard to the horizon and meridian, are alike and identical. This is the case, for instance, with all places lying on any one of those semicircles which are drawn through the arcs of the meridian and horizon ; and each of these semicircles (all of which have position at the same equal distance from each other) marks one temporal hour[2] ; and, as the time occupied in proceeding through the places[3] above described, and arriving at the same position of the horizon and meridian, is rendered unequal to and different from the time of transits in the zodiac ; so, also, the transits of other spaces are made, agreeably to their position, in time again distinct from this.

There is, however, a method by which the proportion of time, occupied in the progress of a succeeding place to a prorogatory and preceding place, in whatever position, whether oriental, meridianal, or occidental, or any other, may be easily calculated. It is as follows :—

When it has been ascertained what degree of the zodiac is on the

---

[1] Or, times to be reckoned in another manner.

[2] On this passage, there has been founded (to use Whalley's words) "what we call Mundane Parallels, or parallels in the world. And, as zodiacal parallels are equal distances from the tropical or equinoctial circles, so mundane parallels are a like equal distance from the horizontal or meridianal points or circles. And as zodiacal parallels are measured by the zodiacal circle, so those mundane parallels are measured by the diurnal or nocturnal arcs : and just so long as the Sun or any other planet is, in proceeding from the cusp of the twelfth House to the cusp of the tenth, the same Sun or other planet will be in proceeding from the cusp of the tenth to the cusp of the eighth House. And the distance between Sun-rising and setting, is the diurnal arc which the meridian cuts in two equal parts. In directions, these mundane parallels have a twofold consideration : first, simple ; secondly, according to the rapt motion of the earth, or the *primum mobile* : all which have been largely explained by the learned Monk, Placidus," &c. That Author has certainly stated, in one of his Theses, that "those seats, or parts of the circle, are to be received, in which the stars, having a different declination, effect equal temporal hours " (p. 22, Cooper's Translation), and he has fully exemplified this principle in other parts of his "Primum Mobile" ; but Ptolemy here speaks only of *one* of the *semi*circles between the horizon and meridian, without reference to any other semicircle, corresponding in distance from the horizon and mid-heaven ; and all that he has said on the subject amounts only to this, that the prorogation is completed when the succeeding place arrives at the same semicircle on which the preceding place had been posited.

[3] The ascendant, mid-heaven, and western horizon ; as mentioned in the preceding paragraph.

mid-heaven, as also which are the preceding and succeeding degrees, the period of whose meeting is to be calculated, the position of the preceding degree, and its distance in temporal hours from the meridian, are next to be noted ; because any part of the zodiac, on becoming distant from the meridian in the same temporal hours, must fall on the same individual semicircle.[1] For ascertaining this distance, the number of ascensions, in a right sphere, found in the intermediate space between the said preceding degree and the mid-heaven, either above or under the earth, is to be divided by the number of the diurnal or nocturnal horary times of the said preceding degree : for instance, if that degree be above the earth, by its diurnal horary times ; and, by its nocturnal, if it be under the earth. It is then to be discovered in what number of equatorial times the succeeding degree will be distant from the same meridian, by as many similar temporal hours as those by which the preceding degree is distant from it. And, to effect this, the hours in question must be noted, and it must first be observed, by the right ascensions again, how many equatorial times the succeeding degree, at its original position, is distant from the degree on the mid-heaven ; and then it must be seen how many equatorial times it will be distant, on coming to the preceding degree's distance in temporal hours from the said mid-heaven : this will be found, by multiplying those hours by the succeeding degree's horary times ; diurnal, if the future position be above the earth, and nocturnal if under ; and the difference in amount, of these two distances, in equatorial times, will present the number of years inquired for.

CHAPTER XV

EXEMPLIFICATION

In order to exemplify the foregoing instructions, let the first point of Aries be supposed as the preceding place, and the first point in Gemini the succeeding ; and let the latitude of the country, to which the operation relates, be such as will cause the longest day to consist of fourteen hours[2] ; and where the horary magnitude of the beginning of Gemini will be about seventeen equatorial times.[3]

Let the first point of Aries be first placed on the ascendant, so that the beginning of Capricorn may be on the mid-heaven above the earth,

---

[1] *Vide* Note [2], p. 95.

[2] This, in the Northern Hemisphere, would be the latitude of Alexandria (where Ptolemy flourished), or, in his own words, that of the 3rd Climate, passing through Lower Egypt, numbered 30° 22'.—*Vide* extracts from the Tables of the Almagest, inserted in the Appendix.

[3] This is the magnitude of the diurnal temporal hour of the first point of Gemini in the latitude prescribed.

and the first point of Gemini be distant from the said mid-heaven 140 equatorial times.[1]   Now, since the first point of Aries is distant six temporal hours from the mid-heaven above the earth, the times of that distance will be found, by multiplying the said six hours by the seventeen equatorial times of the horary magnitude of the first point of Gemini, to be 102.[2] The whole sum of the distance to the mid-heaven above the earth, is 148 times ; and as 148 times exceed 102 by 46, the succeeding place will consequently devolve into the preceding place after 46 times (being the amount of the times of ascension of Aries and Taurus[3]) ; since, in this instance, the prorogatory place is established in the ascendant.

In like manner, let the first point of Aries be next placed on the mid-heaven, culminating ; so that the first point of Gemini, in its first position, may be distant from the said mid-heaven 58 equatorial times.[4] Now, as it is required to bring the first point of Gemini, in its second position, to the mid-heaven, the whole distance is to be reckoned, viz. 58 times, in which Aries and Taurus pass the mid-heaven ; because, again, the prorogatory place was culminating.[5]

In the same way, let the first point of Aries be descending[6] ; so that the beginning of Cancer may occupy the mid-heaven, and the first point of Gemini precede the mid-heaven at the distance of 32 equatorial times.[7] Therefore, as the first point of Aries is on the west, and again distant six temporal hours from the meridian, let these six hours be multiplied by the seventeen times ; which will produce 102, making the sum of the distance[8] of the first point of Gemini, at its future descension, from the meridian.[9] But, as the first point of Gemini, at its first position, was already distant from the meridian 32 times ; which number 102 exceed by 70 ; it will consequently arrive at its

---

[1] By right ascension, as shown by the Extract, inserted in the Appendix, from the Tables of Ascensions in the Almagest. The exact distance, however, according to that Table, is 147° 44′.

[2] Or rather, according to the Table, 102° 39′.

[3] That is to say, of the oblique ascension, which is here required to be reckoned ; because the prorogatory and preceding place is in the ascendant. *Vide* p. 95, and Note [2] in p. 94. And the first point of Gemini, on arriving at the ascendant, will be distant from the mid-heaven 102° 39′ by right ascension ; the 13th degree of Aquarius being then in culmination in the prescribed latitude. The oblique ascensions in the latitude 30° 22′ N. are also shown in the extract referred to in the preceding note : and it thereby appears, that Aries and Taurus ascend in 45° 5′, instead of 46°.

[4] Or, rather, 57° 44′—by right ascension.—*Vide* extract above referred to.

[5] *Vide* p. 95.

[6] Or on the cusp of the 7th House.

[7] Or, rather, 32° 16′—by right ascension again.—*Vide* extract as before.

[8] By right ascension. The amount according to the Table is, however, 102° 39′, as before stated.

[9] On which the 10th degree of Virgo will then be posited.

descension after 70 times, the amount of the excess; in which space Aries and Taurus will have descended, and their opposite signs Libra and Scorpio arisen.[1]

Again, let the first point of Aries have another position, not in any angle,[2] but, for instance, at the distance of three temporal hours past the meridian; so that the 18th degree of Taurus may be on the mid-heaven, and the first point of Gemini be approaching the mid-heaven, at the distance of thirteen equatorial times. The seventeen times must, therefore, be again multiplied by the three hours, and the first point of Gemini, at its second position, will be found to be past the meridian, at the distance of 51 times.[3] The distance of 13 times of the first position and 51 times of the second position are then both to be taken; and they will produce 64 times. In the former instances the prorogatory place performed in the same succession; viz. occupying 46 times in coming to the ascendant, 58 in coming to the mid-heaven, and 70 in coming to the west; so that the present number of times, depending on the intermediate position between the mid-heaven and the west, and being 64, also differs from each of the other numbers, in proportion to the three hours' difference of position. For, in the other cases which proceeded by quadrants,[4] according to the angles, the times progressively differed by twelve, but, in the present case of a minor distance of three hours, they differ by six.[5]

There is, however, another method which may be used, and which is still more simple; for instance, should the preceding degree be on the ascendant, the following intermediate times of ascension,[6] between it and the succeeding degree, may be reckoned; should it be on the mid-heaven, the times of ascension must be reckoned on a right sphere; and, if it be on the west, descending, the intermediate times of descension[7] are to be reckoned. But, should the preceding degree be between any two of these angles, as, for instance, at the distance of Aries, just spoken of, the proper times for each angle must first be considered. And, since the first point of Aries was assigned a position between the two angles of the mid-heaven and the west, the proper times of the distances from

---

[1] By oblique descension and ascension: *Vide* p. 95.—The Table shows the amount to be 70° 23'.

[2] In reference to p. 95, and Note [1] in the same page.

[3] The 18th degree of Cancer being then in culmination.

[4] Or semi-diurnal arcs, each equal to six temporal hours.

[5] The amount of the progressive difference of the times of prorogation, as here mentioned, is of course only applicable to the parallel of declination of the first point of Gemini, in the latitude before quoted. It must necessarily vary in all other parallels of declination, and also in all other latitudes.

[6] Oblique ascension.

[7] The times of oblique descension of any arc of the zodiac are equal to the times of oblique ascension of its opposite arc; as before explained.

these angles to the first point of Gemini[1] would be found to be 58 from the mid-heaven, and 70 from the west. The distances, in temporal hours, of the preceding degree from each of these angles, are then to be ascertained ; and whatever proportion these same temporal hours, contained in such distances between the said preceding degree and each angle, may bear to the temporal hours of the whole quadrant, the same proportion, out of the excess of the times of distance of one angle over those of the other, is either to be added to, or deducted from, the actual number of times of the respective angles. For instance, in the example before set forth, 70 times exceed 58 times by 12 ; and the preceding place was distant from the angles three equal temporal hours, which are the half of six, the number belonging to the whole quadrant. Now, three being the half of six, and 12 being the amount of the excess, the half of 12 is therefore to be taken, giving 6 to be either added to the 58 times, or substracted from the 70 : thus, in either way, produciug 64, the required number of times.

If, however, the preceding place should be distant from either angle two temporal hours, which are the third part of 6, then, in that case, the third part of 12, the amount of the excess, must be taken, viz. 4 : and, if the said two hours be the distance, as calculated from the mid-heaven, the said 4 times are to be added to the 58 times ; but, if it be the distance from the occidental angle, the 4 times are to be subtracted from the 70.

In conformity with these rules now laid down, the amount of the times must necessarily be obtained.[2]

[1] That is to say, at the time of the 1st point of Aries transiting the cusp of each angle respectively.

[2] The calculation of time may be greatly facilitated by the use of a zodiacal planisphere, said to have been invented about thirty years ago by Mr. Ranger, who died without making his invention public. The invention consists of a set of instruments perfectly adapted, as far as relates to the zodiac, for astronomical, as well as astrological, purposes ; and the completeness with which it solves, in the most intelligible and expeditious manner, all the astronomical problems of the zodiac, deserves attention. Whether a similar plansiphere was known in the days of Placidus, I am not aware ; but it is worthy of remark that the following words occur in his " Primum Mobile," and seem almost to have been predicted of Mr. Ranger's planisphere :—" If any one would provide himself with a Ptolemic planisphere, with the horary circles, crepuscules, the zodiac's latitude, and all other things requisite, it would be of very great service towards foreseeing the aspects." (Cooper's Translation, p. 87.) In the Appendix will be found a plate, containing diagrams drawn by the instruments in question, which, though not completely filled up, will show how easily, and, at the same time, how accurately, the measure of time in directions may be ascertained. The said diagrams have been adapted to the " exemplification " here given by Ptolemy ; one of them being laid down for the latitude of Alexandria, and the other for the latitude of southern Britain (51° 30′ N.), with similar positions of the preceding and succeeding places adverted to in the text.

The anæretic and critical influences of all meetings or descensions of prorogators[1] remain to be determined ; beginning, in due order, with such as are accomplished in the shortest time. And whatever else may happen, by means of any affliction or assistance offered (in the manner heretofore prescribed) during the actual transit of the meeting, is also to be decided on, as well as whatever may occur through other circumstances, arising out of the ingresses taking place at the time : because, should the places of both the significators be afflicted, and should the transit of the stars, at the then existing ingress, operate injuriously on the chief ruling places, it is then altogether probable that death will ensue ;[2] and, even though one of the places[3] may be disposed favourably to human nature, the crisis will still be important and perilous ; but, if both the places be so disposed favourably, some debility only, or transient malady, or hurt, will then happen. It is, however, necessary in these cases, to consider also what familiarity, or analogy, the peculiar properties of the places, thus meeting, may bear to the circumstances of the nativity.

In order to obviate the doubts which frequently arise, as to the particular star or place to which the anæretic dominion ought to be assigned, all the meetings should be duly contemplated and considered, each by each ; and thus, after considering those chiefly corresponding with the events already past, and with the future events about to follow, or with the whole altogether, it will be practicable to found an observation on the equality or inequality of their influence.

CHAPTER XVI

THE FORM AND TEMPERAMENT OF THE BODY

THE matters affecting and regulating the duration of life have now been disposed of ; and it becomes proper to enter into further particulars, commencing, in due order, with the figure and conformation of the body ; because Nature forms and moulds the body before she inspires it with a soul. In fact, the body, in its materiality, is endowed with suitable constitutional properties begotten with it, and almost apparent from its very birth ; but the soul afterwards, and by degrees, develops

---

[1] These meetings and descensions are technically termed " directions."

[2] On these words Placidus has the following remark : " The revolutions may possess some virtue, but only according to the constitution of the stars to the places of the prorogators of the nativity, and their places of direction, but no farther ; as Ptolemy was of opinion, and briefly expresses himself in his Chapter of Life. ' Those who are afflicted, both in the places and conclusions of the years, by the revolution of the stars infecting the principal places, have reason to expect certain death.' " (Cooper's Translation, p. 127.)

[3] Of the significators before mentioned.

the appropriate qualities which it derives from the primary cause, and which become known much later than external attributes, and in process of time only.

In regard to the body, therefore, it is in all cases requisite to observe the oriental horizon, and to ascertain what planets may preside or have dominion over it, and also to pay particular attention to the Moon. For, from both these places,[1] and from their rulers, as well as from the natural formation and contemperament appertaining to every species of the human race, and also from the figure ascribed to those fixed stars which may be co-ascending, the conformation of the body is to be inferred. The planets possessing dominion have the chief influence, and the proper qualities of their places co-operate with them. And, in order to simplify these instructions, and as the planets are first to be treated of, each planet is individually to be considered as follows, viz. :

Saturn, when oriental, acts on the personal figure by producing a yellowish complexion and a good constitution ; with black and curled hair, a broad and stout chest, eyes of ordinary quality, and a proportionate size of body, the temperament of which is compounded principally of moisture and cold. Should he be occidental, he makes the personal figure black or dark, thin and small, with scanty hair on the head ; the body without hair, but well shaped ; the eyes black or dark ; and the bodily temperament consisting chiefly of dryness and cold.

Jupiter ruling, when oriental, makes the person white or fair, with a clear complexion, moderate growth of hair, and large eyes, and of good and dignified stature ; the temperament being chiefly of heat and moisture. When occidental, he still causes a fair complexion, but not of equal clearness ; and he produces long straight hair, with baldness on the forehead or on the crown of the head ; and he then also gives a middle stature to the body, with a temperament of more moisture.

Mars, ascending, gives a fair ruddiness to the person, with large size, a healthy constitution, blue or grey eyes, a sturdy figure, and a moderate growth of hair, with a temperament principally of heat and dryness. When occidental, he makes the complexion simply ruddy, and the personal figure of moderate stature, with small eyes ; the body without hair, and the hair of the head light or red, and straight ; the bodily temperament being chiefly dry.

Venus operates in a manner similar to that of Jupiter, but, at the same time, more becomingly and more gracefully ; producing qualities of a nature more applicable to women and female beauty, such as softness, juiciness, and greater delicacy. She also peculiarly makes the eyes beautiful, and renders them of an azure tint.

Mercury, when oriental, makes the personal figure of a yellowish complexion, and of stature proportionate and well-shaped, with small

---

[1] That of the ascendant, and that of the Moon.

eyes and a moderate growth of hair; and the bodily temperament is chiefly hot. If occidental, he gives a complexion white or fair, but not altogether clear; straight, dark hair, a thin and slight figure, some squint or defect in the eyes, and a long visage[1] faintly red; the temperament being chiefly dry.

The Sun and Moon, when configurated with any one of the planets, also co-operate: the Sun adds a greater nobleness to the figure, and increases the healthiness of the constitution; and the Moon, especially when holding or delaying her separation,[2] generally contributes better proportion and greater delicacy of figure, and greater moisture of temperament; but, at the same time, her influence in this latter particular is adapted to the proper ratio of her illumination; as referred to in the modes of temperament mentioned in the beginning of this treatise.[3]

Again, should the planets be matutine, and fully conspicuous,[4] they will cause the body to be large; if in their first station, they will make it strong and vigorous; if they should precede or be in advance, it will be disproportionate; if in their second station, it will be weaker, and, if vespertine, altogether mean and subservient to evil treatment and oppression. At the same time, the places of the planets,[5] as has been already said, co-operate especially in producing the shape of the personal figure, and contribute also towards the temperament.

And further, it is the general tendency of the quadrant comprised between the vernal equinox and the summer tropic to produce good complexions, advantageous stature, fine constitutions, and fine eyes; with a temperament abounding in heat and moisture. The quadrant from the summer tropic to the autumnal equinox tends to produce an ordinary complexion, proportionate stature, a healthy constitution, large eyes, a stout person, with curled hair, and a temperament abounding in heat and dryness. The quadrant from the autumnal equinox to the winter tropic causes yellowish complexions, slender, thin, and sickly persons, with a moderate growth of hair, fine eyes, and a temperament abundantly dry and cold. The other quadrant, from the winter tropic to the vernal equinox, gives a dark complexion, proper stature, straight hair on the head and none on the body, a goodly figure, and a temperament abounding in cold and moisture.

---

[1] The original word is (in the accusative plural) αιγοηους, which Allatius has rendered, by "*pedibus caprinis*," *goat-footed*, as if it were compounded of αιξ *capra* and πους *pes;* but the preferable derivation seems to be from αιξ and ωψ *vultus;* meaning "*goat-faced.*"

[2] From any one of the said planets.

[3] *Vide* Chap. VIII, Book I.

[4] The Greek is ποιουμενοι φασεις; literally "*making apparition*"; but the subsequent context seems to require the meaning I have adopted.

[5] The parts of the signs in which the planets are posited.

To speak, however, more particularly, all constellations of human form, both those within and those without the zodiac, act in favour of giving a handsome shape to the body, and due proportion to the figure; while those not of human form vary its due proportions, and incline it towards their own shape; assimilating it, in some measure, to their own peculiarities, either by enlarging or diminishing its size, by giving it additional strength or weakness, or by otherwise improving or disfiguring it. Thus, for example, Leo, Virgo, and Sagittarius enlarge the person; and Pisces, Cancer, and Capricorn tend to make it diminutive; and thus, again, the upper and anterior parts of Aries, Taurus, and Leo increase its strength and their lower and posterior parts render it weaker: while, on the other hand, Sagittarius, Scorpio, and Gemini act conversely; for their anterior parts produce greater debility, and their posterior parts greater vigour. In like manner, Virgo, Libra, and Sagittarius contribute to render the person handsome and well-proportioned; and Scorpio, Pisces, and Taurus incline it to be misshapen and disfigured.

The other constellations[1] also operate on similar principles; and all these influences it is necessary to bear in mind, in order that the peculiar properties, observed in their joint temperament, may be so compounded as to authorize an inference therefrom, concerning the form and temperament of the body.

CHAPTER XVII

THE HURTS, INJURIES, AND DISEASES OF THE BODY

NEXT in succession to the foregoing chapter, the circumstances relating to bodily hurts, injuries, and diseases, claim to be discussed; and they require to be considered in the following mode.

For the investigation of these circumstances, the two angles on the horizon, both the ascendant and the western, must in all cases be remarked; but more especially the western angle and its preceding house,[2] which is inconjunct with the ascendant. After these angles have been noted, it must be observed in what manner the malefic planets may be configurated with them: for, if both the malefics, or even if one of them, should be stationed bodily on any of the successive degrees composing the said angles, or be configurated with such degrees in quartile or in opposition, some bodily disorders or injuries will attach to the native or person then born: and this will especially happen if, also, both the luminaries, either together or in opposition, or even if one of them, should be angularly posited in the manner described.

---

[1] For the operative qualities of the other constellations, *vide* Chapters X and XI, Book I.

[2] The sixth house.

Because, in such a case, not only a malefic which may have ascended in succession to the luminaries, but also any one which may have pre-ascended, if placed in an angle, has power to inflict certain diseases and injuries, such as may be indicated by the places of the horizon and of the signs, as well as by the natures of the planets themselves ; whether malefics, or others evilly afflicted and configurated with them.

Such parts of the signs, as contain the afflicted part of the horizon, will show in what part of the body the misfortune will exist, whether it be a hurt, or disease, or both : and the natures of the planets, in operating the misfortune, also regulate its particular form or species. For, among the chief parts of the human body, Saturn rules the right ear, the spleen, the bladder, the phlegm, and the bones ; Jupiter governs the hand, the lungs, the arteries, and the seed ; Mars, the left ear, the kidneys, the veins, and the privities ; the Sun rules the eyes, the brain, the heart, the sinews or nerves, and all the right side ; Venus, the nostrils, the liver, and the flesh ; Mercury, the speech, the under-standing, the bile, the tongue, and the fundament ; and the Moon governs the palate, the throat, the stomach, the belly, the womb, and all the left parts.

It generally happens that some casual hurt, or injurious affection of the body, is the utmost that takes effect when the malefics may be oriental, and that considerable diseases occur only when the malefics may be occidental. And a hurt is distinct from a disease, inasmuch as the pain, which it induces at the time, is not afterwards continued ; while a disease is, on the other hand, imposed on the sufferer either constantly or at repeated intervals. These remarks are applicable to all cases ; but, in order to inquire particularly into the nature of the hurt or disease, a further attention must be paid to the figures, or schemes, with which the effects, about to be produced, will for the most part correspond in character.

For instance, blindness of one eye will ensue, when the Moon may be in the before-mentioned angles, either operating her conjunction, or being at the full : it will also happen should she be configurated with the Sun in any other proportional aspect, and be at the same time con-nected with any one of the nebulous collections in the zodiac ; such as the cloudy spot of Cancer, the Pleiades of Taurus, the arrow-head of Sagittarius, the sting of Scorpio, the parts about the mane of Leo, or the urn of Aquarius. Moreover, both eyes will be injured should the Moon be in an angle, and in her decrease, and Mars or Saturn, being matutine, ascend in succession to her ; or, again, if the Sun be in an angle, and these planets pre-ascend before him, and be configurated with both luminaries, whether the luminaries be in one and the same sign, or in opposition ; provided also the said planets, although oriental of the Sun, be occidental of the Moon. Under these circumstances, therefore, Mars will cause blindness by a stroke or blow, or by the sword or by burning ; and, if he be configurated with Mercury, it will be effected either in a place of exercise or sport, or by the assault of robbers. Saturn, however, under the same circumstances, produces blindness by cataract, or cold, by a white film, or by other similar disorders.

Venus, if in one of the angles before-mentioned, and especially if she be in that of the west, and Saturn be in conjunction or in configuration with her, or be changing place with her,[1] while Mars, at the same time, is in elevation above her, or in opposition to her, will produce impotence in the native, if a male ; and, if a female, will render her liable to abortion, or to produce children stillborn, or not capable of being extracted except in mangled parts.   Such misfortunes especially happen under Cancer, Virgo, and Capricorn ; even though the Moon may be in the ascendant, in conjunction with Mars.   And if, under the same circumstances, Venus be also configurated with Mercury, as well as Saturn, Mars again being in elevation above her, or in opposition to her, the native will be either an eunuch or hermaphrodite, or devoid of the natural channels and vents.   And, when these positions occur, should the Sun also partake in the configuration, the luminaries and Venus being all masculinely constituted, the Moon in her decrease, and the malefics brought up in the degrees next successively ascending, the males will be born maimed or crippled, or injured in their private members (particularly under Aries, Leo, Scorpio, Capricorn, and Aquarius) ; and the females will remain childless and unprolific. And it also occasionally happens that the natives, under such a configuration, are likewise injured in the face or eyes.

If Saturn and Mercury, in conjunction with the Sun, be in the before-mentioned angles, the native will have some defect in the tongue, and stammer or speak with difficulty : especially if Mercury be occidental, and both he and Saturn configurated with the Moon.   Should Mars, however, be found together with them, he will for the most part remove the defect in the tongue, after the Moon shall have completed her approach to him.

Further, should the malefics be in angles, and the luminaries, either together or in opposition, be brought up to them ; or, if the malefics be brought up to the luminaries, especially when the Moon may be in her nodes, or in her bend,[2] or in obnoxious signs, such as Aries, Taurus, Cancer, Scorpio, and Capricorn, the body will then be afflicted with excrescences, distortions, lameness or paralysis.

If the malefics be in conjunction with the luminaries, the calamity will take effect from the very moment of birth : but should they be in the mid-heaven, in elevation above the luminaries, or in opposition to each other, it will then arise out of some great and dangerous

---

[1] This seems to imply, if Saturn be in one of Venus's places of dignity, and Venus in one of Saturn's.   Such a counterposition is technically termed " mutual reception."

[2] In her extreme latitude, whether north or south.

E

accident; such as a fall from some height or precipice, an attack of robbers, or of quadrupeds. And thus, if Mars hold dominion, he will produce the misfortune by means of fire or wounds, through quarrels, or by robbers; and if Saturn, it will be caused by a fall, by shipwreck, or by convulsive fits or spasms.

The minor bodily disorders mostly occur on the Moon's being posited in a tropical or equinoctial sign; and, if in that of the vernal equinox, these disorders usually arise from the white leprosy; in that of the summer tropic, from tetters; in that of the autumnal equinox, from leprosy; and in that of the winter tropic, from the eruption of pimples, and similar inconveniences.

Considerable diseases, however, take effect when the malefics may be configurated in the same situations as those before prescribed, yet differing in one respect; that is to say, being occidental of the Sun and oriental of the Moon. In such cases, Saturn will generally produce cold in the bowels, excessive phlegm, rheumatism, emaciation, sickliness, jaundice, dysentry, cough, obstruction, colic, or scurvy; and, in women, besides these diseases, he produces complaints of the womb. Mars will cause expectoration of blood, atrabilarious attacks, pulmonary complaints, sores, and diseases in the private parts (which will be rendered still more painful by surgical burning or incision), such as fistula, hæmorrhoids, or knots in the fundament, and also inflamed and putrifying ulcers. In women, to these calamities, he adds abortion, excision of the fœtus or its mortification.

And, even though these planets should not be properly configurated towards the particular parts of the body, their qualities will still operate. Mercury also will act with them, and contribute to the increase of the evil: thus, if he be in familiarity with Saturn, he will much augment the coldness, and promote the continuance of rheumatism, and the disturbance of the fluids; especially in the chest, throat, and stomach. If in familiarity with Mars, he will tend to produce greater dryness, and will increase ulcers, abscesses, loss of hair, scarified sores, erysipelas, tetters, blackness of bile, insanity, epilepsy,[1] and similar disorders.

Some of the properties, peculiar to disease, arise out of the various character of the signs which may contain the above-mentioned configurations in the two angles. Thus Cancer, Capricorn, and Pisces, and, in short, all signs ascribed to terrestrial animals and fishes, appropriately cause diseases of putridity, tetters, excoriation, scrofula, fistula, leprosy, and the like; while Sagittarius and Gemini produce disease by falling fits and epilepsy. And if the planets happen to be posited in the latter degrees of the signs containing them, the extremities of the

---

[1] Της ιερας νοσου; literally, "the holy disease," which authors have explained to mean epilepsy. Perhaps the disease was anciently called holy, because the patient, when possessed by the fit, seemed to be under the influence of some supernatural agency.

body will then be chiefly affected by the disease or hurt ; which will arise from humours or accidents, producing leprosy, gout, or other infirmities, in the hands and feet.

Under the circumstances above detailed, the disease or hurt will be incurable, provided there shall be not one of the benefics in configuration with the malefics which effect the evil, nor with the luminaries posited in angles ; and even though the benefics may be so configurated, the misfortune will still be incapable of remedy, if the malefics be well fortified, and in elevation above them.

Should the benefics, however, hold principal situations, and be in elevation above the obnoxious malefics, the disease or hurt will then be moderate, and have neither deformity nor disgrace attached to it ; and it will sometimes be altogether prevented and set aside, if the benefics be oriental. Jupiter, for instance, by means of human aid, such as wealth or rank can command, will conceal and soothe hurts and diseases ; and, if Mercury be joined with him, the assistance will be further improved by the addition of skilful physicians and good medicine. Venus, likewise, through the mediation of deities and oracles, will cause hurts to appear in a manner neither ungraceful nor unbecoming, and will ameliorate diseases by medicines granted by the gods.

Lastly, should Saturn be present in the configuration, the afflicted persons will move abroad to show their maladies, and to complain ; and if Mercury also be present, they will do so for the sake of deriving support and profit from the exhibition.

CHAPTER XVIII

THE QUALITY OF THE MIND

THE consideration of circumstances applicable to the body is practised under the foregoing rules.

Of the spiritual qualities, however, all those which are national and intellectual are contemplated by the situation of Mercury ; while all others, which regard the mere sensitive faculties, and are independent of reason, are considered rather by other luminaries of a less subtle constitution and more ponderous body; for instance, by the Moon and such stars as she may be configurated with, as well by separation,[1] as by application.

Now the mind is liable to impulse in a multiplicity of directions, and the investigation of them cannot be summarily nor hastily performed, but must be conducted by means of many various observations : for the different qualities of the signs, containing Mercury and

---

[1] That is to say, in the commencement of her separation from the aspect or conjunction of such stars.

the Moon, or such stars as hold any influence over those two, are well competent to contribute towards the properties of the mind; so likewise are the configurations made with the Sun and the angles, by stars bearing any relation to the point in question; besides, also, the peculiar nature exercised by each star in operating upon the mental movements.

Thus, the tropical signs generally dispose the mind to enter much into political matters, rendering it eager to engage in public and turbulent affairs, fond of distinction, and busy in theology; at the same time, ingenious, acute, inquisitive, inventive, speculative, and studious of astronomy and divination.

Bicorporeal signs render the mind variable, versatile, not easy to be understood, volatile, and unsteady; inclined to duplicity, amorous, wily, fond of music, careless, full of expedients, and regretful.[1]

Fixed signs make the mind just, uncompromising, constant, firm of purpose, prudent, patient, industrious, strict, chaste, mindful of injuries, steady in pursuing its object, contentious, desirous of honour, seditious, avaricious, and pertinacious.

Oriental positions, and those in the ascendant, especially if made by planets in their proper faces,[2] make men liberal, frank, self-confident, brave, ingenious, unreserved, yet acute. Oriental stations, and positions on the mid-heaven, or culminations, make men reflective, constant, of good memory, firm, prudent, magnanimous, successful in pursuing their desires, inflexible, powerful in intellect, strict, not easily imposed upon, judicious, active, hostile to crime, and skilful in science.

Precedent and occidental positions make men unsteady, irreverent, imbecile, impatient of labour, easily impressed, humble, doubting, wavering, boastful, and cowardly, slothful, lazy, and hard to rouse. Occidental stations, and positions on the lower heaven (as well as Mercury and Venus, when making vespertine descension by day, and rising in the night), will render the mind ingenious and sagacious, but not capable of great recollection, nor very industrious; yet inquisitive in occult matters, such as magic and sacred mysteries; also studious of mechanics, and mechanical instruments: addicted to the observation of meteors, to philosophy, to augury by means of birds, and to the judgment of dreams.

Further, should the planets having dominion be in places of their own, and in conditions suitable to their own qualities, the mental properties will be rendered exquisite, unimpeded, and successful: and especially if these planets rule at the same time over both places; that is to say, be by some mode configured with Mercury, and holds

---

[1] The Greek is μεταμελητικους, which means "penitent," or "prone to repentance," or "to subsequent regret." It is difficult to convey its precise meaning in the text.

[2] *Vide* Chapter XXVI, Bo k I.

separation from, or application to the Moon. Should the said planets, however, not be thus constituted, but be posited in places not particularly appropriate to themselves, they will yet, even then, infuse into the composition of the mental energy the properties of their own nature ; but obscurely and imperfectly, and not with such force and strong evidence as in the other case.

The peculiar qualities of planets in dominion, or in elevation, are powerfully impressed upon the mental energy : for instance, persons, who, in consequence of the familiarity of the malefics, become wicked and dishonest, have their impulse to commit evil, free and unrestrained, when the said familiarity is not governed by any contrary influence. But, should a contrary condition impede and govern that familiarity, the impulse will be frustrated, and the culprits will be easily overtaken, and undergo punishment. In like manner, persons endowed with goodness and virtue, by the familiarity between the benefics and the before-mentioned places,[1] and when no contrary influence in elevation may interpose, will exert themselves with cheerfulness and alacrity in performing good actions, will be subject to no injustice, but enjoy the advantages of their honesty and virtue. If, however, this familiarity should be superseded by some contrary condition, the very mildness and humanity of these persons will operate to their disadvantage, exposing them to contempt and accusation, and rendering them liable to be wronged by the multitude.

The foregoing observations, relative to the moral habit, apply generally ; and the particular properties, created in the mental energies by the actual nature of the planets, according to the respective dominion of each, remain to be treated of.

The planet Saturn, therefore, when alone possessing dominion of the mind, and governing Mercury and the Moon, and if posited in glory, both cosmically and with respect to the angles,[2] will make men careful of their bodies,[3] strong and profound in opinion, austere, singular in their modes of thinking, laborious, imperious, hostile to crime, avaricious, parsimonious, accumulators of wealth, violent, and envious : but, if he be not in glory, cosmically, and as regards the angles, he will debase the mind, making it penurious, pusillanimous, ill-disposed, indiscriminating, malignant, timorous, slanderous, fond of solitude, repining, incapable of shame, bigoted, fond of labour, void of natural affection, treacherous in friendship and in family connections, incapable of enjoyment, and regardless of the body.[4] Connected with Jupiter in the mode before-mentioned, being also situated in glory,

---

[1] That of Mercury, and that of the Moon.

[2] This seems to imply, if well placed in elevation ; as, in the mid-heaven, for instance, or in a conspicuous situation ; and in possession of dignities.

[3] Or, persons : the Greek is φιλοσωματους.

[4] Or, persons : μισοσωματους.

Saturn will render the mind virtuous, respectful, well-intentioned, ready to assist, judicious, frugal, magnanimous, obliging, solicitous of good, affectionate in all domestic ties, mild, prudent, patient, and philosophical: but, if thus connected and posited ingloriously, he makes men outrageous, incapable of learning, timorous, highly superstitious, yet regardless of religion, suspicious, averse to children, incapable of friendship, cunning, misjudging, faithless, foolishly wicked, irascible, hypocritical, idle and useless, without ambition, yet regretful, morose, highly reserved, over-cautious, and dull. Conciliated with Mars, and posited in glory, Saturn renders men reckless, over-diligent, free in speech, turbulent, boastful, austere in their dealings, pitiless, contemptuous, fierce, warlike, bold, fond of tumults, insidious, deceitful, and implacable; promoters of faction, tyrannical, rapacious, hostile to the commonwealth, delighting in strife, vindictive, profound in guilt, strenuous, impatient, insolent, mischievous, overbearing, evil, unjust, obstinate, inhuman, inflexible, immutable in opinion, busy, able in office, active, submitting to no opposition, and on the whole successful in their undertakings; but, if thus connected, and not placed in glory, he will make men plunderers, robbers, adulterers, submissive to evil, seeking gain by their turpitude, infidels in religion, void of the common affections, mischievous, treacherous, thievish, perjurers, and sanguinary; eaters of unlawful food, familiar with guilt, assassins, sorcerers, sacrilegious, impious, violators of the tomb, and, in short, thoroughly depraved. Conciliated with Venus, and being again in glory, Saturn makes men averse to women, and renders them fond of governing, prone to solitude, highly reserved, regardless of rank, indifferent to beauty, envious, austere, unsociable, singular in opinion, addicted to divination and to religious services and mysteries; solicitous of the priesthood, fanatical, and subservient to religion; solemn, reverential, sedate, studious of wisdom, faithful in friendship, continent, reflective, circumspect, and scrupulous in regard to female virtue: but, if he be thus conciliated, and not posited in glory, he makes men licentious and libidinous, practisers of lewdness, careless, and impure in sexual intercourse; obscene, treacherous to women, especially to those of their own families; wanton, quarrelsome, sordid, hating elegance; slanderous, drunken, superstitious, adulterous, and impious; blasphemers of the gods, and scoffers at holy rites; calumniators, sorcerers, hesitating at nothing. If conciliated with Mercury, and if in a glorious position, Saturn makes men inquisitive, loquacious, studious of law and of medicine, mystical, confederate in secrecy, fabricators of miracles, impostors, improvident, cunning, familiar with business, quick in perception, petulant, accurate, vigilant, meditative, fond of employment, and tractable: but, if connected with Mercury, and not posited gloriously, he causes men to be frivolous, vindictive, laborious, alienated from their families, fond of tormenting, and void of enjoyment; night-wanderers, insidious, treacherous, pitiless, and

thievish ; magicians, sorcerers, forgers of writings, cheats, unsuccessful
in their undertakings, and quickly reduced to adversity. Such are the
effects of Saturn.

When Jupiter alone has dominion of the mind, and is gloriously
situated, he renders it generous, gracious, pious, reverent, joyous,
courteous, lofty, liberal, just, magnanimous, noble, self-acting, compassionate, fond of learning, beneficent, benevolent, and calculated for
government : and, if posited ingloriously, he will endow the mind with
qualities apparently similar to these, but not of such virtue and lustre :
as, instead, of generosity, he will then cause profusion ; instead of
piety, bigotry ; for modesty, timidity ; for nobleness, arrogance ; for
courteousness, folly ; for elegance, voluptuousness ; for magnanimity,
carelessness ; and for liberality, indifference. Conciliated with Mars,
and being in glory, Jupiter will make men rough, warlike, skilful in
military affairs, dictatorial, refractory, impetuous, daring, free in
speech, able in action, fond of disputation, contentious, imperious,
generous, ambitious, irascible, judicious, and fortunate : but, if thus
connected, and not placed in glory, he makes men mischievous, reckless,
cruel, pitiless, seditious, quarrelsome, perverse, calumnious, arrogant,
avaricious, rapacious, inconstant, vain and empty, unsteady, precipitate, faithless, injudicious, inconsiderate, senseless, and officious ;
inculpators, prodigals, triflers, altogether without conduct, and giving
way to every impulse. When conciliated with Venus, and in a glorious
position, Jupiter will render the mind pure, joyous, delighting in
elegance, in the arts and sciences, and in poetry and music ; valuable
in friendship, sincere, beneficent, compassionate, inoffensive, religious,
fond of sports and exercises, prudent, amiable, and affectionate,
gracious, noble, brilliant, candid, liberal, discreet, temperate, modest,
pious, just, fond of glory, and in all respects honourable and worthy ;
but, if posited ingloriously, when so connected, he makes men luxurious,
soft, effeminate, fond of dancing, indulgent in expenses, incapable of
managing women, yet amorous and lascivious ; mean, slanderous,
adulterous, fond of dress, dissolute, dull, wasteful, without energy,
enervated, fond of personal adornment, womanish in mind, yet
observant of holy rites and ceremonies, faithful, harmless, pleasant,
affable, cheerful, and liberal to misfortune. If connected with Mercury,
and posited in glory, Jupiter will render men fit for much business,
fond of learning, and of geometry and the mathematics ; poetical,
public orators, acute, temperate, well-disposed, skilful in counsel,
politic, beneficent, able in government, pious, religious, valuable in
all useful professions, benevolent, affectionate in their families, ready
in acquiring knowledge, philosophical, and dignified : but when so
connected, and placed ingloriously, he will produce contrary effects,
rendering men frivolous, empty, contemptible, credulous of falsehood,
senseless, fanatical, trifling, petulant, affectors of wisdom, stupid,
arrogant, pretenders in art, magicians, and vacillating : Yet he will

also produce men skilled in various learning, and of strong memory, capable of imparting instruction, and pure in their enjoyments.

Mars alone having dominion of the mind, and placed with glory, makes men noble, imperious, irascible, warlike, versatile, powerful in intellect, daring, bold, refractory, careless, obstinate, acute, self-confident, contemptuous, tyrannical, strenuous, stern and able in government : but, posited ingloriously, he makes men cruel, mischievous, sanguinary, tumultuous, extravagant in expense, boisterous, ruffian-like, precipitate, drunken, rapacious, pitiless, familiar with crime, restless, outrageous, hostile to their families, and infidels in religion. Should he be conciliated with Venus, and posited in glory, he renders the mind cheerful, docile, friendly, complacent, joyous, playful, frank, delighting in songs and dancing, amorous, fond of the arts, and of dramatic personation, voluptuous, brave, libidinous in desire, sensible, cautious, and discreet ; disposed to free sexual intercourse,[1] quick in anger, extravagant in expense, and jealous : but, if he have an inglorious position when thus conciliated, he makes men overbearing, lascivious, sordid, opprobious, adulterous, mischievous, liars, fabricators of deceit, cheats of their own families as well as others, eager in desire, and at the same time soon satiated, debauchers of wives and virgins, daring, impetuous, ungovernable, treacherous, faithless, dangerous, fickle and weak in mind ; and occasionally also wasteful, fond of dress, audacious, and shameless. Connected with Mercury, and placed in glory, Mars renders men skilful in command, cautious, strenuous, active, obstinate, yet versatile, inventive, sophistical, laborious, busy in all things, eloquent, imposing, deceitful, inconstant, overknowing, maliciously artful, quick witted, seductive, hypocritical, treacherous, habituated to evil, inquisitive, fond of strife, and successful ; fair dealers with persons of habits similar to their own, and, in short, altogether mischievous to their enemies, though beneficial to their friends : but, if Mars be posited ingloriously, and thus connected, he makes men prodigal, yet avaricious, cruel, daring, bold, regretful and vacillating ; liars, thieves, infidels in religion, perjurers, and impostors ; seditious, incendiaries, frequenters of theatres, covered with infamy, robbers, housebreakers, sanguinary, forgers of writings, familiar with crime, jugglers, magicians, sorcerers, and assassins.

When Venus rules alone in a position of glory, she renders the mind benignant, good, voluptuous, copious in wit, pure, gay, fond of dancing, jealous, abhorring wickedness, delighting in the arts, pious, modest, well-disposed, happy in dreams, affectionate, beneficent, compassionate, refined in taste, easily reconciled, tractable, and entirely amiable : but, if contrarily posited, she renders the mind dull, amorous, effeminate, timorous, indiscriminating, sordid, faulty, obscure, and ignominious. Conciliated with Mercury, and posited with glory, Venus makes men

---

[1] Προς μιξιν θηλειων και αρρενων διακειμενους.

lovers of the arts, philosophical, of scientific mind and good genius, poetical, delighting in learning and elegance, polite, voluptuous, luxurious in their habits of life, joyous, friendly, pious, prudent, fitted for various arts, intelligent, not misled by error, quick in learning, self-teaching, emulous of worth, followers of virtue, copious and agreeable in speech, serene and sincere in manner, delighting in exercise, honest, judicious, high-minded, and continent in desire as regards women[1]; but, when so conciliated and posited adversely, she will make men oppressive, fit for various arts, evil-tongued, unsteady, malevolent, fraudulent, turbulent, liars, calumniators, faithless, crafty, insidious, practised in evil, uncourteous, debauchers of women, corrupters of youth,[2] fond of personal adornment, dissolute, infamous, notoriously offensive and publicly complained of, yet striving after all things.

Mercury, alone, having dominion of the mind, and being in a glorious position, renders it prudent, clever, sensible, capable of great learning, inventive, expert, logical, studious of nature, speculative, of good genius, emulous, benevolent, skilful in argument, accurate in conjecture, adapted to sciences and mysteries, and tractable : but, when placed contrarily, he makes men busy in all things, precipitate, forgetful, impetuous, frivolous, variable, regretful, foolish, inconsiderate, void of truth, careless, inconstant, insatiable, avaricious, unjust ; and altogether of slippery intellect, and predisposed to error.

To these influences and their effects, as above detailed, the Moon also contributes : for, should she be in the bends of her southern or northern boundary,[3] she will render the properties of the mind more various, more versatile in art, and more susceptible of change : if she be in her nodes, she will make them more acute, more practical, and more active. Also, when in the ascendant, and during the increase of her illumination, she augments their ingenuity, perspicuity, firmness and expansion ; but, when found in her decrease, or in occultation, she renders them more heavy, more obtuse, more variable of purpose, more timid, and more obscure.

The Sun likewise co-operates, when conciliated with the lord of the mental temperament ; contributing, if he be in a glorious position, to increase probity, industry, honour, and all laudable qualities ; but, if adversely situated, he increases debasement, depravity, obscurity, cruelty, obstinacy, moroseness, and all other evil qualities.

---

[1] Προς αρρενας δε κεκιννημενους και ζηλοτυπους.
[2] Παιδων διαφθορεας.
[3] That is to say, in her extreme latitude, whether south or north.

CHAPTER XIX

THE DISEASES OF THE MIND

IN connection with the foregoing discussion on the properties of the mind, the circumstances relating to eminent mental disorders, such as madness, epilepsy,[1] and others of the like formidable nature, duly claim attention.

Now, with reference to these, it is always essential to consider the planet Mercury and the Moon, and to observe in what mode they may be disposed towards each other, and towards the angles, and also towards the malefics : for, if the Moon and Mercury be unconnected with each other, or with the oriental horizon, and provided such planets as may be adversely and noxiously configurated should be in elevation above them, or overrule them, or be in opposition to them, the mental properties will then consequently become impregnated with various disorders : the characters of which may be clearly known by the qualities of the stars thus controlling the places.[2]

It is true that there are many disorders of a moderate nature, capable of being distinguished by what has been already stated, in the preceding chapter, regarding the mental qualities : for it is by the increase and growth of certain of those qualities, that an injurious excess is produced ; and every irregularity of the moral habit, whether by deficiency or superabundance, may be fitly termed a moral disorder. But, at the same time, there are other disorders of so vast and manifold a disproportion, that they quite, as it were, overpower the natural course of the intellect and passions of the mind. And of these greater disorders it is now proposed to treat.

For example, epilepsy generally attaches to all persons born when Mercury and the Moon may be unconnected either with each other, or with the oriental horizon, while Saturn and Mars may be in angles and superintend the scheme ; that is to say, provided Saturn be so posited by day, and Mars by night : otherwise, when the converse may happen in these schemes, viz. when Saturn may have dominion by night, but Mars by day (especially if in Cancer, Virgo or Pisces), the persons born will become insane. And they will become demoniac, and afflicted with moisture of the brain, if the Moon, being in face to the Sun, should be governed by Saturn when operating her conjunction, but by Mars when effecting her opposition ; and particularly when it may happen in Sagittarius and in Pisces.

---

[1] Epilepsy is defined to be " a conclusive motion of the whole body, or some parts of its parts, accompanied with a loss of sense." The knowledge of this latter effect probably induced the author to rank it among diseases of the mind.

[2] Of Mercury, the Moon, and the ascendant.

If the malefics, only, should have ruled the scheme, in the manner described, the said disorders of the mind will become irremediable, although at the same time not eminent, but doubtful, and not openly displayed ; but, should the benefics, Jupiter and Venus, be conciliated, and be posited in eastern parts and in angles, while the malefics may be in western parts, the disorders, although highly conspicuous, will then be susceptible to cure. For instance, under Jupiter's influence, they will be healed by means of medical or surgical aid, and by diet and medicine ; under Venus, by the guidance of oracles and by divine interposition.

Should the benefics, however, be occidental, and the malefics be found in eastern parts and in angles, the disorders will then become not only incurable, but most conspicuous : the epileptic persons will then be subjected to constant fits, and to danger of death ; the insane will become outrageous and unmanageable, breaking away from their families, raving and wandering in nakedness : the demoniacs and those afflicted with moisture of the brain will become furious, uttering mysterious sayings, and wounding themselves.

The several places of position in the scheme also afford co-operation : for instance, those of the Sun and Mars contribute to insanity ; those of Jupiter and Mercury, to epilepsy ; those of Venus, to the fury of enthusiasm ; and those of Saturn and the Moon, to demoniac affections and moisture of the brain.

It is by such configurations, as those just described, that any morbid deviation, occurring in the active or reasoning faculties of the mind, is produced ; but a deviation of the passive, or merely sensitive faculties, is discernible chiefly in the excess and deficiency (as the case may be) of the masculine and feminine genders ; that is to say, in the superabundance, or deficiency, of the power of either gender, to produce a conformation agreeable to its own proper nature : and a knowledge of this latter deviation is to be acquired by means of the following rules.

When the Sun, instead of Mercury, may be with the Moon, and if Mars, together with Venus, be then in familiarity with them, in that case, provided the luminaries only be found in masculine signs, men will excel in their nature, or, in other words, will possess in full plenitude the properties becoming their sex ; while the properties of women, who are thus constituted more masculinely and more actively, will deviate from the usual limits of nature. But, if both Mars and Venus, or if only one of them, be likewise masculinely situated, men will be freely and promptly inclined to natural intercourse and connexion ; and women will be, in like manner, licentious and intemperate in intercourse beyond nature. Their desires will be practised in privacy, and not openly, should only Venus be situated masculinely ; but shamelessly and publicly, if Mars also masculinely placed, together with Venus.

But, if the luminaries only be in feminine signs, women will then possess their natural functions in greater plenitude, and men will deviate from the limits of nature towards effeminacy and wantonness. And, if Venus be femininely posited, women will be lustful and licentious, and men wanton and soft; seeking connexion contrary to nature; yet in privacy and not openly: but, if Mars be posited femininely, they will then put their desires in practice shamelessly and publicly.

The oriental and diurnal positions of Mars and Venus also contribute to more masculine and more reputable qualities; and their occidental and vespertine[1] positions to qualities more feminine, and more sordid.

Lastly, if Saturn be in familiarity with them, he will likewise co-operate, by tending to produce greater impurity and obscenity, and greater evil altogether; but Jupiter, if in familiarity, tends to greater decency and modesty, and altogether to better conduct; and Mercury to greater mobility, diversity, activity, and notoriety of the passions.

---

[1] Εσπερινοι; perhaps, more properly, *nocturnal;* the word being used in contrast to ημερινοι, *diurnal.*

END OF THE THIRD BOOK

BOOK THE FOURTH

CHAPTER I

PROEM

ALL those circumstances have now been set forth, which occur previously to the birth, as well as at the actual birth, and after it, and which it seemed necessary to mention, as conducing to a knowledge of the general quality of the contemperament produced. And of the other points, now remaining, by which extrinsic events[1] are contemplated, those regarding the several fortunes of wealth and of rank claim to be taken first into consideration. Each of these fortunes has a distinct relationship; for instance, that of wealth relates to the body, and that of rank to the mind.

CHAPTER II

THE FORTUNE OF WEALTH

THE circumstances regulating the fortune of wealth are to be judged of from that part alone, which is expressly denominated the Part of Fortune; the position of which is, in all cases, whether arising in the day or in the night, always as far removed from the ascendant as the Sun is distant from the Moon.[2]

When the Part of Fortune has been determined, it must be ascertained to what planets the dominion of it belongs; and their power and connexion, as also the power and connexion of others configurated with them, or in elevation above them, whether of the same or of an adverse condition, are then to be observed: for, if the planets which assume dominion of the Part of Fortune be in full force, they will create much wealth, and especially should the luminaries also give them suitable testimony in addition.

In this manner, Saturn will effect the acquirement of wealth by means of buildings, agriculture, or navigation; Jupiter, by holding some government, or office of trust, or by the priesthood; Mars, by the army and military command; Venus by means of friends, by the

---

[1] That is to say, such events as are independent of the will, and not necessarily consequent on any peculiar conformation of the mind or body.

[2] *Vide* Chapter XIII of the 3rd Book.

dowry of wives, or by other gifts proceeding from women[1]; and Mercury by the sciences and by trade.

Should Saturn, however, when thus in influence over the fortune of wealth, be also configurated with Jupiter, he particularly provides wealth through inheritance; especially, if the configuration should exist in the superior angles, Jupiter being also in a bicorporeal sign and receiving the application of the Moon; for, in such a case, the native will also be adopted by persons unallied to him, and will become heir to their property.

And, further, if other stars, of the same condition as those which rule the Part of Fortune, should likewise exhibit testimonies of dominion, the wealth will be permanent : but, on the other hand, if stars of an adverse condition should either be in elevation above the ruling places, or ascend in succession to them, the wealth will not continue. The general period of its duration is, however, to be calculated by means of the declination of the stars, which operate the loss, in respect of the angles and succedent houses.[2]

CHAPTER III

THE FORTUNE OF RANK

THE disposition of the luminaries and the respective familiarities, exercised by the stars attending them, are to be considered as indicative of the degree of rank or dignity.[3]

For example, should the two luminaries be found in masculine signs and in angles, or even if only one of them be in an angle,[4] they being at the same time specially attended by a doryphory[5] composed of all

---

[1] I have considered the words, γυναικειων δωρεων, as comprising "*the dowry of wives*," as well as other "*gifts from women.*"

[2] That is to say, its duration will depend on the time requisite to complete the arc of direction or prorogation between the stars, operating the loss, and the places which give the wealth. And the calculation is to be made as pointed out in the 14th and 15th Chapters of the 3rd Book.

[3] It seems that there have been different opinions on this point. Placidus makes the following remark on the subject : " I do not take the dignities from the horoscope, but from the Sun and Medium Cœli, according to Ptolemy and others." (Cooper's Translation, p. 121.)

[4] The Perugio Latin, of 1646, says, " If either both luminaries, or only that one of the *chief quality* " (which Whalley defines to be the Sun by day, and the Moon by night) " be in an angle," &c.

[5] *Doryphory. Vide* Chapter V of the 3rd Book. On the present passage, Placidus has the following words : " You are not to observe what is generally alleged by professors, respecting the satellites " (*quasi* doryphory) " of the luminaries, for dignities ; viz. that the satellites are those planets which are found within 30°, on either side of the luminaries ; but that a satellite is [also]

the five planets ; the Sun by such as are oriental, but the Moon by occidental, the persons then about to be born will consequently become kings or princes. And, if the attendant stars themselves should also be in angles, or configurated with the angle above the earth,[1] the said persons will become great, powerful, and mighty in the world : and even yet more abundantly so, provided the configurations, made by the attendant stars with the angles above the earth, be dexter,. But, when both luminaries may not be found in masculine signs as aforesaid, but the Sun only in a masculine and the Moon in a feminine sign, and only one of them posited in an angle, the other concomitant circumstances still existing in the mode above described, the persons about to be born will then become merely chieftains, invested with the sovereignty of life and death.

And if the attendant stars, while the luminaries may be situated in the manner last-mentioned, should be neither actually in angles, nor bear any testimony to the angles, the persons then born, although they will still enjoy eminence, will attain only some limited dignity or distinction ; such as that of a delegated governor, or commander of an army, or dignitary of the priesthood ; and they will not be invested with sovereignty.

If, however, neither of the luminaries be in an angle, and it happen that most of the attendant stars be either themselves in angles, or configurated with the angles, the persons then born will not attain to any very eminent rank ; yet they will take a leading part in ordinary civil and municipal affairs : but, should the attendant stars have no configuration with the angles, they will then remain altogether undistinguished and without advancement ; and provided, further, that neither of the luminaries be found situated in a masculine sign, nor in an angle, nor be attended by any benefics, they will be born to complete obscurity and adversity.

The general appearance of exaltation or debasement of rank is to be contemplated as before stated, but there are many gradations intermediate to those already specified, and requiring observation of the particular interchanges and variations, incidental to the luminaries themselves and their doryphory, and also to the dominion of the planets

any kind of aspect of the stars to the luminaries of what kind soever : which, if it be made by application, its power extends inwardly over the whole orb of light of the aspecting planet, and the more so, as the proximity is greater ; but, by separation, it is not so. This doctrine may be seen in several chapters of Ptolemy ; for, an aspecting star influences the significator, and disposes him to produce effects co-natural to him, by a subsequent direction. But a star of no aspect does not predispose the significator, and produces very little or no effect of its nature, by a subsequent direction ; this is the true doctrine of the stars." (Cooper's Translation, pp. 124, 125.)

[1] The angle of the mid-heaven ; see the first note to this Chapter.

which compose their doryphory. For instance, should the benefics, or stars of the same condition, exercise the chief dominion, the dignities to be acquired will be not only important, but also more securely established ; and, on the other hand, if the chief dominion be claimed by the malefics, or by stars of an adverse condition, the dignities will be more subordinate, and more dangerous and evanescent.

The species of dignity may be inferred by observing the peculiar qualities of the attendant stars. And, if Saturn have chief dominion of the doryphory, the power and authority derived therefrom will lead to wealth and profit : authority proceeding from Jupiter and Venus will be pleasurable, and attended by presents and honours : that proceeding from Mars will consist in commanding armies, in obtaining victories, and in overawing the vanquished : and that proceeding from Mercury will be intellectual, superintending education and study, and directing the management of business.

CHAPTER IV

THE QUALITY OF EMPLOYMENT

THE dominion of the employment, or profession, is claimed in two quarters ; viz. by the Sun, and by the sign on the mid-heaven.

It is, therefore, necessary to observe whether any planet may be making its oriental appearance nearest to the Sun,[1] and whether any be posited in the mid-heaven ; especially, when also receiving the application of the Moon. And if one and the same planet possess both these qualifications, that is to say, make its nearest appearance to the Sun, and be also in the mid-heaven, that one alone must be elected to determine the present inquiry : and, likewise, though the planet should not be thus doubly qualified, but only singly, in whichever respect, even then that planet alone must still be elected provided itself alone should possess such single qualification. If, however, there should be one planet presenting its nearest appearance, and another in the mid-heaven conciliating the Moon, both must then be noticed ; and whichever of two may have greater sway, and possess greater rights of dominion, that one must be preferred. But where not any planet may be found so situated, neither making its appearance as above described, nor being in the mid-heaven, then that one, possessing the dominion of the mid-heaven,[2] is to be considered as lord of the employment : it is,

---

[1] See the 4th Chapter of the 8th Book of the Almagest inserted in the Appendix.

[2] The Greek says merely " that one having the dominion," without specifying the place of dominion : the Latin printed at Perugio, is, however, " *dominum accipe medii cœli*," which is certainly the sense required by the tenor of the previous instructions. Whalley also has similarly rendered it.

however, only some occasional occupation which can be thus denoted; because persons, born under such a configuration, most commonly remain at leisure and unemployed.

What has now been said, relates to the election of the lord of the employment or profession; but the species of the employment will be distinguished by means of the respective properties of the three planets, Mars, Venus, and Mercury, and of the signs in which they may be posited.

Mercury, for instance, produces writers, superintendents of business, accountants, teachers in the sciences, merchants and bankers: also, soothsayers, astrologers, and attendants on sacrifices, and, in short, all who live by the exercise of literature, and by furnishing explanation or interpretation; as well as by stipend and salary, or allowance. If Saturn bear testimony jointly with Mercury, persons then born will become managers of the affairs of others, or interpreters of dreams, or will be engaged in temples for the purpose of divination, and for the sake of their fanaticism. But, if Jupiter join testimony, they will be painters, orators, or pleaders in argument, and occupied with eminent personages.

Should Venus have dominion of the employment, she will cause persons to be engaged in the various perfumes of flowers, in unguents and wines, and also in colours, dyes, and in spices: thus she will produce vendors of unguents, garland-makers,[1] wine-merchants, dealers in medical drugs, weavers, dealers in spices, painters, dyers, and vendors of apparel. If Saturn add his testimony to hers, he will cause persons to be employed in matters belonging to amusement and decoration; and will also produce jugglers, scorcerers and charlatans, and all such as practise similarly. But, if Jupiter join testimony with Venus, persons will become prize-wrestlers, and garland-wearers,[2] and will be advanced in honour through female interest.

Mars, ruling the employment, and being configurated with the Sun, will produce persons who operate by means of fire; for instance, cooks, as well as those who work in copper, brass, and other metals, by

---

[1] Among the ancients, a garland was an indispensable decoration at all public ceremonies, whether civil or religious, and at private banquets. The making of garlands was, therefore, a considerable employment.

[2] It would seem, from "garland-wearers" being placed here in connection with "prize-wrestlers" ($a\theta\lambda\eta\tau a\iota$), that the author intended to point out persons competent to obtain the victors' wreath in public exhibitions. But it appears that the word $\sigma\epsilon\phi a\nu\eta\phi o\rho o\varsigma$, *garland-wearer*, also signifies a person who was annually chosen by the priests to superintend religious ceremonies, an office similar to that of high priest. According to Athenæus, the Stephanephorus of Tarsos was invested with a purple tunic, edged or striped with white, and wore the laurel chaplet, which Plato, in the treatise *de Legibus*, describes as being constantly worn by these officers, although the other priests wore it only during the performance of the ceremonies.

melting, burning, and casting : if Mars be separated from the Sun, he will make shipwrights, smiths, agriculturists, stonemasons, carpenters, and subordinate labourers. If Saturn bear testimony, in addition to Mars, persons will decome mariners, workers in wells, vaults or mines, painters, keepers of beasts or cattle, cooks or butchers, and attendants on baths or on exhibitions. And, if Jupiter join testimony, they will be soldiers, or mechanics, collectors of revenue, inn-keepers, toll-gatherers, or attendants on sacrifices.

Further, should it happen that two arbiters of employment may be found together, and provided they should be Mercury and Venus, they will then produce musicians, melodists, and persons engaged in music, poetry, and songs : they will also produce (especially if changed in their places)[1], mimics, actors, dealers in slaves, makers of musical instruments, choristers and musical performers, dancers, weavers, modellers in wax, and painters. And if Saturn join testimony with Mercury and Venus, the preparation and sale of female ornaments will be added to the aforesaid occupations. But, if Jupiter give testimony, the persons will become administrators of justice, guardians of public affairs, instructors of youth, and magistrates of the people.

Should Mercury and Mars together be lords of the employment, persons will become statuaries, armour-makers, sculptors,[2] modellers of animals, wrestlers, surgeons, spies or informers, adulterers, busy in crime, and forgers. And, if Saturn also bear testimony in addition to Mercury and Mars, he will produce assassins, highwaymen, thieves, robbers lurking in ambush, marauders on cattle, and swindlers. But, if Jupiter afford testimony, he will engage persons in honourable warfare, and in industry ; making them cautious and diligent in business, curious in foreign matters, and deriving profit from their pursuits.

When Venus and Mars exercise the dominion together, persons will become dyers, dealers in unguents and perfumes, workers in tin, lead, gold, and silver, mock combatants or dancers in armour, dealers in medical drugs, agriculturists, and physicians, healing by means of medicine. And if Saturn add testimony to Venus and Mars, he will produce persons attendant on animals consecrated to religion ; also grave-diggers and undertakers, mourners and musicians at funerals, and fanatics occupied in religious ceremonies, lamentations, and blood. But, if Jupiter add testimony, the persons will become regulators of sacrifices, augurs, holders of sacred offices, governors placed over women, and interpreters ; and they will derive support from such occupations.

The properties of the signs, in which the lords of the employment may be posited, are also influential in varying the employment. For

---

[1] Meaning probably " if in mutual reception," which position has been before explained.

[2] Or makers of hieroglyphics—ιερογλυφοι.

example, the signs of human shape promote all scientific pursuits, and
such as are of utility to mankind ; the quadrupedal signs contribute to
produce employment among metals, in business and trade, in house-
building, and in the work of smiths and mechanics : the tropical and
equinoctial signs tend to give employment in translation or interpretation, in matters of exchange, in mensuration and agriculture, and in
religious duties : the terrestrial and watery signs tend to employment
in water, and in connection with water, as well in regard to the nurture
of plants, as to ship-building ; they likewise contribute to employment
in funerals, in embalming and preserving, and also in salt.

Moreover, should the Moon herself actually occupy the place
regulating the employment,[1] and, after her conjunction, continue in
course with Mercury, being at the same time in Taurus, Capricorn, or
Cancer, she will then produce soothsayers, attendants on sacrifices, and
diviners by the basin.[2] If she be in Sagittarius or Pisces, she will make
necromancers, and evokers of dæmons : if in Virgo or Scorpio, magicians,
astrologers, and oracular persons, possessing prescience : and, if in
Libra, Aries, or Leo, she will produce fanatics, interpreters of dreams,
and makers of false vows and adjurations.

From the foregoing rules, the various forms of employment are to be
inferred ; and its magnitude or importance will be manifested by the
existing power of the ruling planets.   For instance, if the said planets be
oriental, or in angles, they will give the person eminence and authority
in his employment ; but, if occidental or cadent, they will render him
subordinate.   And should the benefics be in elevation, the employment
will be important, lucrative, secure, honourable, and agreeable ; but,
on the other hand, if the malefics be in elevation above the lords of the
employment, it will then be mean, disreputable, unprofitable, and
insecure : thus, Saturn brings an adverse influence in coldness or
tardiness, and in the composition or mixture of colours[3] ; and Mars

---

[1] That is to say, the mid-heaven ; as stated in the 4th Chapter of the
3rd Book, and in the commencement of the present Chapter.

[2] This mode of divination, as practised by the Greeks, is mentioned by
Potter. It is likewise described by a learned Doctor of Medicine, Geo. Pictorius
Vigillanus (in his Treatise " de Speciebus Magiæ Ceremonialis," printed at
Strasburgh, 1531), as being used " when the fraudulent vanity of a dæmon
renders things more like each other than eggs are to eggs."   And, according
to this writer, it is practised by exorcising water, and pouring it into a basin,
wherein the vain and refractory dæmon is immersed : the said dæmon will
sometimes remain at the bottom, and sometimes raise himself to the surface,
sending forth a slender hissing ; out of which the desired responses are to be
formed.

[3] Κρασεσι των χρωματων.—These words have been rendered literally, but
they seem to contain some figurative meaning, rather than a literal one.
Perhaps the preferable sense of them is, " by a mixture of views," or "from various
pursuits being blended together."

produces opposition by audacity and publicity in enterprise : and both planets are alike hostile to proficiency and prosperity.

The general period, at which any increase or diminution of the employment may take place, must, again in this case also, be determined by the disposition of the stars, which operate the effect towards the oriental and occidental angles.

CHAPTER V

MARRIAGE

THE consideration of circumstances relating to marriage, or the co-habitation of husband and wife, as sanctioned by law, succeeds to the foregoing details, and must be pursued in the following method.

With regard to men, it is to be observed in what manner the Moon may be disposed ; for, in the first place, if she be found in the oriental quadrants, she will cause men either to marry early in life, or, after having over-passed their prime, to marry young women ; " but, should she be situated in either of the occidental quadrants, men will then marry either late in life, or to women advanced in age[1] " : and if she be found under the Sun's beams, and configurated with Saturn, she then entirely denies marriage. Secondly, should she be in a sign of single form, and in application to only one of the planets, she will cause men to marry only once ; but, if she be in a bicorporeal or multiform sign, or in application to several planets, she will cause them to be married several times ; and, provided also that the planets, which thus, either by adjacency or by testimony,[2] receive her application, be benefic, men will then obtain good wives ; but if, on the contrary, the said planets be malefic, bad. For example, if Saturn receive the Moon's application, the wives whom he will provide will be troublesome and morose ; but, if Jupiter receive it, they will be decorous and economical ; if Mars, bold and refractory ; if Venus, cheerful, handsome, and agreeable ; and, if Mercury, sensible, prudent, and clever. Moreover, should Venus be found connected with Jupiter, Saturn,[3] or Mercury, she will render wives provident, and attached to their husbands and children ; but, if she be found connected with Mars, they will be irascible, unsteady, and indiscreet. Thus far in reference to the marriage of men.

But, in the case of women, the Sun must be observed, instead of the Moon : and, should he be posited in the oriental quadrants, women will be married either in their own youth, or to men younger than

---

[1] The words marked with inverted commas are not in the Greek ; they are found, however, in two Latin translations ; that of Basle, 1541, and that of Perugio, 1646.

[2] In other Editions, " whether by conjunction or aspect."

[3] "*Saturn.*" Not found in the Elzevir edition, but in others.

themselves; but, if he be in the occidental quadrants, they will either be married late in life, or to men who have passed their prime, and are advanced in years. And should the Sun be in a sign of single form, or configurated with only one oriental planet, he will cause them to enter into matrimony only once; but, if in a bicorporeal or multiform sign, or configurated with several oriental planets, he will then cause them to be often married. And Saturn, being configurated with the Sun, will provide husbands steadfast, advantageous, and industrious; Jupiter, such as are honourable and noble-minded; Mars, severe husbands void of affection and intractable; Venus, amiable and hand-some husbands; and Mercury, such as are provident and expert in business. But, if Venus be found connected with Saturn, she will indicate dull and timid husbands; "if with Jupiter, the husbands will be good, just, and modest[1]; " if with Mars, hasty, lustful, and adulter-ous; and if with Mercury, they will be extravagantly desirous of young persons.[2]

In regard to the Sun, those quadrants which precede the ascending and descending points of the zodiac, and, in respect of the Moon, those which are measured from her conjunction and opposition[3] to her intermediate quarters, are called oriental quadrants: the occidental quadrants are, of course, those lying opposite to the oriental.

Whenever both nativities, viz. that of the husband and that of the wife, may exhibit the luminaries configurated together in concord, that is to say, either in trine or in sextile to each other, the cohabitation will most usually be lasting; especially if the said concord exist by means of interchange[4]; but its duration will be also much more securely established, provided the Moon in the husband's nativity should corre-spond or agree with the Sun in the wife's nativity.[5] If, however, the relative positions of the luminaries be in signs inconjunct, or in opposi-tion, or in quartile, the cohabitation will be speedily dissolved upon slight causes, and the total separation of the parties will ensue.

And should the configuration of the luminaries, when made in con-cord, be aspected by the benefics, the cohabitation will continue in respectability, comfort, and advantage; but, on the other hand, it will abound in strife, contention, and misfortune, if the malefics be in aspect to the said configuration.

In like manner, even though the luminaries may not be favourably

---

[1] The words thus marked " " are not found in the Elzevir edition, but appear in the Latin one of Basle, 1541.

[2] Περι παιδας επιθυμητικους.

[3] That is to say, from the new and the full Moon.

[4] By mutual recepton; according to Whalley, and also according to the Latin copy of Perugio, 1646.

[5] Meaning, probably, if the Moon in the husband's nativity should be in the same position as the Sun in the wife's nativity, or harmoniously configurated with that position.

configurated in concord, should the benefics still offer testimony to them, the cohabitation will then not be entirely broken off, nor totally destroyed for ever, but will be again renewed, and re-established as before. But if, on the contrary, the malefics bear testimony to such discordant disposition of the luminaries, a dissolution of the cohabitation will take place, accompanied by scorn and injury. Should Mercury alone be conjoined with the malefics, it will be effected by means of some public inculpation ; and if Venus also be found with them, it will be on the ground of adultery, or sorcery, or some similar offence.

There are, however, other varieties in the married state, which are to be contemplated by means of Venus, Mars, and Saturn. And should these planets act in familiarity with the luminaries, the cohabitation will be appropriate and domestic, and authorised by law ; because Venus holds a certain affinity both to Mars and Saturn : her affinity to Mars, for instance, consists in each having exaltation in a sign belonging to the other's triplicity,[1] and it operates in the cases of youthful and vigorous persons : while her affinity to Saturn arises from their respective houses being in the signs, again also, belonging to each other's triplicity,[2] and relates to persons of more advanced age.

Hence, if Venus be in concurrence with Mars, she will produce entire love and affection in the cohabiting parties ; and if Mercury also coincide with the said planets, such affection will become publicly notorious. Should Venus be found in a sign mutually common and familiar, such as Capricorn, or Pisces,[3] she will effect marriages between brothers and sisters and kindred by blood : and, provided she be also in the presence of the Moon, when the native may be male, she will cause him to connect himself with two sisters, or other near relatives ; but, if the native be a female, a similar contract on her part, with two brothers or near relatives, will be indicated, when Venus may be also with Jupiter.[4]

Again, if Venus be with Saturn, the cohabitation will be established entirely in happiness and constancy ; and if Mercury be present with them, it will be profitable ; but, should Mars be present, it will be unsettled, calamitous, and afflicted by jealousy. And if Mars be configurated on equal terms with Venus, Saturn, and Mercury, he will effect marriage between persons of equal age ; but, on the other hand, should he be more oriental, marriage will take place with a younger man or woman ; and, if more occidental, with an older person. Should Venus and Saturn be found in signs common to each other, that is to

---

[1] The exaltation of Venus being in Pisces, and that of Mars in Capricorn. *Vide* Chapters XXI and XXII, Book I.

[2] Libra being Venus's house, and in Saturn's triplicity ; and Capricorn being Saturn's house, and in Venus's triplicity. *Vide* Chapters XX and XXI, Book I.

[3] *Vide* Note [1] in p. 126.   [4] Instead of the Moon.

say, in Capricorn and Libra,[1] marriage will be contracted between
persons kindred by blood : and, when the said position may happen in
the ascendant, or in the mid-heaven, provided the Moon also should
present herself there, men will become connected with their mothers,
or maternal aunts, or with their mothers-in-law ; and women with
their own sons, or the sons of their brothers, or with their daughters'
husbands. But if, instead of the Moon, the Sun should be in concurrence with the said position, and especially should it happen that
the planets in question may be occidental, men will then connect
thenselves with their daughters, or the wives of their sons ; and women
with their fathers, or paternal uncles, or the husbands of their daughters.

When the aforesaid configurations,[2] although not existing in signs
of affinity to each other,[3] should be found in feminine places, they will
render the parties obscene, lustful and shameless ; for instance, when
found in the anterior and hinder parts of Aries, and near the Hyades of
Taurus, about the urn of Aquarius, in the hinder parts of Leo, and in
the face of Capricorn. And should the last-named planets, Venus and
Saturn, be posited in angles, they will then, if posited in the first two
angles, the eastern and southern, produce a total exposure of the
passions, and cause them to be publicly canvassed ; but, if in the last
two angles, the western and northern, they will produce eunuchs, or
persons unprolific, and not possessing the proper channels of nature.

The passions, liable to operate in males, are to be considered by
observation of Mars : for should he be separated from Venus and Saturn,
but yet, at the same time, be supported by the testimony of Jupiter,
he will make men pure and decorous in sexual intercourse, and incline
them to natural usages only : and, if he attach himself to Saturn only,
he will render them cold in blood and dull in appetite ; if, however,
when Saturn and Mars may be thus connected together, Venus and
Jupiter should also be configurated with them, men will then become
easily excited and eager in desire, although they will still be continent,
and restrain themselves in order to avoid reproach. But should Saturn
be absent, and Mars be with Venus alone, or even although Jupiter
also be with her, men will become highly licentious, and attempt to
gratify their desires in every mode.[4] And further, if Venus be found

---

[1] *Vide* Note [2] in p. 126.   [2] Of the planets before specified.

[3] These are such signs as are connected with each other in any manner
similar to that before described, as connecting Capricorn with Pisces, and with
Libra ; or, in other words, signs common to the planets configurated.

[4] The following also occurs here : " και ει μεν ο εις των ασερων δυτικος, ο δε
ετερος ανατολικος εσι, και προς ανδρας και γυναικας εσονται διακειμενοι, ουχ'
υπερβολικως δε, ει δε αμφοτεροι οι ασερες δυτικοι ευρεθωσι, προς μονον το
θηλυ εσονται καταφερεις. θηλυκων δε των ζωδιων υπαρχοντων εν οις οι
ασερες, και αυτοι παοχειν ανεξονται τα του θηλυος. ει δε αμφοτεροι
ανατολικοι ωσι, προς μονον το αρρεν ερμητικως εξουσι. των δε ζωδιων
αρσενικων οντων, προς πασαν αρσενικην ηλικιαν."

more occidental, men will connect themselves with low women, female servants, and aliens or vagabonds; but, should Mars be found occidental, with women of rank, and gentlewomen; or with women living with their husbands, or under the protection of men. Thus far with regard to males.

In the case of females, Venus requires attention : for, if she be configurated with Jupiter, or with Mercury, she will cause women to be temperate and pure in sexual intercourse ; still, however, when she may be thus connected with Mercury, if Saturn be not present also, she will cause them to be easily excited to desire ; although they will control their desires, and avoid reproach. But, should Venus be conjoined or configurated with Mars alone, she will render women licentious and lustful ; and if, to both these planets, when thus conjoined or configurated, Jupiter also present himself, Mars being at the same time under the rays of the Sun, women will then mingle in intercourse with servants, and persons meaner than themselves, or with aliens, or vagabonds : but, should it happen that Venus may be under the rays of the Sun, they will then connect themselves with their superiors or masters. And, further, should the planets be in feminine places, or configurated femininely, they will be content with their passive faculties only.[1]

Saturn, in being conciliated with such positions as those now described, tends to produce greater obscenity ; Jupiter, greater decency ; and Mercury, greater publicity, and greater fickleness, or instability.

CHAPTER VI

CHILDREN

THE next point to be investigated is that concerning children : and, to accomplish this, observation must be made of the planets posited in, or configurated with the place on the zenith,[2] or its succedent house, which latter is called the place of the good dæmon. And should it happen that not any planets may be present in the said places, nor configurated with them, it will then be necessary to take into consideration such as may be in opposition thereto.

Now the Moon, Jupiter, and Venus are esteemed as givers of offspring ; but the Sun, Mars, and Saturn are considered as denying children altogether, or as allowing but few : while Mercury, being in quality common to both parties, lends co-operation to that with which he may be configurated, and gives offspring, when oriental, but withholds, when occidental.

---

[1] To this the following sentence succeeds : εαν δε αρρενικως διακειμενοι ωσιν οι ασερες, και προς το ποιειν.

[2] The angle of the mid-heaven.

To speak briefly, if the planets, which grant progeny, be so posited as described,[1] and placed singly, the gift of progeny will be single only[2]; but should they be in bicorporeal or in feminine signs, they will grant double offsprings[3]: so likewise if they should be in prolific or seminal signs, such as Pisces, Cancer, and Scorpio, they will grant twins, or even more. And provided they should also be masculinely constituted, as well by configuration with the Sun, as by being in masculine signs, they will grant male children; but otherwise, if femininely constituted, female.

But, although the said planets, even if beneath the malefics in elevation, or, even if found in barren places, or in signs such as those of Leo and Virgo, will still grant children; yet such children, thus indicated, will neither be healthy, nor continue in life. Should it happen, however, that the Sun and the malefics may be in entire possession of the places above mentioned, viz. that on the zenith, or the succedent house allotted to the good dæmon; and provided they be, at the same time, in masculine or barren signs, and the benefics be not in elevation above them, a total privation of offspring is thereby indicated; but, should they be in feminine or prolific signs, or supported by the testimony of the benefics, children will then be granted; yet they will be liable to disease, and short-lived.

If, however, planets of each condition should be configurated with, and have prerogative in prolific signs, there will then ensue a loss of either all the children, or only few, or else the major part of them; in the same proportion as that in which the planets, bearing testimony to either condition, may preponderate on one side rather than the other; by excelling in number, or in influence, in consequence of being posited more orientally, more genuinely in angles, higher in elevation, or successively ascending.

When the lords of the aforesaid signs[4] may be such as are givers of offspring, and be either oriental, or in places proper to themselves, the children thus granted will become eminent and illustrious: but, if occidental, or in places not proper to themselves, the children will then become undistinguished and abject. Should the said lords also be in concord with the part of fortune, and with the ascendant, they will render the children amiable, and cause them to be beloved by their parents, and to inherit their parents' substance: but, if found inconjunct, and not in concord with the said parts, the children will then become odious and mischievous to their parents, and will forfeit the inheritance of their substance.

---

[1] The meaning, apparent from the commencement of the chapter, is this: "Should such planets be in the mid-heaven or its succedent house, or configurated with either." [2] Μοναδικην, single, or one at a birth.

[3] Διδυμογωνιαν, double, or two at a birth.

[4] That on the mid-heaven, and that on the eleventh house.

Further, should the planets which grant progeny be appropriately configurated with each other, they will promote brotherly love, and mutual regard and affection among the children; but, if inconjunct, or in opposition, they will excite in them mutual hatred, deceit, and treachery.

The general investigation regarding children is to be conducted in the foregoing method : but, in order to enquire into particular circumstances consequent on the above, it will be necessary to assume, as an ascendant, the position of each planet which gives offspring, and to observe the separate schemes ; drawing inferences therefrom as in the case of a nativity.

CHAPTER VII

FRIENDS AND ENEMIES

WITH respect to friendship and enmity, it may be observed that great and lasting familiarities, or disagreements, are respectively called sympathies and enmities ; while the smaller, such as arise occasionally, and subsist for a short time only, are denominated casual intimacies and strifes : the whole are to be contemplated according to the following rules.

Indications of great and lasting friendships, or enmities, may be perceived by observation of the ruling places, exhibited in the respective nativities of both the persons, between whom the friendship or enmity may subsist. It is consequently essential to observe the places of the Sun, the Moon, the ascendant, and the part of fortune ; for, should all these in both nativities be in the same signs, or should either all or most of them be counterchanged in position in each nativity, and especially should the two ascendants be within the distance of seventeen degrees from each other,[1] they will create fixed and indissoluble friendship. On the other hand, should they be in signs inconjunct, or in opposition, they will produce great and lasting enmity. If, however, they be not constituted in either of the modes above mentioned, but merely configurated in signs,[2] they will then produce minor friendship ; provided such configuration exist by trine or sextile; but, if by quartile, they will excite minor enmity, so as to take effect at certain particular times, in which the friendship remains, as it were, inactive and subdued, while the malefics transit the configuration : and, in a similar manner, enmity also will be softened and abated, when the benefics may enter upon the configuration.[3]

---

[1] Or, regard each other within the distance of seventeen degrees.

[2] That is to say ; if the places of the Sun, &c., in one nativity be configurated with such parts of the zodiac as are occupied by the Sun, &c., in the other nativity.

[3] Of any of the four places above described.

The friendship and enmity, which men bear towards each other, may be classed under three general heads. One kind is suggested by spontaneous wilfulness; another, by the idea of profit; and another, by pain and pleasure mutually excited.

And, therefore, should either all or most of the aforesaid places be in familiarity with each other, friendship of all the three kinds will be established: so, also, should the places be entirely without familiarity, similar enmity will be established. If, however, familiarity, or absence of familiarity (as the case may be), exist only as regards the places of the luminaries, friendship or enmity will then be established by spontaneous will; and friendship thus produced is the best and most secure; while, on the other hand, enmity so arising is, in like manner, the worst and most dangerous. The friendship, or enmity, consequent on the familiarity or non-familiarity of the respective parts of Fortune, will be established on the idea of profit; and that, consequent on a similar disposition of the respective ascendants, will arise from pain or pleasure mutually excited between the parties.

It will, however, be necessary to pay still further attention to the places in question, in order to observe whether any and what planets may be in elevation above them, or in aspect to them; because, among all the said places, that particular one, to which any planet in elevation, or in succession, may be adjacent, whether in the same sign, or in the next, will possess the more powerful influence over friendship or enmity: and whichever place may have its aspecting planets more powerfully benefic, will operate in a greater degree[1] to advantage in friendship, and to the relaxation of enmity. The foregoing instructions are applicable to such friendships or enmities as are great and lasting.

But, in the case of others, which subsist only occasionally, and which have been defined as casual intimacies and strifes, it is essential to make observation of the motions of the planets, as exhibited by each nativity; that is to say, the times are to be calculated, on the completion of which the motions of the planets of one nativity will cause them to enter on certain places of the other nativity; for it is at such periods that certain particular friendships and enmities occur, continuing for a short time, until the said ingress of the planets shall have passed over.

For instance, Saturn and Jupiter, when making ingress upon each other's places, produce friendship by certain agreements, or engagements, relating either to agriculture or to inheritance: Saturn and Mars create contention and treachery spontaneously entertained: Saturn and Venus, friendship between kindred; liable, however, soon to grow cool: Saturn and Mercury, friendship on account of business, or profit, or some secret art or mystery.

Jupiter and Mars create friendship in the direction of affairs, and by means of dignities; Jupiter and Venus also create friendship by means

---

[1] Than the rest of the places.

of female persons, or attendants on religion, or on oracles : Jupiter and Mercury, friendship by means of eloquence and science, and philosophical inclinations.

Mars and Venus cause friendship in the course of amours, adultery, and fornication : Mars and Mercury excite hatred and strife by offences committed in business and trade, or by sorcery.

And Venus and Mercury produce communion by means of the arts and sciences, by a mutual interest in literature, or by female persons.

It is in this manner that the planets operate in producing friendship or enmity. And their comparative intensity or relaxation of vigour is to be distinguished by the situation of the places, which they occupy, with regard to the four principal and ruling places[1] : for, should they be posited in angles, at the places of the respective parts of Fortune, or at those of the luminaries, they will render the casual intimacies or strifes more eminent and remarkable ; but, if they be remote from these places, their effects will not be highly conspicuous. The comparative degree of injury or advantage, liable to be received, is to be discerned by means of the good or evil properties of such planets as may be thus in aspect to the aforesaid places.

With respect to servants,[2] the sign of the evil dæmon[3] is considered as the place to which the disposition ruling over them must be referred ; and it is to be observed what planets are in aspect to that place, both at the actual time of nativity, and at that of any ingresses made upon it, or oppositions to it ; and also, especially, whether the lords of the said sign may be configurated in familiarity with the ruling places of the nativity, or not in familiarity.

CHAPTER VIII

TRAVELLING

THE circumstances indicative of travel are to be considered by means of the situation held by both the luminaries, in respect to the angles, and especially, by means of that held by the Moon. For, should she be descending, or cadent from the angles, she will cause journeys and changes of residence : Mars, also, if descending, or cadent from the zenith, will sometimes do the same, provided he may occupy a situation in quartile, or in opposition to the luminaries. And, if the part of Fortune, also, should happen to be placed in signs which produce travelling, the course and practice of the whole life will be engaged in foreign lands.

---

[1] Those of the Sun, Moon, Ascendant, and part of Fortune, as before mentioned.

[2] "——and the attachment, or disagreement, subsisting between them and their masters " ;—so Allatius, and the Latin translation printed at Perugio.

[3] The twelfth house.

And further, provided the benefics superintend the aforesaid places, or ascend in succession to them, the engagements abroad will be honourable and lucrative, and the return home speedy and unobstructed : but if, on the contrary, the malefics superintend or ascend in succession to those places, the journey outward will then lead to peril and misfortune, and the return will be replete with difficulty. But it is, at the same time, necessary in all cases to consider the contemperament also, and to observe such of the existing configurations as are more predominant.

It most usually happens, that, if the luminaries be posited in the cadent houses of the oriental quadrants, the travel will take place in the eastern or southern quarters of the world ; and that, if placed in western situations, or in an occidental quadrant, travel will be then prosecuted in the northern or western parts. And, should the signs, which operate travel, be themselves single in form, or should the planets, having dominion of them, be singly posited, the journeys will then take place after long intervals, and occasionally only : but, if the said signs be bicorporeal, or double in form or figure, travel will be constantly repeated and continued.

Thus, when Jupiter and Venus may be in dominion over the luminaries, and over the places producing travel, they will render the journeys agreeable, as well as free from danger : for the traveller will be joyfully forwarded on his way by the magistrates of the country, and by the concurrent assistance of friendly persons ; the state of the atmosphere will also be favourable, and he will meet with abundance of accommodation. And, provided Mercury also be present with the planets above-specified, utility, profit, presents and honours will likewise be derived from the journey.

Saturn and Mars, if controlling the luminaries, and, especially, if placed distant from each other,[1] will produce great dangers, and at the same time render the journey fruitless and unavailing. Should they be in watery signs, the dangers will arise by shipwreck, or among deserts and wilderness[2] ; if in fixed signs, by precipices, and adverse blasts of wind ; in tropical and equinoctial signs, by want of food and other necessaries, and by some unwholesome state of the atmosphere ; in signs of human form, by robbery, treachery, and various depredations ; and, if in terrestrial signs, by the attack of wild beasts, or from earthquakes. And, should Mercury also lend concurrence, the traveller will incur further danger from accusations made against him, as well as from reptiles and venomous stings or bites.

The question, whether the events will be advantageous or injurious in quality, must, however, be further considered by observation (made

---

[1] The probable meaning is, "if not acting in concert " : but the Latin of Perugio says, "*si sint oppositi secundum longitudinem.*"

[2] There seems a misprint here in the original : δυσωδιων, " foul vapours," instead of δυσοδων, " wildernesses."

in the forms already detailed), of the peculiar properties of the places, in which the lords of employment, of wealth, of the body, or of rank, may be posited. And the periods, at which travelling will take place, are to be considered by the occasional ingress of the five planets.[1]

CHAPTER IX

THE KIND OF DEATH

IT now remains to treat of the kind and species of death. It is, however, first to be determined, by the rules already delivered regarding the duration of life,[2] whether death will ensue from an oriental or occidental position of the predominating influence. And, if death ensue from some oriental position, or meeting of rays, the place of such meeting must be observed, and by means of that place the kind of death is to be distinguished; if from the descension, or setting, of the significator, or prorogator, the place of descension[3] must be considered: because death is to be expected conformable in character to the influences, whatever they may be, which preside over the said places; or, if not any influences should directly preside, it will then be conformable to the influences, of whatever kind, which may be brought first in succession to the places in question: the configuration of the stars, the property of the aforesaid anæretic places, and the nature of the signs and of the terms,[4] are, also, all of them co-operative.

Thus, for example, if the dominion of death be vested in Saturn, he will produce death by means of lingering diseases; cough, rheumatism, flux, ague, disorder of the spleen, dropsy, colic, and complaints in the womb; and, in short, by all such diseases as proceed from the superabundance of cold.

Jupiter effects death by quinsey, inflammation of the lungs, apoplexy, spasm, pains in the head, morbid performance of the heart, and by all diseases arising from the superabundance of air, and from immoderate and impure respiration.

Mars causes death by constant fevers, semitertians, sudden and spontaneous wounds, diseases of the kidneys, expectoration of blood, and hæmorrhages of various kinds; by miscarriage, or abortion, and by childbirth, by erysipelas, and, in short, by such diseases as proceed from abundant and immediate heat.

Venus produces death by disorders of the stomach, and of the liver,

[1] On the places indicative of travelling.
[2] *Vide* the 14th Chapter of the 3rd Book; on the number of the modes of prorogation.
[3] That is to say, the sign and degree on the occidental horizon.
[4] See a subsequent note, p. 135, which gives an instance of the mode in which Placidus applied the power of the terms, in an anæretic direction.

by scurvy and dysentry : also by consumption or wasting away,[1] and by fistula and poison, and by all diseases incident on the superabundance or poverty of moisture, and its corruption.

Lastly, Mercury causes death to proceed from fury, madness, melancholy, epilepsy, falling fits, coughs, and obstructions, and by such diseases as arise from superabundant or disproportionate dryness.

When the lords of death may fully possess their own peculiar and natural properties, and when neither of the malefics may be in elevation above them, death will ensue in the modes above detailed, and in the ordinary course of nature. But a violent and remarkable death will occur when both the malefics, either in conjunction, or in quartile or opposition to each other, may be lords of the anæretic places ; or if both, or only one of the two, should attack either both the luminaries, or even only the Sun or the Moon. In such a case, the evil character of the death will proceed from the concurrence of the malefic influence, and its magnitude or remarkable nature from the additional testimony of the luminaries : its quality, also, will be known by means of the rest of the planets and stars in configuration, and by the signs which contain the malefic influence.[2]

Hence, if it happen that Saturn be in fixed signs, and in quartile or opposition to the Sun, and contrary in condition, he will produce death by suffocation, occasioned either by multitudes of people, or by hanging or strangulation : so, likewise, should he be occidental, and the Moon be succedent to him, he will operate the same effects. If he be posited in places or signs of bestial form, the native will be destroyed by wild beasts : and, if Jupiter also offer testimony, being at the same time badly afflicted, the death will then occur in public, and by day ; for example, by being exposed to combats with wild beasts. If Saturn be posited in opposition to either of the luminaries in the ascendant,[3] he

---

[1] Δια σηψεων. Perhaps more properly, putridity or rottenness. The Perugio Latin translation renders it by " cancer."

[2] Placidus, in treating of the nativity of Lewis, Cardinal Zachia, uses these words : " This example also teaches us what the sentiments of Ptolemy were concerning a violent death ; when, in a peremptory place, both the enemies meet together, it is to be understood, that in the nativity the violence is some-times first preordained from the unfortunate position of the Apheta ; at other times quite the contrary. But, because the direct direction happened to be in the terms of Mercury, the sickness was attended with a delirium and lethargy, so that you may perceive this to have been the true cause of the native's death." (Cooper's Translation, pp. 198, 199.)

[3] Ειδε ανθωροσκοπησει προσοιον δηποτε των φωτων : which Allatius has translated, " if he should be in the ascendant opposed to either of the lumin-aries " (si in horoscopo alteri luminum opponatur) ; but the Latin copy of Basle, 1541, as well as that of Perugio, 1646, give the passage as now rendered. And it appears in a subsequent place, p. 201 (where the word ανθωροσκοπων occurs), that it can only be properly translated " in opposition to the ascendant."

will cause death in prison : if he be configurated with Mercury, and
especially if near the constellation of the Serpent in the sphere, and in
terrestrial signs of the zodiac, be will produce death by venomous
wounds or bites, and by reptiles and wild beasts. And, should Venus
also attach herself to Saturn and Mercury thus combined, death will then
ensue by poison or female treachery. If Saturn be in Virgo or Pisces, or
watery signs, and configurated with the Moon, he will operate death
by means of water, by drowning and suffocation ; and, if found near
Argo, by shipwreck. Should he be in tropical or quadrupedal signs, and
the Sun be either in conjunction with him, or in opposition ; or if,
instead of the Sun, Mars should so present himself, death will be caused
by the fall of houses or buildings ; and, if posited in the mid-heaven,
death will happen by falls from heights or precipices. These are the
various effects of Saturn, when configurated as described.

Mars, if in signs of human form, and posited in quartile or in opposition to the Sun or Moon, and contrary in condition, will operate death
by slaughter, either in civil or foreign war, or by suicide : if Venus add
her testimony, death will be inflicted by women, or by assassins in the
employment of women : and, should Mercury also be configurated with
them, death will happen from robbers, thieves, or highwaymen. If
Mars be in mutilated or imperfect signs, or near the Gorgon[1] of Perseus,
he will produce death by decapitation, or by mutilation of limb. If
found in Scorpio or Taurus, he will cause death by surgical amputation,
burning or searing, or also by spasms or convulsions. Should he be found
in the mid-heaven, either above or below the earth, death will be inflicted by crucifixion or impalement, and especially if he be in the vicinity of Cepheus or Andromeda. If descending, or in opposition to the
ascendant,[2] he will produce death by fire : and, if in quadrupedal
signs, by falls and fractures. Should Jupiter, however, bear testimony
to Mars, and be at the same time afflicted, death will ensue from the
wrath of princes and kings, and from judicial condemnation.

If it happen that the malefics be in concurrence with each other in the
first instance, and afterwards in mutual opposition, in any of the aforesaid situations, the evil character of the death will be yet further
augmented ; but its species or quality, and its dominion, will depend
upon that one which may be in occupation of the anæretic place. And,
if both the malefics claim prerogative in the anæretic places, the bodies
of persons who thus die will be cast abroad without interment, and will
be devoured by beasts and birds : these circumstances will especially
ensue, when the malefics may be found in signs similar in form to beasts
and birds ; and provided not any one of the benefics should offer
testimony to the place below the earth,[3] nor to the anæretic places.

---

[1] Caput Medusæ.   [2] Ανθωροσκοπων. Vide note [3] in p. 135.
[3] That is to say, the lower heaven, or imum-cœli. Whalley has translated
it, " above the earth," instead of " below " ; mistaking υπο for υπερ.

Lastly, death will occur in foreign lands, when it may happen that the planets controlling the anæretic places may be posited in cadent houses ; especially if the Moon be present in the said places also, or if she be found in quartile or in opposition.[1]

CHAPTER X

THE PERIODICAL DIVISIONS OF TIME

In addition to the foregoing brief observations, applicable to the various forms of death, further attention is demanded with respect to the division of time, which requires to be contemplated in its natural order and succession.

Now as, in all genethlialogical cases, a certain common and general arrangement, affecting the region or country and the race or generation, is pre-supposed to be in operation, to which arrangement particular inferences, relating to the form of the body, the properties of the mind, and national habits and variations, must each be subservient ; and as, in these respects, certain causes more general and predominating are pre-supposed in existence before particular causes, due care must consequently be taken, in order to make an inference consistent with the course of nature, to observe always the original and predominating cause, and never to lose sight of it ; lest some similarity in nativities (if any such should exist) might induce an assertion when the original predominating cause proceeding from the region itself has been overlooked, that the native of Æthiopia will be born of white complexion, and with long and straight hair ; or, on the other hand, that the native of Germany or of Gaul will be black in complexion, and have curled

---

[1] On this chapter Whalley makes the following annotations : " One direction, how malevolent soever, rarely kills ; and, in most nativities, there is required a train of malevolent directions to concur to death : where several malevolent directions concur so together, without the aid of intervenings of the benevolents, they fail not to destroy life.

" In such trains of directions, the author here distinguisheth between the killing planet and the causer of the quality of death ; for one planet doth not give both. The foremost of the malevolent train is the killing place, and shows the time of death ; but the following directions, though benevolent, show the quality. If the train fall altogether, and none follow, for the quality observe those which precede, though at a distance and benevolent also ; for, though the benevolent contribute to the preservation of life, yet they frequently specify the disease which is the cause of death. And with these, our author tells us, concur the configurating stars, the quality of the stars and signs, and the terms in which the lords happen. In violent deaths, the genethliacal positions of the lights are to be observed, and how the malefics affect them, and [how they] are also concerned by directions in the quality or death." See also Chap. XIV, Book II.

F

hair; or, that the said nations are polished in manners, and cultivate learning, but that the people of Greece are barbarous and illiterate: and so, in short, of any other countries; without duly considering the national differences and variations in their several courses of life. So also, with regard to the division of time, it is in the same manner essential to consider the different qualities of the several ages of life, and to pre-determine the appropriate fitness of every age to such events as may be expected: in order to avoid the gross error which might arise from a merely vague consideration of the subject, by attributing to infancy some deed or circumstance of too complete a nature and belonging rather to manhood, or by ascribing to extreme old age the procreation of children, or some other action belonging to youth; and to adapt, on the contrary, to each separate age such circumstances as seem, by due observation of the periods, to be suitable and appropriate thereto.

The mode of consideration[1] applicable to human nature is universally one and the same; and it is analogous to the arrangement of the seven planetary orbs.[2] It, therefore, duly commences with the first age of human life, and the first sphere next above the earth, that of the Moon; and it terminates with the final age of man, and the last of the planetary spheres, which is that of Saturn; and, in fact, it accordingly happens that the appropriate qualities of each sphere take effect in a corresponding age of life, each age being subjected to one particular sphere. These observations are necessary, because the general divisions of time must be considered by means of the spheres, as a primary arrangement; although minor distinctions are to be made by means of the existing peculiarities found in nativities.

Hence, the first age of infancy, which endures for four years, agreeing in number with the quadrennial period of the Moon, is consequently adapted to her; being in its nature moist and incompact, presenting rapidity of growth, being nourished by moist things, and possessing a highly variable habit. Its mental incompleteness is likewise in accordance with its familiar relation to the Moon, and her operative influence.

The age after this continues for ten years, and accommodates itself to the second sphere, that of Mercury. In this period, the intellectual and reasoning faculties of the mind begin to take their character, imbibing the seeds of learning, and developing, as it were, the elements and germs of the genius and abilities, and their peculiar quality. The mind is also roused to discipline and instruction, and to its first exercises.

Venus corresponds with the next and third age, which lasts throughout the following eight years, the number of her own period: from her, the movement of the seminal vessels originates, as well as an unrestrained impetuosity and precipitancy in amours.

---

[1] With respect to the periodical divisions of time.

[2] It will, of course, be remembered, that the Sun, in the Ptolemaic astronomy, is counted as a planetary orb.

The fourth and adult age next succeeds, and is subject to the fourth sphere, that of the Sun : it endures for nineteen years, according to the Sun's number. Authority of action now commences in the mind, the career of life is entered upon, distinction and glory are desired, and puerile irregularities are relinquished for more orderly conduct, and the pursuit of honour.

Mars, next after the Sun, claims the fifth age, that of manhood, agreeing in duration with his own period, viz. fifteen years. He induces greater austerity of life, together with vexation, care, and trouble.

Jupiter occupies the sixth sphere, and influences the maturer age, during the twelve years corresponding to his own period. He operates the relinquishment of labour, of hazardous employment and tumult, and produces greater gravity, foresight, prudence, and sagacity, favouring the claim to honour, respect, and privilege.

Saturn, moving in the last sphere, regulates the final old age, as agreeing with its chilliness. He obstructs the mental movements, the appetites and enjoyments ; rendering them imbecile and dull, in conformity with the dullness of his own motion.

The common properties attributable to the various times of life are subject, in a general manner, to this previous adaptation ; but there are particular periods, arising from the respective peculiarities of nativities, which also require determination, and must be ascertained from the ruling prorogations ; that is to say, from the whole of them, and not from any single one only, as in the case of the duration of life. For example, prorogation made from the ascendant is to be applied to events affecting the body, and to travelling, or change of residence ; that from the part of Fortune, to incidents affecting the substance or wealth; that from the Moon, to actions of the mind, and to communion[1] and cohabitation ; that from the Sun, to dignities and glory ; and that from the mid-heaven, to other particular circumstances of life, such as employment, friendship, and the possession of children. So that thus, at one and the same time any single planet, whether benefic or malefic, will not possess the sole dominion ; for many conflicting events frequently occur at the same period, and a person may, at one and the same time, lose a kinsman, yet inherit his substance; or be at once ill in health, yet prosperous and advantageously established in regard to fortune ; or be struggling with adversity and in want, yet, notwithstanding, be also a father and beget children ; or he may experience other similar contrarieties : because individuals are subject to occurrences which may affect either the body, the mind, the rank, or the condition of wealth, and which are not altogether fortunate or unfortunate at the same period. Something of the kind will, however, frequently happen in cases of perfect good fortune or distress, when meetings of all the benefics or malefics may concur in all or most of the prorogations. Still such cases

---

[1] The Latin copy of Basle, 1541, says, " to marriages."

are but rare, because human nature in general is not subjected to the extremity either of good or evil, but rather to their moderate alteration and counter-change.

The prorogatory places must, therefore, be separately distinguished in the mode before pointed out ; and the planets meeting the prorogations must again be all taken into consideration : not only those which may be anæretic (as in the case of the duration of life), nor those only which may be configurated bodily,[1] or in opposition or quartile, but also those in trine or sextile. And, first, the times in each prorogation will be governed by the planet occupying or configurated with the actual prorogatory degree itself : if, however, there be found no planet thus constituted, the nearest preceding planet will govern the times until another, which may be in aspect to the degree following in the order of the signs, shall take them ; and this one, again, will do the same until the next in succession shall take them.[2] The like rule obtains with respect to any other planets received into dominion, and with respect to those in occupation of the terms.

Further, in prorogations of the ascendant, the degrees of distances will be equal in number to the ascensional times of the particular latitude ; but, in prorogation, from the mid-heaven, to the times of culmination ; and, in other prorogations, they will be in proportion to the ascensions, or descensions, or culminations, and will depend on their proximity to the angles ; as has been already said in treating of the duration of life.[3]

The arbiters of general times are to be determined by the foregoing method ; but arbiters of annual periods as follows : viz. after the number of years which have elapsed since the birth has been ascertained, the amount is to be projected from each place of prorogation, in the succession of the signs, at the rate of one sign for a year,[4] and the lord

---

[1] "*Bodily*," or in conjunction.

[2] On this passage, Whalley remarks, " we are to observe in direction, that the star in exact ray with the prorogator shall be ruler until the prorogator meets another ray ; that then the planet whose ray it is shall take the dominion, and so on. But if no planet aspect the hyleg (prorogator) exactly, that which casts its rays before the prorogator is to be taken for ruler of the time, till another planet's ray comes in by direction. And the lord of the term, in which the direction falls, must be considered as a co-partner in this dominion."

[3] *Vide* Chap. XIV, Book 3.

[4] The Greek is simply εἰς τα επομενα κατα ξωδιον ; but the context proves that the entire meaning must be as now given, although the Latin translation of Perugio renders it " one year to each degree." Whalley explains that by annual periods " the author intends profections : for the taking of which, for every year from the birth, add one sign to the sign in which the aphetics are at birth, and the sign which ends at the year desired is the sign profectional for that year, and the lord of that sign is chronocrator (arbiter) for that year ; so far as the degrees of that sign reach. For example, if a prorogator at birth

of the last sign[1] is to be assumed as arbiter. And, with regard to periods reckoned by months, the same rule is to be observed : for in this case also, the number of the month, as counted from the month of the nativity, is to be projected from such places as possess the dominion of the year, in the proportion of twenty-eight days per sign. So, likewise, in the case of periods reckoned by days, the number of the day, counted from the day of birth, must be projected from the monthly places of dominion, allowing for each sign two days and a third.[2]

It is, however, necessary to notice the ingresses made on places allotted to different periods ; for they take effect in no small degree on the events of the period. Thus, the ingresses made by Saturn, on places of general periods, require special observation ; those made by Jupiter, on places of annual periods ; those made by the Sun, Mars, Venus, and Mercury, on monthly places ; and the Moon's transit over daily places. It must also be remembered, that arbiters of general periods are chiefly paramount over the events ; and that, to their influence, the arbiters of particular periods (each of whom acting by its own proper nature) present either co-operation or obstruction ; and that the ingresses also operate on events, by increasing or diminishing their force and extent.[3]

The general characteristic property, and the duration of the period, will be indicated by the place of prorogation, as also by the lord of the general times, and by the planet in possession of the terms ; by means of the familiarity subsisting, from the actual birth, between each planet, and the places of which they may have respectively and originally taken dominion. The arbiters of time will also give indication whether the event will be good or evil, by means of their own naturally benefic or malefic property and temperament, and by their original familiarity or variance with the place of which they have become lords. But the period, at which the event will become more strongly evident, is shown

be in 15° of Gemini, to 15° of Cancer serves the first year ; but the first six months are ruled by Mercury, and the last six by the Moon and Jupiter ; and so on.

[1] The Latin translation of Basle, 1541, says, "the lord of that sign in which the number shall terminate."

[2] Whalley says here, "let a sign be added for each month to the sign of the year. So, in the example before proposed, the last 15° of Gemini, and the first 15° of Cancer, shall serve for the first month : the last 15° of Cancer and the first 15° of Leo, for the second month ; and so on. And for days, from 15° of Gemini to 15° of Cancer, rules two days and eight hours after birth, &c."

Placidus is of opinion, "that Ptolemy, speaking of annual places, is to be understood of the places of secondary directions ; and that when he speaks of the menstrual, he hints at the places of progressions." (Cooper's Translation, pp. 25 and 57.)

[3] Placidus says, that "active ingresses, if they be similar, to the pre-ordained effects, cause them to influence ; if dissimilar, they either diminish or retard ; as Ptolemy has it in the last Chapter of Book IV." (Cooper's Translation, p. 27.)

by the relative positions of the annual and monthly signs towards the places wherein the causes exist, and also by the ingresses of the planets.[1]

The mode in which the Sun and Moon may be disposed, in reference to the signs relating to annual and monthly periods, is also indicative. For example, should they, from the date of the nativity, be posited in concord with the operative places, and keep a position of concord at the ingresses, they will produce good ; but, if adversely posited, evil. And also, if they be not in concord with the said places, and provided they be contrary in condition, and in opposition or in quartile, to the transits, they will cause evil : should they, however, not be in quartile, nor in opposition, but otherwise configurated, their influence then will not be equally malefic.

Should it happen that the same planets may be lords of the times,[2] as well as of the ingresses, the effect will be extreme and unalloyed, if of a favourable nature ; and more particularly unmitigated, if evil. And should the said planets be not only lords of the times, but likewise hold dominion from the date of the nativity, and provided also that all the prorogations, or most of them, should tend to, or depend on, one and the same place, or, should the prorogations not be so constituted, yet notwithstanding, if the meetings occurring at the periods be found to be either all, or most of them, benefic or malefic, they will wholly produce, in all respects, good or evil fortune, respectively.

It is in this method, which preserves a natural order and succession, that times and seasons require to be contemplated.

---

[1] Placidus observes, that "the primary directions of the significators to their promittors, and the lords of the terms, Ptolemy calls the General Arbiters of Times, because they pre-ordain the general times of their effects ; which, as its motion is slow and its perseverance long, discovers its effects after a very long time ; that is, after months and years. In order that we may know, in this extent of time, on what particular month and day the effects appear, Ptolemy proposes these motions for observation, wherein, when the majority of the causes agree together, then doubtless the effect is accomplished, or most clearly manifests itself." (Cooper's Translation, p. 109.) And he says afterwards, in speaking of secondary directions, progressions, ingresses, &c., "these subsequent motions of the causes demand our greatest attention." (*Ibid.*, p. 110.) In the Appendix to the same book, at p. 438, the proper equation of time, or measurement of the arcs of direction, is also treated of, in reference to the 16th canon of Placidus, which is as follows :—

"*To equate the Arc of Direction.* Add the arc of direction to the right ascension of the natal Sun ; look for this sum in the table of right ascensions under the ecliptic, and take the degree and minute of longitude corresponding with that sum ; then, in the best ephemeris, reckon in how many days and hours the Sun, from the day and hour of birth, has arrived at that degree and minute. The number of days indicate as many years ; every two hours over, reckon a month." (*Ibid.*, p. 55.)

[2] Whether general or annual.

And now, in adverting to the scope allotted to this work in its commencement, all further adaptation of the forms of events liable to take effect at particular times will here be relinquished ; because the operative influences which the stars exercise in all events, whether general or particular, may be arranged in proper order, if care be taken that the causes set forth by the Rules of Science, and the causes arising from any existing commixture, be duly combined and blended together.

THE END

APPENDIX

NO. I

THE various constellations of the fixed stars having now been duly described, their aspects remain to be investigated.

Independently of the steadfast and immutable aspects which the said stars preserve among themselves, either rectilinearly, or triangularly, or by other similar forms,[1] they have also certain aspects considered as referring exclusively to the planets and the Sun and Moon, or parts of the zodiac ; certain others to the earth only ; and others, again, to the earth, the planets and the Sun and Moon, or parts of the zodiac, combined.

With regard to the planets only, and parts of the zodiac, aspects are properly considered as made to them by the fixed stars, when the said planets and fixed stars may be posited on one and the same of those circles which are drawn through the poles of the zodiac ; or, also, if they be posited on different circles, provided a trinal or sextile distance between them may be preserved ; that is to say, a distance equal to a right angle and a third part more, or a distance equal to two-thirds of a right angle ; and provided, also, that the fixed stars be on such parts of the circle as are liable to be transited by any one of the planets. These parts are situated within the latitude of the zodiac, which circumscribes the planetary motions. And as far as the five planets are concerned, the aspects of the fixed stars depend upon the visible mutual conjunctions, or configurations, made in the forms above prescribed ; but, with respect to the Sun and Moon, they depend on occultations, conjunctions, and succedent risings of the stars. Occultation is when a star becomes invisible by being carried under the rays of the luminary ; conjunction, when it is placed under the luminary's centre ; and succedent rising, when it begins to reappear on issuing out beyond the rays.

In regard to the earth only, the aspects of the fixed stars are four in number, and are known by the common term of angles : to speak, however, more particularly, they are the oriental horizon, the meridian or mid-heaven above the earth, the occidental horizon, and the meridian or mid-heaven below the earth. And in that part of the earth where the equator is in the zenith, the whole of the fixed stars are found to

---

[1] That is to say, by the opposition, trine, &c.

rise and set, and to be above as well as below the earth, once in each revolution ; because the situation of the poles of the equator, being in this manner on the plane of the horizon, thereby prevents the constant visibility or invisibility of any one of the parallel circles. But in other parts of the earth, where the pole of the equator is in the zenith, the fixed stars can never set nor rise ; because the equator itself is then on the plane of the horizon, and circumscribes the two hemispheres (which it thus creates, one above and the other below the earth) in such a manner, that in one revolution every star must twice transit the meridian, some of them above, others below the earth. In other declinations, however, between these extreme positions of the equator, as just mentioned, there are certain of the circles always visible, and others never visible ; consequently, the stars intercepted between the first of such circles and the poles can neither rise not set, but must, in the course of one revolution, twice transit the meridian ; above the earth, if the said stars be on a circle always visible ; but below the earth, if on a circle never visible. The other stars, however, situated on the greater parallels, both rise and set, and are found in each revolution once on the meridian above the earth, and once on that below the earth. In all these cases, the time occupied in proceeding round from any angle to the same again, must be everywhere equal in its duration, for it is marked by one sensible revolution ; and the time occupied in passing from either meridianal angle to the angle diametrically opposite, is also everywhere equal ; because it is marked by the half of one revolution. So, also, the passage from either horizontal angle to its opposite angle is again effected in the same equal portion of time, wherever the equator may be in the zenith, for it is then likewise marked by the half of an entire revolution ; because on such a position of the equator, all the parallels are then divided, as well by the horizon as by the meridian, into two equal parts. But in all other declinations, the time of passage of a semicircle above the earth is not equal to that of its passage below the earth, except only in the case of the equinoctial circle itself, which, in an oblique sphere, is the only one divided by the horizon into two equal parts, all others (its parallels) being bisected into dissimilar and unequal arcs. It follows, accordingly, that the time contained in the space between rising or setting, and either meridian, must be equal to the time between the *same* meridian and rising and setting ; because the meridian divides equally such portions of the parallels as are above or under the earth. But in proceeding in an *oblique* sphere, from rising or setting to *either* meridian, the time occupied must be unequal ; and in a right sphere, equal, because the entire portions above the earth are, in a *right* sphere only, equal to those below the earth ; whence, for instance, in a right sphere, whatever stars may be together on the meridian must also all rise and set together, until their progress becomes perceptible by the poles of the zodiac ; while, on the other hand, in an oblique sphere, whatever stars may be together on the meridian can neither all rise together nor set together ; for the more southern stars must always rise later than those which are more northern, and set earlier.[1]

The aspects made by the fixed stars, in regard to the planets or parts of the zodiac, and the earth combined, are considered, in a general manner, by the rising, or meridianal position, or setting of the same fixed stars in conjunction with any planet or part of the zodiac ; but their aspects are properly distinguishable, by means of the Sun, in the nine following modes :—

1. The first is called matutine subsolar, when the star is found together with the Sun in the oriental horizon. Of this aspect, one species is called the oriental, invisible, and succedent rising ; when the star, at the commencement of its occultation, rises immediately after the Sun : another is called the precise oriental co-rising ; when the star is found in partile conjunction with the Sun in the oriental horizon : another is the oriental, precedent, and visible rising ; when the star, beginning to appear, rises before the Sun.

2. The second aspect is termed matutine location in the mid-heaven ; when the star is found on the meridian, either above or below the earth, while the Sun is on the oriental horizon. And of this aspect, one species is called a succedent and oriental location in the mid-heaven, invisible ; when, immediately after the Sun's rising, the star shall be found on the meridian : another is the precise oriental location in the mid-heaven ; when, exactly as the Sun rises, the star is at the same time on the meridian ; another is the oriental precedent location in the mid-heaven ; when the star first shall come to the meridian above the earth, and the Sun may then immediately rise.

3. The third, called matutine setting, is when the Sun may be actually in the oriental horizon, but the star in the occidental. One of the forms of this aspect is called the oriental, succedent setting, invisible ; when the star sets immediately after the Sun's rising : another is the precise oriental co-setting, when the star sets at the moment of the Sun's rising : another is the oriental, precedent, and visible setting, when the Sun does not rise until immediately after the setting of the star.

4. The fourth aspect is named meridianal subsolar, and takes place when the Sun is actually on the meridian, but the star on the oriental horizon. Of this, one is diurnal and invisible ; when the star rises while the Sun is posited on the meridian above the earth : another is nocturnal and visible ; when the star rises while the Sun is placed on the meridian below the earth.

5. The fifth is called meridianal location in the mid-heaven ; when the Sun, as well as the star, may be at the same time on the meridian. Of this aspect, two sorts are diurnal and invisible ; when the star is on the meridian above the earth, together with the Sun, or on that below

---

[1] On this side of the equator.

the earth, diametrically opposite to the Sun. Two also are nocturnal, and of these, one is invisible ; when the star is on the meridian under the earth, together with the Sun : the other, however, is visible ; when the star is on the meridian above the earth, diametrically opposite to the Sun.

6. The sixth is meridianal setting ; when the star is found on the occidental horizon, while the Sun is on the meridian. Of this, one species is diurnal and invisible ; when the star sets while the Sun is above the earth on the meridian : the other is nocturnal and visible ; when the star sets while the Sun is on the meridian below the earth.

7. The seventh aspect is called vespertine subsolar ; when the star is found on the oriental horizon, while the Sun is posited on the occidental horizon. One form of this aspect is the vespertine succedent rising, visible ; when the star rises immediately after sunset : another is the precise vespertine co-rising ; when the star rises and the Sun sets at one and the same time : another is the precedent, vespertine rising, invisible ; when the star rises immediately before the Sun sets.

8. The eighth is named vespertine location in the mid-heaven ; when the star is on the meridian, either above or below the earth, while the Sun is placed on the occidental horizon. Of this aspect, one kind is called a visible vespertine location in the mid-heaven ; when the star is found there immediately after sunset : another is the precise vespertine location in the mid-heaven ; when the star is found there at the moment of sunset ; another is the vespertine precedent location in the mid-heaven, invisible ; when the star arrives there immediately before sunset.

9. The ninth aspect is called vespertine setting ; when the star, together with the Sun, is on the occidental horizon. One form of this aspect is the vespertine, succedent and visible setting ; when the star, at the commencement of its occultation, sets immediately after the Sun : another is the precise vespertine setting ; when the star sets at the same moment with the Sun : another is the precedent, invisible setting ; when the star, before it emerges from its occultation, sets before the Sun.

NO. II

ALMAGEST ; BOOK II. EXTRACT FROM CHAP. IX

Of Circumstances regulated by Ascensions

In any climate whatever, the magnitude of a given day or night is to be computed by the number of ascensional times proper to that particular climate. For example, the magnitude of the day will be ascertained by numbering the times between the Sun's zodiacal degree and the degree diametrically opposite, in the succession of the signs ; and that of the night, by numbering the times, from the degree diametrically opposite to the Sun, onwards, in the order of the signs, to be degree actually occupied by the Sun : because, by dividing the respective amounts of these times so obtained, by fifteen, the number of equatorial hours belonging to each space will be exhibited ; and if the division be made by twelve, instead of fifteen, the result will show the numbers of degrees equivalent to one temporal hour of either of the said spaces respectively.[1]

The magnitude of any temporal hour may be, however, more easily found by referring to the annexed Table of Ascensions, and taking the difference between the respective aggregate numbers, inserted therein under the heads of the equinoctial parallel or right sphere, and of any particular climate for which the magnitude of the temporal hour is required ; and, if the said hour be a diurnal hour, the aggregate times as stated against the zodiacal degree occupied by the Sun ; but, if nocturnal, those stated against the degree diametrically opposite, are to be compared ; and the sixth part of the difference between them is to be added, if the said degree be in the northern signs, to the fifteen times of an equatorial hour ; but subtracted therefrom, if in the southern signs. The amount thus obtained will be the required number of degrees of the temporal hour in question.[2]

And if it be required to reduce the temporal hours of any given day or night, in a certain climate, into equatorial hours, they must be multiplied by their proper horary times, whether diurnal or nocturnal,

---

[1] Thus (according to the Table inserted at p. 152), in the climate or latitude of Lower Ægypt, the times of ascension between the first point of Gemini and the first point of Sagittarius, diametrically opposite, are 205° 18', which, being divided by 15, give 13 hours 41 minutes and a fraction of equatorial time, as the length of the day of the first point of Gemini. And the same number of times of ascension, divided by 12, give 17° 6' and a fraction of the equator, as the length of the diurnal temporal hour. In the latitude of Southern Britain, the times of ascension between the same points as above mentioned are 236° 2', which, divided by 15, give 15 hours 44 minutes and a fraction of equatorial time, as the length of the day of the first point of Gemini ; and, if divided by 12, they produce 19° 40' and a fraction of the equator, as the length of the diurnal temporal hour.

[2] Thus, the aggregate times of ascension, in a right sphere, of the first point of Gemini are 57° 44' ; and, in the climate of Lower Ægypt, 45° 5' : the sixth part of the difference between them is 2° 6' and a fraction, which, added to 15°, again makes the diurnal temporal hour of the first point of Gemini equal to 17° 6' and a fraction of the equator. In the climate of Southern Britain, the aggregate times of ascension of the first point of Gemini are 29° 43' : the sixth part of the difference between that sum and 57° 44' of right ascension is 4° 40' and a fraction, which, added to 15°, makes the diurnal temporal hour of the first point of Gemini, in South Britain, equal to 19° 40' and a fraction of the equator, as before shown.

as the case may be ; the product is then to be divided by fifteen, and
the quotient will necessarily be the number of equatorial hours in the
climate in question, on the given day or night.[1] On the other hand,
equatorial hours are also to be reduced into temporal hours by being
multiplied by fifteen, the product of which is to be divided by the horary
times proper to the given day or night in the said climate.

The degree ascending in the ecliptic, at any given temporal hour,
may also be ascertained by multiplying the number of temporal hours
since sunrise, if the given hour be diurnal, but if nocturnal, since sunset,
by their proper horary times ; and the product is to be added, in the
succession of the signs, to the aggregate number (as shown by the ascensions proper to the climate) of the Sun's degree, if the given hour be
diurnal, but, if nocturnal, to that of the degree diametrically opposite,
and that particular degree of the ecliptic which shall correspond with
the total number thus found in the ascensions of the climate will be the
degree then ascending.[2]

But, in order to ascertain the degree on the meridian above the earth,
the number of temporal hours since the preceding noon are also to be
multiplied by their proper horary times, and the product is to be added
to the aggregate number of the Sun's right ascension ; and that degree
of the ecliptic, with which the total number as found in the aggregate

---

[1] For example,

Diurnal horary times of the first point of Gemini, in the latitude of Alexandria	17° 6′ 30″
Number of temporal hours	12

15)205 18 0

Diurnal equatorial hours of the first point of Gemini in the latitude of Alexandria	13 41 12

Diurnal horary times of the first point of Gemini in the latitude of Southern Britain	19° 40′ 10″
Number of temporal hours	12

15)236 2 0

Diurnal equatorial hours of the first point of Gemini in the latitude of Southern Britain	15 44 8

[2] Let the first point of Gemini be on the meridian above the earth ; the
number of temporal hours since sunrise will then be 6, by which 17° 6′ 30″
are to multiplied. The product will be 102° 39′ : this, added to 45° 5′, the
aggregate number of the first point of Gemini in the latitude of Alexandria,
will give 147° 44′, which, in the ascensions of the climate in question, will
correspond to the 3d degree of Virgo, and show that to be the degree ascending.
In the latitude of Southern Britain the total number would still amount to
the same, viz. 147° 44′, but it would show 7° and about 30′ of Virgo to be
ascending.

times of right ascension shall correspond, will then be on the meridian.[1]
The degree on the oriental horizon will, however, also show what
degrees occupies the meridian; for, by subtracting 90 times (the
amount of the quadrant) from the aggregate number ascribed to the said
ascending degree in the Table proper to the climate, the number so
reduced will be found, in the aggregate times of the Table of Right
Ascension, to correspond with the degree on the meridian. And again,
on the other hand, by adding 90 to the aggregate times ascribed by
right of ascension to the degree on the meridian above the earth, the
degree ascending may be obtained, for it will be that degree which
corresponds to that total number, as stated in the Table proper to the
climate.[2]

The Sun always preserves an equal distance in equatorial hours from
all parts of the same meridian; but his distance in equatorial hours
from different meridians varies according to the degrees of distance
between meridian and meridian.

The foregoing extracts have been made to show the entire agreement
between the astronomy of the Tetrabiblos and that of the Almagest.
The Tables herein given from the latter work are, of course, now, in
some degree, superseded by others of modern calculation, infinitely
more complete.

[1] Let the first point of Gemini be three temporal hours past the meridian;
these hours reduced to degrees, in the latitude of Alexandria, will give 51° 19′,
which, added to the right ascension of the first point of Gemini, make 109° 3′,
showing the 18th degree of Cancer on the meridian. In the latitude of Southern
Britain, these hours would produce 59°, which, added to the right ascension,
would make 116° 44′, and show the 25th degree of Cancer on the meridian.

[2] Thus, in the latitude of Alexandria, when the first point of Gemini is
three temporal hours past the meridian, the 16th degree of Libra will be on
the ascendant, and the aggregate times of ascension of that degree in the said
latitude are 109° 3′: by subtracting 90 from this sum, the remainder will be
19° 3′, the right ascension of the mid-heaven answering to the 18th degree
of Cancer. In the latitude of Southern Britain, the 18th degree of Libra would
be on the ascendant, of which degree the aggregate times of ascension in that
latitude are 206° 44′, from which, if 90 be subtracted, the remainder will
be 116° 44′, the right ascension of the mid-heaven answering to the 25th degree
of Cancer. The converse of these operations seems too obvious to need
explanation.

TABLE OF LATITUDES, AS SHOWN BY THE DURATION OF THE LONGEST DAY

[From the Almagest.]

LONGEST DAY.		LATITUDE.		LONGEST DAY.		LATITUDE.	
H.	M.	D.	M.	H.	M.	D.	M.
12	0	0	0	16	15	50	15
12	15	4	15	16	30	²51	35
12	30	8	25	16	45	52	50
12	45	12	30	17	0	54	1
13	0	16	27	17	15	55	0
13	15	20	14	17	30	56	0
13	30	23	51	17	45	57	0
13	45	27	40	18	0	58	0
14	0	¹30	22	18	30	59	30
14	15	33	18	19	0	61	0
14	30	36	0	19	30	62	0
14	45	38	35	20	0	63	0
15	0	40	56	21	0	64	30
15	15	43	5	22	0	65	30
15	30	45	1	23	0	66	0
15	45	46	51	24	0	66	10
16	0	48	32				

¹ Alexandria.   ² Southern Britain.

Extract from the Table of Ascension (Contained in the Almagest), Calculated for every Tenth Degree of the Zodiac.

SIGNS.	Tenth Degree.	In a Right Sphere under the Equator, Diurnal Arc 12 Hours:		3rd Climate, thro' Lower Ægypt, Lat. 30° 22' N. Diurnal Arc 14 Hours.		8th Climate thro' Southern Britain, Lat. 51° 30' N. Diurnal Arc 16 Hs. 20 Mts:	
		Times of Ascen:	Aggregate Times.	Times of Ascen.	Aggregate Times:	Times of Ascen.	Aggregate Times:
		D. M.	D. M.	D. M.	D. M.	D. M.	D. M.
Aries . . .	10	9.10	9.10	6·48	6.48	4. 5	4. 5
	20	9.15	18.25	6.55	13.43	4.12	8. 17
	30	9.25	27.50	7.10	20.53	4.31	12.48
Taurus . .	10	9.40	37.30	7.33	28.26	4.56	17.44
	20	9.58	47.28	8. 2	36.28	5.34	23.18
	30	10.16	57.44	8.37	45. 5	6.25	29.43
Gemini . .	10	10.34	68.18	9.17	54.22	7.29	37.12
	20	10.47	79. 5	10. 0	64.22	8.49	46. 1
	30	10.55	90. 0	10.38	75. 0	10.14	56.15
Cancer . .	10	10.55	100.55	11.12	86.12	11.36	67.51
	20	10.47	111.42	11.34	97.46	12.45	80.36
	30	10.34	122.16	11.51	109.37	13.39	94.15
Leo . . .	10	10.16	132.32	11.55	121.32	14. 7	108.22
	20	9.58	142.30	11.54	133.26	14.22	122.44
	30	9.40	152.10	11.47	145.13	14.24	137. 8
Virgo . . .	10	9.25	161.35	11.40	156.53	14.19	151.27
	20	9.15	170.50	11.35	168.28	14.18	165.45
	30	9.10	180. 0	11.32	180. 0	14.15	180. 0
Libra . . .	10	9.10	189.10	11.32	191.32	14.15	194.15
	20	9.15	198.25	11.35	203. 7	14.18	208.33
	30	9.25	207.50	11.40	214.47	14.19	222.52
Scorpio . .	10	9.40	217.30	11.47	226.34	14.24	237.16
	20	9.58	227.28	11.54	238.28	14.22	251.38
	30	10.16	237.44	11.55	250.23	14. 7	265.45
Sagittarius .	10	10.34	248.18	11.51	262.14	13.39	279.24
	20	10.47	269. 5	11.34	273.48	12.45	292. 9
	30	10.55	270. 0	11.12	285. 0	11.36	303.45
Capricornus .	10	10.55	280.55	10.38	295.38	10.14	313.59
	20	10.47	291.42	10. 0	305.38	8.49	322.48
	30	10.34	302.16	9.17	314.55	7.29	330.17
Aquarius .	10	10.16	312.32	8.37	323.32	6.25	336.42
	20	9.58	322.30	8. 2	331.34	5.34	342.16
	30	9.40	332.10	7.33	339. 7	4.56	347.12
Pisces . . .	10	9.25	341.35	7.10	346.17	4.31	351.43
	20	9.15	350.50	6.55	353.12	4.12	355.55
	30	9.10	360. 0	6.48	360. 0	4. 5	360. 0

No. III.

THE CENTILOQUY, OR HUNDRED APHORISMS OF CLAUDIUS PTOLEMY[1];
OTHERWISE CALLED, THE FRUIT OF HIS FOUR BOOKS

I.   JUDGMENT must be regulated by thyself, as well as by the science ; for it is not possible that particular forms of events should be declared by any person, however scientific ; since the understanding conceives only a certain general idea of some sensible event, and not its particular form.   It is, therefore, necessary for him who practices herein to adopt inference.   They only who are inspired by the deity can predict particulars.

II.   When an enquirer shall make mature search into an expected event, there will be found no material difference between the event ifself and his idea of it.

III.   Whosoever may be adapted to any particular event or pursuit, will assuredly have the star indicative thereof very potent in his nativity.

IV.   A mind apt in knowledge will discover truth more readily than one practised in the highest branches of science.

V.   A skilful person, acquainted with the nature of the stars, is enabled to avert many of their effects, and to prepare himself for those effects before they arrive.

VI.   It is advantageous to make choice of days and hours at a time well constituted by the nativity.   Should the time be adverse, the choice will in no respect avail, however favourable an issue it may chance to promise.

VII.   The mingled influences of the stars can be understood by no one who has not previously acquired knowledge of the combinations and varieties existing in nature.

VIII.   A sagacious mind improves the operation of the heavens, as a skilful farmer, by cultivation, improves nature.

[1] Moxon's Mathematical Dictionary says, that the " Centiloquium is a book containing one hundred astrological aphorisms, commonly ascribed to Ptolemy, as its author, but by some to Hermes Trismegistus."   This account, however, seems to be inaccurate ; for the Centiloquy attributed to Osiris's contemporary and counsellor (eulogized by Lilly as having been " one of the wisest of all mortal men, and as ancient as Moses "), is very different from that known by the name of the Καρπος, or " Fruit of the Tetrabiblos."   Whether this latter Centiloquy be really the work of Ptolemy is another question : it has been usually edited as his, but some of the aphorisms seem to relate to horary questions only, which are not adverted to in the Tetrabiblos, and there are others also which do not appear to result from the doctrine of that book.

IX.　In their generation and corruption forms are influenced by the celestial forms, of which the framers of talismans consequently avail themselves, by observing the ingresses of the stars thereupon.

X.　In the election of days and hours, make use of the malefics, to the same moderate extent as the skilful physician would use poisons in order to perform cures.

XI.　A day and hour are not to be elected until the quality of the object proposed shall be known.

XII.　Love and hatred prohibit the true accomplishment of judgments ; and, inasmuch as they lessen the most important, so likewise they magnify the most trivial things.

XIII.　In every indication made by the constitution of the heavens, secondary stars, whether auxiliary or injurious thereto, are also to be used.

XIV.　The astrologer will be entangled in a labyrinth of error, when the seventh house and its lord shall be afflicted.

XV.　Signs cadent from the ascendant of any kingdom are the ascendants of that kingdom's enemies. But the angles and succedent houses are the ascendants of its friends. It is the same in all doctrines and institutions.

XVI.　When the benefics may be controlled in the eighth house, they bring mischief by means of good men : if, on the other hand, they be well affected, they will prevent mischief.

XVII.　Give no judgment as to the future life of an aged person, until the number of years he may live shall have been reckoned.

XVIII.　If, while a benefic may ascend, both the luminaries should be in the same minute,[1] the native will be equally and highly prosperous all things which can befall him. So, likewise, if the luminaries be mutually opposed by the east and west. But the contrary effect will be produced, should a malefic be on the ascendant.

XIX.　The efficacy of purgation is impeded by the Moon's conjunction with Jupiter.

XX.　Pierce not with iron that part of the body which may be governed by the sign actually occupied by the Moon.

XXI.　When the Moon may be in Scorpio or Pisces, purgation may be advantageously used, provided the lord of the ascendant be coupled with some star posited below the earth. If he be coupled with a star placed above the earth, the potion swallowed will be vomited up.

XXII.　Neither put on nor lay aside any garment for the first time, when the Moon may be located in Leo. And it will be still worse to do so, should she be badly affected.

---

[1] Of the same degree and sign.

XXIII. Aspects between the Moon and stars give the native much activity ; and, if the stars be in power, they indicate an efficient, but if weak an inert, excitation to action.

XXIV. An eclipse of the luminaries, if in the angles of the nativity, or of an annual revolution, is noxious ; and the effects take place according to the space between the ascendant and the place of eclipse. And as, in a solar eclipse, a year is reckoned for an hour, so likewise, in a lunar eclipse, a month is reckoned for an hour.

XXV. The progression of a significator, posited in the mid-heaven, is to be made by right ascension ; of another posited in the ascendant, by the oblique ascension of the particular latitude.

XXVI. There is obvious concealment in the case, if the star significative of any particular affair be in conjunction with the Sun, either under the earth or in a place foreign to its own nature. On the other hand, there is manifestation, should the star be raised to elevation out of its depression, and be located in its own place.

XXVII. Venus gives pleasure to the native in that part of the body which may be ruled by the sign she occupies. It is the same with other stars.

XXVIII. When the Moon may not hold a familiarity with two planets, as is desirable, care should be taken to connect her, if possible, with some fixed star combining their qualities.

XXIX. The fixed stars grant extremely good fortune, unconnected with the understanding ; but it is most commonly marked by calamities, unless the planets also agree in the felicity.

XXX. Observe the creation of the first king of any dynasty ; for if the ascendant at that creation should agree with the ascendant of the nativity of the king's son, he will succeed his father.

XXXI. When the star ruling over any kingdom shall enter into a climacterical place, either the king, or some one of the chief men of his kingdom, will die.

XXXII. Concord between two persons is produced by an harmonious figuration of the stars, indicative of the matter whereby good will is constituted, in the nativity of either person.

XXXIII. Love and hatred are discernible, as well from the concord and discord of the luminaries, as from the ascendants of both nativities : but obeying signs increase good will.

XXXIV. If the lord of the place of the new Moon be in an angle, he is indicative of the events liable to happen in that month.

XXXV. When the Sun arrives at the place of any star, he excites the influence of that star in the atmosphere.

XXXVI. In the foundation of cities, consider the fixed stars which may seem to contribute thereto ; but in the erection of houses, observe the planets. The kings of every city which has Mars in culmination will most commonly perish by the sword.

XXXVII. If Virgo or Pisces be on the ascendant, the native will create his own dignity ; but if Aries or Libra is on the ascendant, he will cause his own death. The other signs are to be contemplated in the same way.

XXXVIII. Mercury, if established in either house of Saturn, and in power, gives the native a speculative and inquisitive intellect : if in a house of Mars, and especially if in Aries, he gives eloquence.

XXXIX. Affliction of the eleventh house, in the creation of a king, indicates damage in his household and his treasury : affliction of the second house denotes the detriment of his subject's wealth.

XL. When the ascendant is oppressed by the malefics, the native will delight in sordid things, and approve ill-favoured odours.

XLI. Beware the affliction of the eighth house and its lord, at a time of departure ; and that of the second house and its lord, at a time of return.

XLII. Should a disease begin when the Moon may be in a sign occupied at the birth by some malefic, or in quartile or opposition to any such sign, such disease will be most severe ; and if the malefic also behold the said sign, it will be dangerous. On the other hand, there will be no danger if the Moon be in a place held at the time of birth by some benefic.

XLIII. The malefic figures of a nation are strengthened by adverse figurations of existing times.

XLIV. It is an evil case if the ascendant of a sick person resist the figuration of his own nativity ; and if the time should not bring up any benefic.

XLV. If the ascendant, or principal significators, be not in human signs, the native himself will be also estranged from human nature.

XLVI. In nativities much happiness is conferred by the fixed stars ; and also by the angles of the new Moon, and by the place of a kingdom's Part of Fortune, should the ascendant be found in any of them.

XLVII. If a malefic in one nativity fall on the place of a benefic in another nativity, he who has the benefic will suffer damage from him who has the malefic.

XLVIII. If the mid-heaven of a prince be the ascendant of his subject, or if their respective significators be configurated in a benevolent form, they will continue long inseparable. It will be the same, also, should the sixth house of a subject or servant be the ascendant of his prince or master.

XLIX. If the ascendant of a servant be the mid-heaven in his master's nativity, the master will place so much confidence in that servant as to be ruled by him.

L. Overlook none of the hundred and nineteen conjunctions; for on them depends the knowledge of worldly operations, whether of generation or of corruption.

LI. Make the sign occupied by the Moon at the time of birth the sign ascending at the conception; and consider that in which she may be posited at the conception, or the opposite one, as the sign ascending at the birth.

LII. Men of tall stature have their lords of nativity in elevation, and their ascendants in the beginnings of signs; but the lords of men of short stature will be found in declination.[1] It must also be seen whether the signs be right or oblique.

LIII. The lords of nativity of slight or thin men have no latitude, but those of stout or fat men have; and, if the latitude be south, the native will be active; if north, inactive.

LIV. In the construction of a building, the principal rulers, if coupled with a star below the earth, will impede the erection.

LV. Mars' evil influence over ships is diminished if he be neither in the mid-heaven nor in the eleventh house; but if in either of those places, he renders the ship liable to be captured by pirates. And if the ascendant be afflicted by any fixed star of the nature of Mars, the ship will be burned.

LVI. While the Moon is in her first quarter, withdrawing from her conjunction with the Sun, the bodily humours expand until her second quarter: in her other quarters they decrease.

LVII. If, during a sickness, the seventh house and its lord be afflicted, change the physician.

LVIII. Observe the place of an aspect, and its distance from the ascendant of the year; for the event will happen when the profection may arrive thither.

LIX. Before pronouncing that an absent person shall die, observe whether he may not become intoxicated; before declaring that he shall receive a wound, see whether he may not be let blood; and before saying that he shall find treasure, examine whether he may not receive his own deposit; for the figures of all these things may be similar.

LX. In cases of sickness, observe the critical days, and the Moon's progress in the angles of a figure of sixteen sides. If those angles be well affected, it is favourable for the invalid; if they be afflicted, unfavourable.

---

[1] Or in obscure situations.

LXI. The Moon is significative of bodily matters, which, in respect of motion, resemble her.

LXII. By marking exactly the beginning of a conjunction,[1] judgment may be made of the variation of the weather in the ensuing month. It will depend upon the lord of the angle of every figure, for he controls the nature of the atmosphere ; assuming also at these times the quality of the existing weather.

LXIII. In the conjunction of Saturn and Jupiter, pronounce according to the nature of that one which may be higher in elevation. Follow the same rule with other stars.

LXIV. After ascertaining the lord of the inquiry, see what power he may have in the annual revolution, or in the ascendant of the new Moon ; and pronounce accordingly.

LXV. In the least conjunction, the difference of the mean conjunction, and in the mean conjunction the difference of the greatest conjunction.[2]

LXVI. Consider no profection by itself alone, but make reference also to the qualifications and impediments of the stars.

LXVII. Years are diminished by the imbecility of the receiver.

LXVIII. A malefic, when matutine, signifies an accident ; when vespertine, a disease.

LXIX. The native's sight will be impaired if the Moon be opposed to the Sun, and joined with nebulous stars ; and if the Moon be in the western angle, and both the malefic stars in the eastern angle, the Sun being in an angle also, the native will become blind.

LXX. Insanity is produced if the Moon have no connection with Mercury ; and, if neither of them be connected with the ascendant, Saturn being in occupation of the angle by night, but Mars by day, especially if in Cancer, Virgo, or Pisces, a dæmoniac affection will be produced.

LXXI. If both luminaries may be in masculine signs, in the nativities of males, their actions will be consonant with nature ; but if so placed in the nativities of females, they increase their action. And Mars and Venus, if matutine, incline to the masculine gender ; if vespertine, to the feminine.

LXXII. Matters of education are to be considered by the ascending lords of triplicity ; matters of life, by the lords of the conditionary luminary's triplicity.

---

[1] Of the Sun and Moon.

[2] On this aphorism Partridge has said, " how Ptolemy meant it to be understood, I know not ; and so I leave it."

LXXIII. If the Sun be found with the Gorgon's head (*Caput Medusæ*), and not aspected by any benefic star, and if there be no benefic present in the eighth house, and the lord of the conditionary luminary be opposed to Mars, or in quartile to him, the native will be beheaded. If the luminary culminate, his body will be maimed or mangled ; and if the aspect in quartile be from Gemini or Pisces, his hands and feet will be amputated.

LXXIV. Mars, if ascending, uniformly gives a scar in the face.

LXXV. If the Sun be in conjunction with the lord of the ascendant, in Leo, and Mars have no prerogative in the ascendant, and if there be no benefic in the eighth house, the native will be burned.

LXXVI. If Saturn hold the mid-heaven, and the conditionary luminary be opposed to him, the native will perish in the ruins of buildings, provided the sign on the lower heaven be an earthly sign ; if it be a watery sign, he will be drowned or suffocated by water : if a human sign, he will be strangled by men, or will perish by the halter or the scourge. Should there, however, be a benefic in the eighth house, he will not suffer death, although he will be brought near it.

LXXVII. Profection of the ascendant is to be made for matters affecting the body ; of the Part of Fortune, for extrinsic circumstances ; of the Moon, for the connection between the body and the spirit ; and of the mid-heaven, for the employment or profession.

LXXVIII. A star often dispenses influence in a place in which it has no prerogative, thus bringing unexpected advantage to the native.

LXXIX. Whoever has Mars in the eleventh house, does not govern his master.

LXXX. If Venus be in conjunction with Saturn, and have any lord of house in the seventh house, the native will be of spurious origin.

LXXXI. Times are reckoned in seven ways ; viz. by the space between two significators ; by the space between their mutual aspects ; by the approach of one to the other ; by the space between either of them and the place appropriated to the proposed event ; by the descension of a star, with its addition or diminution ; by the changing of a significator ; and by the approach of a planet to its place.

LXXXII. When a figure may be equipoised, observe the horoscope (or figure) at the new or full moon, and, if that also be equipoised, be not hasty in giving judgment.

LXXXIII. The time of obtaining a grant indicates the affection between the applicant and his prince ; but the seat[1] shows the nature of the office ;—

[1] Or part of heaven indicating the grant.

LXXXIV. And if Mars be lord of the ascendant at the time of entering on possession, and posited in the second house, or coupled with the lord of the second, he brings much mischief.

LXXXV. Should the lord of the ascendant be configurated with the lord of the second house, the prince will spontaneously create many charges.

LXXXVI. The Sun is the source of the vital power; the Moon, of the natural power.

LXXXVII. Monthly revolutions are made in twenty-eight days, two hours and about eighteen minutes. Judgment is also made by some persons by means of the Sun's progress; that is to say, by his partial equations to that degree and minute which he might hold at the beginning.

LXXXVIII. In making profection of the part of Fortune for a whole annual revolution, a space equal to that between the Sun and Moon is to be reckoned from the ascendant.

LXXXIX. Consider the grandfather's affairs from the seventh house and the uncle's from the sixth.

XC. Should the significator be in aspect to the ascendant, the hidden event or object will correspond in its nature with the ascendant; but if the ascendant be not so aspected, the nature of the event will accord with that of the place in which the significator is posited. The lord of the hour shows its colour; the place of the Moon its time; and, if above the earth, it will be a novel thing; if below, old. The part of Fortune indicates its quantity, whether long or short. The lords of the terms, and of the lower heaven and mid-heaven, and of the Moon, shows its substance or value.

XCI. Should the ruler of a sick person be combust, it is an evil portent; and especially if the part of Fortune be afflicted.

XCII. Saturn, if oriental, is not so highly noxious to a sick person; nor Mars, if occidental.

XCIII. Judgment is not to be drawn from any figure until the next conjunction shall have been considered: for principles are varied by every conjunction; and therefore, to avoid error, both the last and the next should be combined.

XCIV. The place of the more potent significator indicates the thoughts of the inquirer.

XCV. The stars rising with the tenth house prove how far the native may be fitted to the occupation which he follows.

XCVI. In an eclipse, such significations as are made nearest the angles, show the events decreed. The nature of the stars in accordance with the eclipse, plants as well as fixed stars, and also the appearances co-ascending, are likewise to be considered, and judgment is to be given accordingly.

XCVII. The event inquired about will be speedily accomplished, should the lord of the new or full Moon be in an angle.

XCVIII. Shooting stars, and meteors like flowing hair, bear a secondary part in judgments.

XCIX. Shooting stars denote the dryness of the air; and, if they are projected to one part only, they indicate wind therefrom: if to various parts, they indicate diminution of waters, a turbulent atmosphere, and incursions of armies.

C. If comets, whose distance is eleven signs behind the Sun, appear in angles, the king of some kingdom, or one of the princes or chief men of a kingdom, will die. If in a succedent house, the affairs of the kingdom's treasury will prosper, but the governor or ruler will be changed. If in a cadent house, there will be diseases and sudden deaths. And if comets be in motion from the west towards the east, a foreign foe will invade the country: if not in motion, the foe will be provincial, or domestic.

END OF THE CENTILOQUY

NO. IV

THE ZODIACAL PLANISPHERE

THE Reader is desired to refer to the Plate at end of book containing diagrams of the Zodiacal Planisphere, which has been spoken of in the Note in p. 99.

Fig. 1 is the Planisphere adjusted for the northern latitude of 30° 22' (where the longest day consists of fourteen equatorial hours), agreeably to the "Exemplification" given by Ptolemy in Chapter XV, Book 3. It represents that portion of the celestial sphere which is contained between the tropics: the central horizontal line is the equator; the curved line extending longitudinally from east to west is the ecliptic; the central perpendicular line is the meridian, or cusp of the 10th house; the other short lines, cutting the equator transversely, are the cusps of the other houses; that of the 1st house being the eastern horizon; that of the 7th, the western horizon. Hence, the distance from the 1st house to the meridian, or from the meridian to the 7th house, shows the semi-diurnal arc of any parallel of declination in the ecliptic; and the distance of the 7th house to the 4th, or from the 4th to the 1st, shows the semi-nocturnal arc. The distance from the cusp of one house to that of the next, taken on the same parallel, is also equal to two temporal hours; thus, for instance, in the latitude above quoted, the semi-diurnal arc of 0° ♊ is 6 h. 50 m., or 102° 39' of the equator; consequently the diurnal temporal hour is equal to one equatorial hour and eight minutes, or to 17° 6' of the equator.

In his first example, Ptolemy directs 0° ♈ to be placed on the ascendant, so that the beginning of ♑ may be on the mid-heaven; 0° ♊ must, therefore, fall on the point A, distant from the mid-heaven 147° 44' of the equator, as measured by the line AB; because every point in the sphere always preserves one and the same parallel with the equator; and 0° ♊, in passing to the mid-heaven, must proceed along the line AB. In the present case, however, it is required to know how long 0° ♊ will be in coming to the ascendant, the given position of 0° ♈. Now 0° ♊ will be on the ascendant when it arrives at the point G; therefore the distance from A to C is the amount of the prorogation between 0° ♈ (when posited on the ascendant) and 0° ♊, and it is equal to 45° 5' of the equator. In the second example, 0° ♈ is placed on the mid-heaven, which position must be at D, so that 0° ♊ must necessarily be at E; and the distance from E to B, equal to 57° 44' of the equator, is the prorogation between 0° ♈ and 0° ♊, when 0⁴ ♈ is on the mid-heaven. In the third example, 0°♈ is supposed to be on the 7th house, descending, at F, so that ♋ is on the mid-heaven, and 0° ♊ at the point G, in advance of the mid-heaven 32° 16' of the equator, as shown by the distance BG. Now it is required to bring 0° ♊ to the 7th house (the place of 0° ♈), and it will be there on arriving at H, distant from B 102° 39' of the equator; but as 0° ♊ is already at G, the distance from G to H, equal to 70° 23' of the equator, is the amount of the prorogation between 0° ♈ and 0° ♊, when 0° ♈ is on the 7th house. The fourth example places 0° ♈ at I, three temporal hours past the meridian; 0° ♊ therefore falls on the point K, at the distance of 13 equatorial degrees before the meridian or mid-heaven, and will be three temporal hours past the meridian (the position of 0° ♈) on arriving at L, distant 51 equatorial degrees from the mid-heaven: the whole distance from K (the first position of 0° ♊) to L, its second position, equal to 64 degrees of the equator, is therefore the prorogation between 0° ♈ and 0° ♊, when 0° ♈ is past the meridian at the distance of three temporal hours. Ptolemy has also instanced two other positions for 0° ♈; viz. at two temporal hours past the meridian, and at two temporal hours before the occidental angle; or, in other words, on the cusp of the 9th house, and on that of the 8th. Now, if 0° ♈ be on the cusp of the 9th house, it must be at M, and 0° ♊ will be at N, distant 62 equatorial degrees from Q, which is also on the cusp of the 9th. If 0° ♈ be on the cusp of the 8th, it must be at O, and 0° ♊ will be at P, distant 66 equatorial degrees from R, which is also on the cusp of the 8th: these two several numbers of degrees will be the respective prorogations between 0° ♈ and 0° ♊, when 0° ♈ is placed on the 9th and 8th houses.

Ptolemy's "Exemplification" has been followed thus minutely in order to show how perfectly Mr. Ranger's invention is adapted to assist (if not to supersede) arithmetical calculation ; for, after the Planisphere has once been accurately laid down, a line drawn parallel to the equator, from the significator to the promittor, or to the promittor's pole of position, and measured by degrees of the equator, will accomplish the whole operation of ascertaining the amount of prorogation.

Fig. 2 is the Equator extended, *in plano*, on a scale proportionate to the planispheres in Figs. 1 and 3 : it is divided into 360 degrees, and into equal time, as measured by the 24 hours of the earth's daily rotation on its axis, and by smaller portions of four minutes each, corresponding with degrees of the equator.

Fig. 3 is the Planisphere set for the latitude of Southern Britain, 51° 30′ N., where the longest day is 16 h. 30 m., the semi-diurnal arc of 0° ♊ being consequently 7 h. 52 m., or 118° of the equator, and its diurnal temporal hour equal to one hour and nearly nineteen minutes of equatorial time, or to 19° 40′ of the equator. In applying Ptolemy's examples, given in Chapter XV, Book 3, to this latitude, it will follow that, when 0° ♈ may be on the ascendant, 0° ♊ will be at A, and will subsequently arrive at the ascendant at C, after the passage of 29° 43′ of the equator. When 0° ♈ may be on the mid-heaven at D, 0° ♊ will be at E, and will arrive at B, on the mid-heaven, after the passage of 57° 44′ of the equator, as in Fig. 1. When 0° ♈ may be on the 7th house, at F, 0° ♊ will be at G, and will come to the 7th house, at H, after the passage of 85° 45′ of the equator. If 0° ♈ be three temporal hours past the meridian, at I, 0° ♊ would be at K, again 13 equatorial degrees before the meridian, as in Fig. 1, and will be three temporal hours past the meridian, a position similar to that assumed for 0° ♈, on arriving at L, distant from the mid-heaven 59 equatorial degrees ; thus making the whole distance, from K to L, 17 equatorial degrees. If 0° ♈ be on the 9th house, at M, 0° ♊ will be at N, distant from Q (also on the 9th house) about 67 equatorial degrees. If 0° ♈ be on the 8th house, at O, 0° ♊ will be at P, distant from R (also on the 8th house) about 76 equatorial degrees.

By taking the trouble to calculate the distances between the several positions given by Ptolemy, the Reader may satisfy himself of the sufficiency of this Planisphere for the purpose for which it was first projected ; viz. for the more expeditious measurement of the arcs of direction. The Tables of Ascensions, extracted from the Almagest, in p. 152, will show that the arcs, as measured in Figs. 1 and 2 of the plate, exactly tally with the amounts of distance obtained by calculating arithmetically, according to the respective latitudes, as quoted in the Tables.

The slight view which has been here given of the Zodiacal Planisphere invented by Mr. Ranger, must not be considered as pretending to offer a complete idea of its powers : they are so manifold and various, that another volume would be required to detail them fully ; and it has now been used only in order to give a better illustration of Ptolemy's examples of the spaces of prorogation than mere words can do. To persons conversant with the mathematical part of astronomy, the facility with which a complete representation of zodiacal latitude, declination, the poles of position, crepusculine circles, and other phenomena, may be made by this Planisphere, will be sufficiently obvious from the accompanying Figures.

FINIS

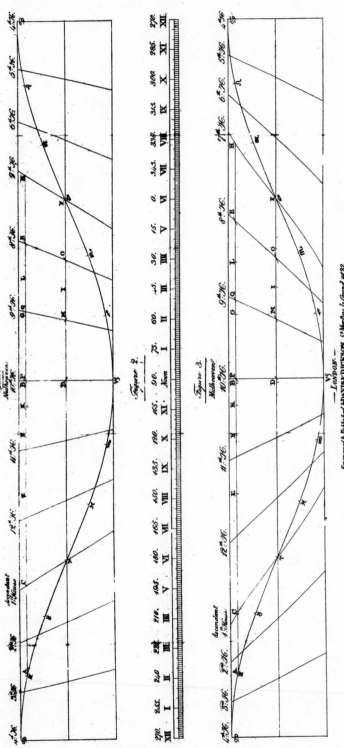

Figure 2.

Figure 3.

— LONDON. —

Engraved & Published by DAVIES & DICKSON, St. Martin le Grand, No 32.